Consumer Psychology

Consumer Psychology

Cathrine V. Jansson-Boyd

Open University Press

Open University Press
McGraw-Hill Education
McGraw-Hill House
Shoppenhangers Road
Maidenhead
Berkshire
England
SL6 2QL

email: enquiries@openup.co.uk
world wide web: www.openup.co.uk

and Two Penn Plaza, New York, NY 10121-2289, USA

First published 2010

A catalogue record of this book is available from the British Library

ISBN-13: 978-0-33-522928-4 (pb) 978-0-33-522927-7 (hb)
ISBN-10: 033522928X (pb) 0335229271 (hb)

Library of Congress Cataloging-in-Publication Data
CIP data applied for

Typeset by RefineCatch Limited, Bungay, Suffolk
Printed in the UK by Bell and Bain Ltd., Glasgow

Fictitious names of companies, products, people, characters and/or data that may be used herein (in case studies or in examples) are not intended to represent any real individual, company, product or event.

Mixed Sources
Product group from well-managed
forests and other controlled sources
www.fsc.org   Cert no. TT-COC-002769
© 1996 Forest Stewardship Council

FSC

The **McGraw·Hill** Companies

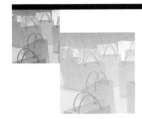

Contents

Preface

This book sets out to provide readers with aspects of Consumer Psychology that are essential to understanding consumer behaviour. To date, there have not been many books with the words 'Consumer Psychology' in their titles. Those that have included them have often been more marketing-oriented than focused on psychology. However, this book focuses on the psychology of consumers and additionally draws upon marketing-related research that can aid the understanding of how consumers think and behave.

Because there has not been one 'typical' or 'standard' type of textbook used universally by consumer psychologists in their teaching around the world, lecturers have often 'made up' their own Consumer Psychology modules. This has been particularly evident in Europe where modules vary greatly in their contents even though the name is the same. Therefore, it is likely that some lecturers may feel that the contents of this book do not cover all the topics that they would like it to. However, this book incorporates the topics that are most commonly included in Consumer Psychology courses around the world, so it will appeal equally to readers in different countries.

New and exciting research within the discipline of Consumer Psychology is constantly emerging. Consequently, the field of Consumer Psychology is moving very quickly, meaning that individuals with a particular interest in this area should make use of research journals in addition to this textbook. Even though this book includes some up-to-date research, it is more about presenting an overall rounded view of Consumer Psychology, which comprises new as well as older 'traditional' theories and perspectives.

The book consists of thirteen chapters that are all structured in the same way. Each chapter covers a different subject area. First, an introductory paragraph briefly outlines what the reader can expect from the chapter. Throughout the chapter, key concepts are highlighted in bold, so that the reader knows what they ought to familiarize themselves with. The key concepts are fully explained in the glossary at the end of the chapter. Also at the end is a short summary followed by either a class exercise or five discussion questions. Both the class exercises and the questions are intended to stimulate further thinking and debate.

Chapter 1 briefly introduces Consumer Psychology and how its foundation is grounded in scientific methods. Additionally, there is also an outline of how Consumer Psychology has grown as a scientific discipline in parallel with the development of the consumer society in which we live today. The history focuses on the period between the mid-seventeenth century and the mid-twentieth century. What is particularly interesting is that psychological investigations into specific aspects of consumption are nothing new. Furthermore, it also reveals that some very well-known psychologists who are commonly studied in psychology undergraduate degrees, have conducted consumer-related research.

Chapter 2 introduces memory and learning. It outlines key aspects of memory such as short-term and long-term memory, as well as how consumers remember and forget information. Moreover, it delineates behavioural, cognitive and social learning approaches. It is essential for a consumer psychologist to have a good understanding of both the areas of memory and learning.

Just like Chapter 2, the third chapter also covers cognitive aspects of psychology. In this chapter perception and attention are discussed. You will become familiar with how humans perceive stimuli, how perception is linked to attention and what can be done to capture consumers' attention.

Chapter 4 discusses how people can define who they are (or try to define who they are) through consumption. It explores how people form their identity and whether or not this can be done through the use of goods that have symbolic meaning.

How emotions can guide consumer behaviour is looked at in Chapter 5. Most aspects of consumption are guided in one way or another by how people feel. It is simply impossible for consumers to detach themselves from how they feel. The effects of emotions are often subconscious and it can therefore be difficult to establish when they play a part in consumer behaviours. Chapter 5 looks at how emotions impact upon cognitive processes such as attention and recall, as well as how they affect decision-making. Additionally, the chapter also deals with persuasive theories of emotion that shed some light on whether or not consumers may be persuaded by factors they encounter in a consumer environment.

Chapter 6 explores the area of attitudes. It looks at how they are formed and why people change them. An outline of whether or not attitudes can predict behaviour is also included. Furthermore, the chapter finishes with an outline of how the mass media can influence people's attitudes.

Chapter 7 introduces the psychology of advertising. A lot has been written about advertising and it is therefore beyond the scope of this chapter to look at all the possible angles of how to make an advert effective. The chapter focuses on how the Elaboration Likelihood Model can be used to explain when advertising is at its most persuasive and, as a result, can favourably alter consumers' attitudes. Moreover, the role of humour, sex, music, fear and shock tactics is also presented.

What motivates consumers to purchase products and services is covered in Chapter 8. This chapter explores motivation as well as looking at common theories of motivation.

Decision-making and brand loyalty are the topics of Chapter 9. It explains how decision-making is affected by different types of heuristics and looks at whether or not consumers can and do make rational decisions. The chapter also outlines what brand loyalty means as well as why consumers become loyal to brands.

Chapter 10 elaborates upon the Internet and how it has become incredibly popular since it first emerged. Naturally, the chapter looks at Internet consumption. This includes how consumers conduct searches on the web and how they make decisions online. Because using the Internet is a consumer activity in itself, the chapter also looks at aspects that may seem less obviously linked to consumption, namely, how it is used as a social tool.

How children differ from adult consumers is covered in Chapter 11. A wide range of other consumer aspects are also covered in this chapter, including how mainstream media (e.g. television) can affect children's thoughts and behaviour, the use of computers, and how well children understand advertising. A lot has been written about children as consumers, especially about the influence of television upon aggressive behaviour. This chapter introduces some key aspects of this subject area. For particularly keen students, it would be highly recommended that they conduct additional reading as it is simply impossible to cover all angles in one chapter.

Chapter 12 examines whether or not there is a link between consumption and happiness. It starts by defining what happiness is and how it can be measured. The chapter then continues by outlining how consumption can be disadvantageous by looking at people who are highly materialistic and those who become addicted to gathering possessions. In the latter part of the chapter a more positive side to consumption is presented. Then the chapter reveals how different types of consumption can make people feel happier overall.

In the final chapter, Chapter 13, the topic of how consumption affects our environment is explored. This chapter looks at how consumers view environmentally friendly products, and whether or not it is possible to reduce consumption of goods and services that are detrimental to our environment.

The thirteen chapters of this book present and review essential topics of Consumer Psychology, by revisiting old key studies as well as discussing recently conducted research. Generally, the book draws on multiple areas of psychology but focuses mainly on the traditional ones such as cognitive, behavioural and social approaches. Some areas of research do not feature extensively in this book, for example, cognitive neuropsychological studies.

Recently, cognitive neuroscience studies have also been applied to Consumer Psychology. This is a very new and exciting development of Consumer Psychology that often makes use of fMRI (functional magnetic resonance imaging). Aspects of cognitive neuroscience studies are briefly mentioned. The reason for not including extensive amounts of such research is partially due to the fact that it is not yet commonly taught in a consumer psychological context. However, it is worth acknowledging that such research is on the rise and is likely to contribute to a better understanding of consumer behaviour in the future. But until this happens it is more practical for students to focus their time and energy on subject areas that are currently deemed to be essential to Consumer Psychology.

Acknowledgements

I thank Nigel Marlow for introducing me to the field of Consumer Psychology. He was a very inspirational lecturer while I studied for my undergraduate course. Without his enthusiasm I doubt that I would have continued my career as a psychologist.

Thank you also to Nigel, Peter Bright, Clare Mackie and Alexander for providing me with feedback on some of the chapters.

Several companies have very kindly granted me permission to reprint images that demonstrate certain aspects of Consumer Psychology. For that I am very grateful, the companies are: Cosmos Communications, Ogilvy & Mather, United Colors of Benetton, Citigroup, Peta, NBC Universal, Mercedez-Benz, and Northern Foods.

The team at McGraw-Hill deserve to be acknowledged. Ruben Hale, Katy Hamilton and Monika Lee, thank you for your support throughout this project.

My final acknowledgements have to be to the two most important people in my life, Alex and Oscar. Without you, my life would be incomplete.

CHAPTER 1

Consumer Psychology

What it is and how it emerged

Introduction

Consumer Psychology is now (more than ever) highly applicable to the world in which we live. Consumption has indoctrinated Western culture and it is now an integral part of society. Consequently, from a business and people point of view, it is important that psychologists have a clear understanding of how it affects human behaviour. So what is Consumer Psychology? How are individuals influenced by consumption? When did scientists start researching consumer psychological questions? Who were the researchers who created the underpinnings for Consumer Psychology as we know it today? These are all questions that will be addressed in this chapter.

What is Consumer Psychology?

Consumer Psychology is about understanding why and how individuals and groups engage in consumer activities, as well as how they are affected by them. A large part of this discipline is focused on the cognitive processes and behaviour involved when people purchase and use products and services. Without knowing how people process information and how they subsequently act, it would be difficult to explain consumer behaviour.

Consumer Psychology is an interdisciplinary subject area and it combines theories and research methods from Psychology, Marketing, Advertising, Economics, Sociology and Anthropology. There are many areas of specialization and throughout the years they have been rapidly growing. Some of the more commonly researched areas include decision-making, consumer judgement, perception and attention, information processing, motivational determinants of consumer behaviour, attitude formation and change, and influences of advertising upon consumer responses. The aforementioned areas are most commonly linked to how marketers, manufacturers and advertisers can attempt to influence consumer decisions to purchase a particular brand or product.

However, there are also areas of consumer research that are not necessarily linked to the increase of sales of products and brands. Such areas include the impact of consumption on children, how products may shape an individual's identity, and how consumption affects the environment.

When learning about Consumer Psychology, it is important to establish a broad understanding of why consumers behave and think the way they do. The more you know, the easier it is to explain consumer behaviour.

Applying scientific methods

Many people seem to believe that consumption is just common sense and that you do not need scientific methods to prove what they already know but this could not be further from the truth. What individuals think they know is often incorrect. At other times scientific studies are also very useful in that they can be used to explain concepts that consumers are unable to express in words, such as how a particular point-of-purchase display affected them when shopping in a supermarket, or whether or not they are influenced by television commercials. It is important to remember that Consumer Psychology is first and foremost a scientific discipline and consequently should always be treated as such.

When conducting research, Consumer Psychologists (just like any other psychologist) make use of a wide range of research methods, both quantitative and qualitative. It is beyond the scope of this book to go into any detail of research methods but all students with a genuine interest in psychology should ensure that they are well acquainted with the range of research methods that can be applied to the field of Consumer Psychology. Without a clear understanding of how researchers reach their conclusions, it can be difficult to appreciate the real value of the outcome from the research studies.

Why study Consumer Psychology?

In everyday life, people are repeatedly exposed to different aspects of consumption. Advertising, travelling on a train, grocery shopping, watching television, listening to music, surfing the Internet, clothes shopping, and reading a book are all examples of things that people consume. Almost all behaviours that humans engage in are directly or indirectly linked to consumption (Tatzel, 2003). Even traditional holidays such as Christmas are these days mainly about consumption. What was originally a religious holiday has mainly been overtaken by aspects of consumption with the quintessential example of this being Santa Claus delivering presents (Belk, 1993). Basically there is no way of escaping the fact that consumption is a part of humans' everyday lives (Kasser & Kanner, 2003). Hence, without studying how consumption affects individuals and groups, one can never truly say that we understand humans.

The scale on which people consume (particularly in Westernized societies) makes it evident that consumption needs to be carefully studied by all those with an interest in human behaviour whether as psychologists, marketers, consumer behaviourists, anthropologists, or sociologists. For example, in the USA, the average person uses approximately 1333 kg of paper and eats 593 kg of meat annually (Goodwin, Nelson, Ackerman, & Weisskopf, 2005). The American population also spends $8 billion per annum on cosmetics (*Human Development Report*, United Nations, 1998), and consumes $25 billion litres of mineral water (Earth Policy Institute, 2002). In Norway, each household spends around £3860 a year on food and drinks and £1830 on clothing and footwear (Statistics Norway, 2007). UK retail sales have shown that these items can be worth around £5 billion over a three-month period (National Statistics, 2007).

Other sales figures that show people's willingness to engage in consumption activities include that all Europeans put together spend around £5 billion on ice cream every year (*Human Development Report*, United Nations, 1998). Globally it has been estimated that 1.12 billion households have one or more televisions, there are over 531 million cars in use, and around £18 billion is spent on bottled water (Worldwatch Institute, 2004).

The aforementioned figures clearly show that we are living in a consumer-driven society. Consequently it is not difficult to see how consumption infiltrates individuals' lives in many various ways.

How consumption affect people's lives

A number of research studies conducted by psychologists have repeatedly shown that consumption is an integral part of people's lives. For example, it has been found that consumer activities can impact upon people's identities and how individuals convey their social status through the use of certain products and services (e.g. Dittmar, 2008a).

Other aspects of consumption that impact upon people's lives include how men and women choose to 'groom' themselves. This includes anything from wearing perfume to going under the knife to change one's physical appearance in some way. Never before has the phrase 'beauty is only skin deep' been more inappropriate. Most people, if you ask them, tend to agree that physical beauty is superficial and that it should not be as important as a person's intellectual, emotional and spiritual qualities. However, the consumer society we live in is pushing consumers in a different direction. The media is constantly subjecting us to images of ideal beauty which makes people feel that they are not good/beautiful/thin/young enough (e.g. Dittmar & Howard, 2004; Lever, Frederick, & Peplau, 2006) and consequently they spend money on both beauty products and cosmetic surgery. 'Grooming'-related issues and the relationship between consumption and identities will be discussed in more detail in Chapter 4.

Social and developmental scientists have also produced a lot of research demonstrating how children are affected by mainstream media (e.g. Bushman & Huesmann, 2001). The focus of such research has often been on whether or not television violence makes children more aggressive (e.g. Huesmann, 1986, 1988; Huesmann, & Miller, 1994). Even though research within this area is not black and white, there is clear evidence that children can at times become more aggressive if exposed to aggressive media images. However, there is often not a straightforward relationship between aggressive children and television violence, even when they are affected by it, and this will be discussed further in Chapter 11.

It is not only children who are affected by the media but also adults. People's opinions, values and beliefs about others are often moulded by what they are exposed to by the media. For example, television commercials can affect the way people view others (e.g. Davies, Spencer, Quinn, & Gerhardstein, 2002), and consumption of pornography can affect men's attitudes towards rape (e.g. Zillmann & Bryant, 1984). Further examples can be found in Chapter 6.

Naturally, media exposure (and in particular advertising) also influences how consumers view particular products and services and whether or not they will purchase them. These days the psychology of advertising is one of the more commonly researched areas of Consumer Psychology. There is now a good understanding of what captures consumers' attention (e.g. Bolls & Muehling, 2003), how it is possible to make consumers consciously think about what they have seen advertised (e.g. Petty & Cacioppo, 1986a), and when it is most suitable to show commercials on television (e.g. Bushman & Bonacci, 2002). See Chapter 7 for a more detailed account of the psychology of advertising.

It has taken a considerable time for Consumer Psychologists to get to the stage we are at today, where we have a good understanding of how the consumer society impacts upon people, how specific consumption behaviours can be explained and what cognitive processes are involved in the various stages of consumption. Numerous researchers, both psychologists and marketers, have contributed along the way. In parallel with the constantly growing consumer society, researchers increasingly try to apply scientific evidence to various aspects of consumption. In order to appreciate how we reached the point we are at today, it is useful to have some background knowledge of the early research contributions as well as familiarizing oneself with how the consumer society rapidly grew into what it is today.

How the science of Consumer Psychology grew in parallel with the consumer society

According to historians, the culture of consumption in Europe started before the Industrial Revolution (Fairchilds, 1998). This was notable in a variety of countries and in social classes such as the Dutch peasants (De Vries, 1975) and in urban and rural English settings (Shammas, 1990). Between the mid-seventeenth century and throughout the eighteenth century, an increase in consumption was significant even though it was not necessarily applicable to all individuals throughout Europe. However, this was to change with the Industrial Revolution as it meant that people from all walks of life in different countries started consuming much more than they previously had.

In the 1800s, the Industrial Revolution spread throughout Europe and the USA. Fundamental changes occurred in transportation, metal manufacture, textile, and agriculture as well as in the social structure. This meant that there was an increase in food supplies and raw materials and the new and more efficient technology that emerged made it possible to increase the overall production levels of many products.

In parallel with the continuous consumption growth, many scientists realized that it is important to understand how the consumer society affects individuals, in order to truly understand human beings. Whether they sought to understand the impact of consumption for social, economic, or humanistic reasons, they have all contributed directly or indirectly to the discipline now referred to as Consumer Psychology.

Consumer Psychology as a field in its own right may be relatively new, but the application of psychology to consumer-related issues has been going on for a lot longer than many realize. Because it is an interdisciplinary area a number of scientists from many different research disciplines have contributed to our understanding of consumption matters today. It is impossible to mention them all here, so what follows is a brief outline of some individuals and events that form the underpinnings of Consumer Psychology as a discipline.

1840–1920

The rise of advertising and experimental psychology

After the Industrial Revolution in Europe during the mid to late eighteenth century, it was inevitable that all consumer-related industries would grow and change rapidly. With the increase in production, competition was fierce between manufacturers and hence the pressure was on to promote the available products. Consequently, during the 1840s a man called Volney Palmer opened the first advertising agency in the world (Fox, 1984). It offered limited services and did not exactly resemble what we consider an advertising agency today. Their main duties appeared to be as brokers for advertising space in newspapers. However, it was not long before the advertising agency's duties expanded and shortly afterwards several others were established that offered a range of advertising-related services.

With a wider range of products now more easily available, it was also thought that shopping could be made more convenient for the customer. Even though there had been a number of smaller shops selling different types of products, the range on offer tended to be rather limited. Instead it was thought that bigger shops where most kind of things could be bought would simplify the shopping experience for consumers. So, in 1852, the world's first department store, Le Bon Marché, opened in Paris. It was one of the first places to announce that haggling was no longer allowed and also had a money back guarantee. Soon others followed, with the likes of Macy's opening in New York in 1878, and the world rapidly became accustomed to larger stores with bigger product selections.

It was also during this period that the world's first experimental psychology laboratory was established. It was set up in Leipzig in 1879 by a German psychologist named Wilhelm Wundt. Often referred to as 'the father of experimental psychology', he was one of the founders of the first major school of thought in psychology – structuralism (Hothersall, 1984).

Structuralism focused on understanding the structure of the mind and Wundt believed that psychologists should focus on immediate conscious experience. Throughout his career he investigated many different areas of psychology, but attention may be the most relevant area to Consumer Psychology. Wundt viewed attention as the part of perception that reflects what humans are consciously aware of. He also had a string of students, some of whom such as James Cattell and E.B. Titchener became well-known psychologists in their own right (Hothersall, 1984).

The importance of material possessions

In the late 1800s scientists started to realize that material possessions play an important role in people's lives. This is evident from William James's writing in 1890 when he proclaimed that possessions contribute to the understanding of who you are. He wrote:

> In its widest possible sense . . . a man's Self is the sum total of all that he can call his, not only his body and his psychic powers, but his clothes and his house, his wife and children, his ancestors and friends, his reputation and works . . . If they wax and prosper, he feels triumphant, if they dwindle and die away, he feels cast down.
>
> (James [1890] 1950, pp. 291–292)

The quote from his book *The Principles of Psychology* demonstrates how he believed that individuals' self-concept would partially be dependent upon owning the right kind of possessions.

James, who was an academic at Harvard University, was originally trained in Philosophy. He was one of the early pragmatists who theorized about consciousness, and in particular focusing on how it enables people to adjust to their environment. It was such a train of thought that also became the foundation for industrial psychology, which studies people at work.

Academics become interested in advertising

With the advertising industry growing rapidly, a string of academics also became interested in the subject area. Harlow Gale is considered to be the founder of the psychology of advertising (Eighmey & Sar, 2007) as he was the first to conduct experiments on the effects of advertising (Kuna, 1976). Gale was interested in the effects of advertising on attention and memory and conducted a series of surveys and experiments to test this (Eighmey & Sar, 2007). A previous student of Wundt in Leipzig (Benjamin & Baker, 2004), he became a lecturer at the University of Minnesota in 1895 where he stayed until 1903. It was during his time in Minnesota that he ran one of the first experimental psychology laboratories in the USA.

During the early years of studying advertising, experimental psychologists affirmed previous theories that consumers were non-rational individuals who were easily influenced (Kuna, 1976). One person in particular was a supporter of this theory, Walter Dill Scott, also one of Wundt's students. He believed that sentimentality, emotions and sympathy all made consumers more open to suggestions made by advertisers (Schultz & Schultz, 2004). In 1903, Scott published a book entitled *The Theory of Advertising* in which he actively propagated the links between advertising and psychology, and stated that the aim of advertising should be to capture people's attention (Schultz & Schultz, 2004). However, curiously, Scott never published any of his work in academic journals, perhaps casting some doubt on how rigorous his work really was.

Coca-Cola is taken to court

In 1909, one of Coca-Cola's trucks containing Coca-Cola syrup was seized by the US government. The Coca-Cola Company was later charged with selling a drink containing a harmful ingredient, caffeine. As the company prepared to face trial in 1911 they realized that the research evidence they intended to present in court mainly consisted of physiological responses to caffeine but very little on how it affected behaviour. Hence they contacted a psychologist by the name of Harry Hollingworth to conduct studies on how caffeine influenced human behaviour.

In order to investigate the effects of caffeine, Hollingworth set up a series of studies designed to test the effects of caffeine on sensory, cognitive and motor functioning. Most of these tests were conducted with his wife Leta. Hollingworth had been James Cattell's student at Columbia University so he was familiar with Cattell's mental tests and could therefore easily apply them to his research for Coca-Cola (Arthur & Benjamin, 1999).

None of the studies by the Hollingworths showed that caffeine had a detrimental impact on cognitive or behavioural performance, even when consumed in much larger doses than would normally be found in a bottle of Coke (Benjamin, Rogers, & Rosenbaum, 1991). As a result, Coca-Cola won the original trial but lost when it was taken to the Supreme Court. Even though Hollingsworth had been hesitant to undertake the work commissioned by Coca-Cola, the rigour of his experimental work was recognized and it was the starting point for his successful academic career. After his work with Coca-Cola, he continued to research how advertisements affect purchase behaviour, which is what he had been doing prior to the trials. Shortly thereafter Hollingworth also wrote a book on the subject area in 1913, entitled *Advertising and Selling: Principles of Appeals and Responses.*

The assembly line is invented and there is continued interest in advertising research

The manufacturing process was to become a lot easier and quicker when Henry Ford, the owner of Ford Motors Company, invented the assembly line in 1913. Ford wanted to manufacture his Model T car cheaply so that cars would no longer be affordable to only the higher income classes. Prior to the assembly line concept, products of all kinds had been more expensive. However, the assembly line ensured that all sorts of products could be produced relatively cheaply in their hundreds, thousands and eventually millions. With the rapid growth in manufacturing practices, competition between products and brands became even fiercer and now more than ever producers needed advertisers to help ensure that their products would sell. When Ford invented the assembly line, he undoubtedly helped establish the consumer society in which we live today.

With advertising quickly establishing itself as an important part of society, it was perhaps not surprising that there was also a continuing interest in how to make it effective and how it affected individuals. In 1914, a book was published that was to be read by many people in the advertising industry in the USA. The author was Daniel Starch and the book was entitled *Advertising: Its Principles, Practice and Technique*. Starch's book on advertising emphasized the links between attention and response (Starch, 1914), something that is still discussed today in advertising journals. He had started his career as an academic but soon came to realize that his real interest was in market research, so he left the academic world and instead set up his own company that specialized in measuring the effectiveness of advertising. Not long after *Advertising: Its Principles, Practice and Technique* was released, Starch also wrote a follow-up entitled *Principles of Advertising*. In the latter book he discussed how the 1880s was a time when advertising had rapidly expanded and that the amount of advertising in some monthly publications had grown as much as 450 per cent (Starch, 1923).

Interest in the applications of advertising continued to grow and it was not only manufacturers who could see its potential. Politicians also became interested when they realized that 'how to sell products' could be applied to sell their own ideas. This was particulary evident during World War I when propaganda campaigns were used as tools to encourage people to continue fighting. For example, the British and Americans spread rumours about the appalling behaviour of the Germans, such as making soap out of enemy soldiers (Jowett & O'Donnell, 1986; Peterson, 1939). This was done so that people would feel that they could not possibly let such a gruesome nation win the war and hence think that it was worth continuing to fight. Many so-called 'atrocity stories' were used, and while some did contain an element of truth, many were concocted solely for the benefit of the British and American governments. Nevertheless, they appeared to be effective, confirming the usefulness of advertising and propaganda.

Since there was no sign of declining interest in the effectiveness of advertising, more books were published on the subject. In 1916, Henry Foster Adams' book entitled *Advertising and its Mental Laws* was published. Adams tackled many different areas in his book, such as the use of statistical analysis to examine people's responses to advertising, gender differences, attention, memory and aesthetics. He was an advocate for using empirical results when trying to understand how advertising works, not too dissimilar to many of the modern books published in recent years.

1920–1938

In the 1920s a number of things happened that contributed significantly to the development of the consumer society in which we live today. In 1920, the first American radio station started broadcasting (Barnow, 1975). The automobile became increasingly common, especially in the USA, and consequently new service institutions such as drive-in restaurants were created, the first of which was opened in 1921, in Dallas (Green, 1992). Additionally, mail-order catalogues became a great success during the 1920s (Boorstin, 1973) and the market was flooded with new products such as washing machines, toasters and irons (Cowan, 1983; Lupton, 1993). The year 1920 would also see a leading academic psychologist join an advertising firm.

John B. Watson

The founder of behaviourism, John B. Watson was the first prominent psychologist to apply psychological methods to advertising (Kreshel, 1990). Watson seemed particularly suited to persuade people to consume different types of products. He believed that individuals could be conditioned into being anything, and if humans could be made into whatever he desired, surely it would not be difficult to get them to buy specific products and brands. Hence, in 1920, he joined America's largest advertising agency, J. Walter Thompson, after having been forced to leave academia after the scandal of having an affair with one of his research students.

In his academic career he had experimented with Ivan Pavlov's classical conditioning technique, most notably in the Little Albert experiment (Watson & Rayner, 1920). Watson (1919) believed that using the systematic application of the principles of classical conditioning, it would be possible to create any kind of human being that he wished to. Such beliefs were summed up in an earlier, now famous statement, when he stated:

> Give me a dozen healthy infants, well-formed, and my own specified world to bring them up in, and I'll guarantee to take any one at random and train him to become any type of specialist I might select – doctor, lawyer, artist, merchant-chief and yes, even beggarman and thief – regardless of his talents, penchants, tendencies, abilities, vocations, and race of his ancestors.
>
> (Watson, 1913)

It was hardly strange that such ideas appealed to the advertising industry.

Many have claimed that Watson had a huge impact upon advertising (e.g. MacGowan, 1928; Winkler & Bromberg, 1939). Some have suggested that his greatest contribution was the development of testimonial advertising which is when a prospective customer may be favourably influenced to try a product when it has been praised by someone else (Buckley, 1989). However, not everybody is convinced that Watson changed the way advertising was used. It may be that he was more of a marketing ploy for the firm that hired him, in that he helped establish an even better reputation for the advertising agency (Kreshel, 1990).

The psychology of advertising continues to grow

In the mid-1920s yet another book showing an interest in applying psychology to consumption related matters was published. The book was entitled *Psychology in Advertising* and was written by Albert T. Poffenberger (1925). Poffenberger was very interested in applied psychology and his first book on psychology and advertising was soon followed by a second, *Applied Psychology: Its Principles and Methods* (1927). The latter was widely used and published in several editions (Wenzel, 1979).

Just as Hollingworth had, Poffenberger had also conducted his graduate studies in psychology at Columbia University where James Cattell was one of his mentors. So it is not surprising that Poffenberger's earlier work included a book that he co-authored with Hollingworth in 1917, entitled, *The Psychology of Taste and Applied Psychology* (Wenzel, 1979).

During his career he was appointed Secretary of the American Psychological Association's (APA) New York branch in 1915 and held the posts of vice-chairman as well as chairman for the Division of Anthropology and Psychology of the National Research Council between 1931 and 1933. Poffenberger also helped established the *Journal of Social Psychology* in 1930 and was appointed APA president in 1934 (Wenzel, 1979).

Another psychologist who also contributed to the understanding of advertising was Nixon. His research mainly focused on the links between attention and advertising. Initial studies of tracking eye movements can be attributed to H.K. Nixon (1924) as he was trying to establish what part of an advertisement consumers look at. To test this, he hid behind a curtain and carefully observed the eye movements of individuals while they were reading. Needless to say, eye-tracking techniques have come a long way since Nixon's days. From his studies he came to conclude that pictures used in print advertisements can guide consumer's attention to the text and that there was little attentional difference between colour and black and white ads (Nixon, 1924, 1926).

Emerging diversity of consumer-related research areas

Towards the end of the 1920s and during the 1930s a string of publications focusing on different consumer psychological areas emerged as scientists showed an increased interest in consumer-related issues. Areas of investigation included how easily different types of advertising were recalled (e.g. Brutt & Crockett, 1928; De Wick, 1935; Guest & Brown, 1939), if people had preferences for certain types of glass containers (Hovde, 1931), and whether there was a relationship between advertisement size and attention (Ferguson, 1934, 1935). Other researchers looked at the impact of radio advertising upon people's attitudes (Cantril & Allport, 1935), and whether personality affects sales performance (Dodge, 1938). It was also at this time that the *Journal of Marketing* was established (*Journal of Marketing*, 2008).

It was not just research that was flourishing during the late 1930s but also consumption in general. Just prior to World War II, consumption of a number of products had higher sales figures than they ever had. For example, cotton production increased worldwide and reached a new all-time high (Roche, 1994) and direct-mail order catalogues became a great success (Boorstin, 1973) which has largely been credited to two men: A. Montgomery Ward and Richard Warren Sears. However, even though sales figures for certain products were looking up, this was all to change when the war started.

1939–1970

World War II

Kurt Lewin, a social psychologist, was born in Prussia (now part of Poland) and studied for his doctorate at the University of Berlin. In 1930, he was invited to spend a six-month period as a visiting lecturer at Stanford University and due to the unsettling events happening in Europe he decided to settle in the USA. His first permanent position in the USA was at the Cornell School of Home Economics in 1933 from which he moved in 1935 when he accepted a position at the University of Iowa (Hothersall, 1994).

In World War II, the Department of Agriculture in the US called upon Kurt Lewin to help convince Americans to eat high protein foods such as hearts, kidneys and livers. With a food shortage appearing inevitable, it was more important than ever to ensure that nothing edible and nutritious was wasted. Lewin had a strong conviction that psychological theories were best implemented in applied settings (Lewin, 1944), so it would seem that he was the ideal candidate for the job.

The Department of Agriculture wanted to ensure that the nation stayed healthy and with shortages of other foods, the only solution was to encourage people to eat meat products that previously had often been thrown away. Lewin's solution was to compare how to most effectively get housewives involved in wanting to eat intestinal meats. He set up a study in which two groups of housewives were invited to take part. The first group were repeatedly told that it was beneficial for them to eat intestinal meats. Rather than being asked what they thought about it, they were lectured to, while the other group were invited to participate in a small group discussion. During the discussion they were asked by a leader to help solve the food shortage problem by focusing on whether or not others like them could be persuaded to take part in an intestinal meat programme. It was found that 32 per cent of those who participated in the discussion later on served intestine for dinner (Lewin, 1947). Hence, Lewin demonstrated that level of involvement could increase the likelihood of being persuaded.

Even though times were hard during the war, the consumer society continued to grow, even if this did not affect all corners of the world and perhaps not always in an expected way. This was the time when the world was exposed to commercial television broadcasting. On the 1st of July in 1941, an American TV station called WNBT started broadcasting programmes incorporating TV commercials (Kirkeby, 2004). But commercial broadcasting was to be severely reduced in 1942. Even though Americans might not have had the pleasure of commercial TV after 1942, it was still reported that 58 per cent of all the families in America had at least one car (Lebergott, 1993), so not all consumption pleasures died out totally.

After World War II

After World War II consumption around the world gradually started picking up again and consequently a renewed interest in advertising also emerged. Then a man called Ernest Dichter decided to introduce Freudian concepts into the US advertising industry. Dichter was interested in understanding consumers' unconscious minds as he thought that consumer spending was reflected by their unconscious desires. Dichter was born in Vienna and immigrated to America in 1937. After less than 10 years in New York, he set up the Institute for Motivational Research. Dichter's ideas were made famous in a best-selling book that was written by Vance Packard (1957). The book revealed the role of psychologists in developing selling techniques that were not always evident to the consumer, so Packard called them 'hidden persuaders'.

It was also around about this time that George Katona pioneered the use of how to apply survey research to consumer buying. Katona was born in Hungary in 1901 and trained in psychology, but later became more interested in economics. Katona was one of the co-founders of the Survey Research Center at the University of Michigan where he worked between 1946 and 1972. It was also during this time that he researched consumers' expectations of financial issues which were summarized in the 'Index of Consumer Sentiment' (ICS). The ICS has since been used in many studies and it indicates whether consumers are optimistic or pessimistic about the financial future (Wärneryd, 1999). Through the use of the ICS, Katona found that when consumers felt confident, they were more willing to enter into new credit agreements (Lea, 1999).

Governments promote consumer societies

With World War II now part of history, governments around the world were looking at ways to strengthen their economies. One obvious way of doing so was to increase consumer spending, so in the 1950s politicians were busy promoting the benefits of living in a consumer society (Hilton, 2007). This again led to an increase in advertising and this was one of the reasons why a lot of research was conducted during the 1950s and 1960s on questions related to attitudes and persuasion (e.g. Hovland, Janis, & Kelley, 1953; Janis et al., 1959).

This was also when the UK opened its first commercial television station, ITV. In 1955, ITV went on air and even though the channel initially did not have as many viewers as hoped for, by 1958, they had 5 million viewers. ITV ruled the airwaves as the only commercial television station in the UK for a considerable period of time but this came to an end in 1982 when Channel 4 was launched (*Marketing*, 2005). Since the 1950s there has been a rapid growth in commercial channels around the world. For example, TV3 started broadcasting in Scandinavia in 1987, 2×2 started broadcasting in Russia in 1990, while Croatia's first private commercial television station, Nova, was launched in 2000.

The continuous growth of consumption made it almost inevitable that psychologists with an interest in consumer-related topics would want their own organization. In 1960, Division 23 of the American Psychological Association was established. It was then called the Consumer Psychology Division and it was only in 1988 that the name changed to The Society for Consumer Psychology (which is its current name).

During the 1960s a string of well-known consumer behaviour books also were published (e.g. Engel, Kollat, & Blackwell, 1968) and the *Annual Review of Psychology* published the first article reviewing Consumer Psychology as a subject area and the article was written by Dik Twedt (1965). The rest, as they say, is history!

Summary

Consumer Psychology is the study of human behaviour and thought processes in relation to products and services as well as how people are affected by consumer activities. How individuals are influenced by consumption may be seen by how they choose their material possessions. By choosing the 'right' kind of products, they can display their identities to others. Another example of how consumption can influence people's lives is through the media that they are exposed to. Researchers have found that this has the capacity to impact upon the values and beliefs that people hold.

The road to understanding consumer behaviour has been long and is still being built. The consumer society in which we live today was rapidly moulded once the Industrial Revolution started. In parallel with the growth of consumption, a string of scientists have contributed valuable research that became the underpinnings of Consumer Psychology. In the late 1800s Wundt researched attention, James acknowledged that possessions affect who you are and Gale investigated the effects of advertising on attention. In the early 1900s Hollingworth, Watson and Poffenberger were some of the people who added to the ever growing amount of consumption-related research, and Lewin, Dichter and Katona were significant contributors in the latter part of the century.

Discussion questions

1 Why is it important to have a clear understanding of research methods when studying Consumer Psychology?
2 Is it good or bad to live in a consumer society?
3 When was the consumer society in which we live in today, established?
4 Are material possessions important?
5 How did the invention of the assembly line change consumer behaviours?

CHAPTER 2

Consumer memory and learning

Introduction

This chapter introduces you to how our memory system works, and the different ways in which consumers can learn about products and services. It is important to have an understanding of both areas if one wishes to truly understand consumer behaviour. Knowing how memory works helps marketers to understand why consumers forget certain marketing messages, and what can be done to help them remember product information. Awareness of different methods of learning can shed some light on what can be done to ensure that consumers are 'taught' to engage in specific types of consumption behaviour.

Consumer memory

Memory is an active mental system that receives, stores, organizes, alters and recovers information (Baddeley, 1990). Without understanding how our memory works, it will not be possible to fully appreciate how consumers reason, make decisions and solve problems, since most consumer decisions are dependent on memory (Alba, Hutchinson, & Lynch, 1991). Memories are personal records of past experiences which can help us to learn new information, affect how we perceive stimuli (Palmeri & Gauthier, 2004), and at times, guide our behaviour (Dougherty, Gronlund, & Gettys, 2003). It is therefore unfortunate for marketers and advertisers that consumers tend to have poor memories for brand names, prices and attribute information (Keller, 1987; Meyers-Levy, 1989; Morwitz, Greenleaf, & Johnson, 1998).

Purchase decisions are often made hours, days, weeks or even months after the consumer was originally exposed to the product information and with limited memories of specific product attributes, advertising has only a limited impact upon the decisions made. For consumers to remember any product- or service-related information at a later date, they need to encode and store that information. The

process of **encoding**, **storage** and **retrieval** (when information is remembered) suggests that our minds function in a similar fashion to a computer (see Figure 2.1).

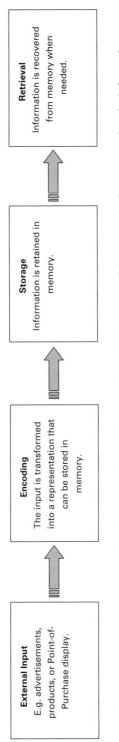

| **External Input**
E.g. advertisements, products, or Point-of-Purchase display. | → | **Encoding**
The input is transformed into a representation that can be stored in memory. | → | **Storage**
Information is retained in memory. | → | **Retrieval**
Information is recovered from memory when needed. |

The human memory processes function in a similar fashion to a computer in that they follow a particular pattern whereby information needs to be transformed into something comprehensible before it can be stored and then retrieved.

FIGURE 2.1 Memory processes.

When encoding information, the consumer transforms the stimuli they encounter into a representation that can be stored in memory. At this stage it is important that they fully recognize and understand the stimuli they have encountered. If the stimuli are ambiguous, the consumer may find it difficult to make sense of the information and consequently fail to store it in their memory. After having encoded the information, the consumer then stores the information in their memory so that it can later be retrieved when they need to access it. Retrieval of product information (or any other type of information) starts with the activation of a node. A node is a particular piece of information that has been stored in long-term memory. When the node is activated, it is transferred from long-term memory to short-term memory so that a person becomes conscious of the product-related information.

Memory systems

Several theories of memory are based on the assumption that our memory consists of three components: sensory memory, short-term memory, and long-term memory (e.g. Atkinson & Shiffrin, 1968). Not all psychologists support the idea of three separate components but it remains one of the most influential models of memory (Matlin, 1998) and many information processing systems are built on this premise (e.g. Bettman, 1979; Sternthal & Craig, 1982). Together the three components are thought to be necessary in order for us to process, store and later access information relevant to our ongoing behavioural goals (see Figure 2.2).

Sensory stores

The sensory stores allow us to store information received through different input modalities (i.e. vision, touch, smell, taste, and hearing) for very brief periods of time. The information lingers for some time after the end of stimulation, enabling the individual to extract the most important features for further analysis. For example, a person might be bombarded with a multitude of different visual and auditory stimuli while walking through a busy shopping district. Most of this cacophony of sights and sounds are of no particular significance, but there may be a tune heard through a specific shop door that captures the person's attention – even though it is only heard for a second or two. In such cases, the stimulus may warrant further investigation.

It has been found that visual information decays within approximately 0.5 seconds (Sperling, 1960) while auditory information lasts for around 2 seconds (Darwin, Turvey, & Crowder, 1972). Provided the information exposed to is of interest and consequently retained for further processing, it is then transferred to short-term memory.

Short-term memory (STM)

Short-term memory (STM) is a system for storing information for brief periods of time and it has a limited capacity (but not as limited as the sensory stores). It deals with the information that is currently being processed. The limitations of the STM were

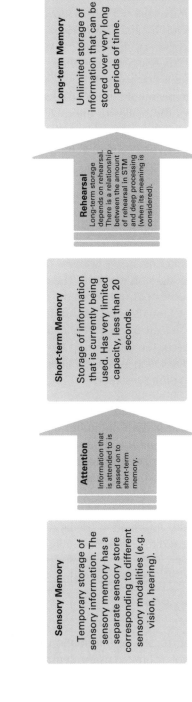

Sensory Memory

Temporary storage of sensory information. The sensory memory has a separate sensory store corresponding to different sensory modalities (e.g. vision, hearing).

Attention

Information that is attended to is passed on to short-term memory.

Short-term Memory

Storage of information that is currently being used. Has very limited capacity, less than 20 seconds.

Rehearsal

Long-term storage depends on rehearsal. There is a relationship between the amount of rehearsal in STM and deep processing (when its meaning is considered).

Long-term Memory

Unlimited storage of information that can be stored over very long periods of time.

The three components of memory demonstrate how there is a relationship between sensory memory, attention, short-term memory, rehearsal and long-term memory.

FIGURE 2.2 Three components of memory.

demonstrated by George Miller (1956) when he conducted a series of digit span tests. In his studies, participants were asked to repeat in the correct order a series of digits that they had heard. Miller found that most could repeat seven digits without making mistakes but most people find it very difficult to repeat more than that. From his studies he concluded that STM has a capacity of seven digits, give or take two digits either way. Hence the STM appears to have the capacity to deal with 'seven plus or minus two' pieces of information at any given time. However, it is possible to increase the amount of information that the STM is capable of dealing with by grouping information together into meaningful units of information, this is known as **chunking**. Regardless of whether the pieces of information are small or large, people still recall approximately seven items at any time (Newell & Simon, 1972).

When people are presented with more information than the STM can deal with, they tend to more readily recall information that was either presented at the beginning or at the end. This is known as the **order effect** (McCrary & Hunter, 1953). Glanzer and Cunitz (1966) demonstrated the order effect when they presented their participants with a list of words and asked them to recall the words in any order they liked. The findings demonstrated that participants generally recalled the first (*primacy effect*) and the last (*recency effect*) few words especially well. From this, they concluded that the primacy effect occurred because the first few words had, through rehearsal, already entered long-term memory. The recency effect occurred because the last few words were still held in short-term memory at the time of recall, but the words in the middle of the list were lost from memory because they were replaced by the later words. This clearly has implications for advertisers and marketers in that they ought to present the information they hope that consumers will remember first or last in their marketing messages, although this will necessarily depend on the amount of information presented.

Long-term memory (LTM)

Unlike STM, long-term memory (LTM) does not have a limited capacity – it is essentially infinite – and once our memories have reached the long-term store, they are there for a very long period of time, perhaps forever (for differences between STM and LTM, see Figure 2.3). Information is transferred from STM to LTM provided

Properties	Short-Term Memory	Long-Term Memory
Capacity	Seven items plus or minus two	Unlimited
Duration	Eighteen seconds	Permanent
Information loss	Rehearsal failure	Retrieval failure
Coding	Acoustic (connected to sound)	Semantic (connected to meaning)

FIGURE 2.3 Differences between short-term and long-term memory.

that a person thinks about the meaning of stimuli encountered and relates it to other information already stored in LTM. The more integrated the information is in LTM, the easier it will be to remember.

The structure of LTM is like a massive integrated spider's web. Each consumer-related piece of information that is stored is also directly or indirectly linked to other pieces of information also stored in LTM so that they form an associative network (Anderson, 1983, 1993). For example, the first thing that springs to mind when you hear the brand name Mercedes may be 'exclusive cars'. However, as you continue to think about it, you may also be thinking about Formula One (as Mercedes are one of the sponsors), then Lewis Hamilton (as he is one of the Formula One drivers), then Naomi Campbell (because she attended a few Formula One races), then other supermodels, and so forth. The longer you think about it, the less directly associated the thoughts may become. But nevertheless they are directly or indirectly related to the original piece of information encountered (see Figure 2.4 for an example of a cognitive associative network). The proximity of the relationship between certain associations and brand names or products can be tested by what is known as **response-time methods** (e.g. Collins & Loftus, 1975; Herr, Farquhar, & Fazio, 1996). In such tests, statements are typically presented and the participants are requested to press either a true or a false button as quickly as they can, depending whether they believe the statements are correct or not. Longer response times indicate that the associations are further away from what is being tested and shorter times that there is a close association between the two. The method is also useful in mapping out consumers' cognitive representations of particular brands and products.

Associations can be formed between anything and they may happen consciously or subconsciously. Just by thinking about two concepts simultaneously we can form an association between them even though they may not have been related to start off with. Our associative mental networks play a part in what is known as the **priming effect** which is when existing information is used to guide our judgements about other pieces of information that we come across. For example, after watching violence on the news it seems much more likely that people's lives will be affected by violent events (Fischhoff, Lichtenstein, Slovic, Derby, & Keeney, 1981).

How information is organized has an impact upon how easily information can be stored in, and retrieved from, LTM. Researchers have found that when multiple items of information are comprehensible and clearly linked together, they are more easily remembered than if they were not (Bransford & Johnson, 1972). Pieces of information that are clearly grouped together enhance memory performance. This was found in a study where participants were presented with a list of different types of minerals and were afterwards asked to recall as many as possible. Most participants could only name a few of the minerals from the list, However, recall was greatly improved when minerals on the list were grouped together into specific categories such as rare, precious stones and masonry stones (Bower, Clark, Lesgold, & Winzenz, 1969).

The multi-store model of memory is simplified in that it only really provides the

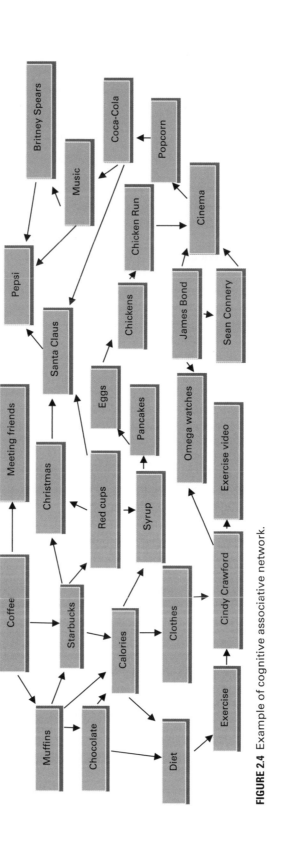

FIGURE 2.4 Example of cognitive associative network.

very basics of how memory works. There is evidence that the STM is not a unitary store (e.g. Warrington & Shallice, 1972) and instead it appears that it consists of separate subsystems (e.g. Baddeley & Hitch, 1974). This has also been suggested for LTM in that it may consist of several long-term memory systems which focus on particular types of information. For example, there may be an **episodic memory** (memories of specific events that happened at a particular place and at a particular time) and **semantic memory** (memories of general factual knowledge about the world) (Tulving, 1972, 1983). In particular, the distinction between an episodic and semantic memory is commonly acknowledged by consumer researchers and practitioners. Commercials often try to trigger episodic memories by focusing on experiences that are shared by a large number of people. In this way consumers' experiences become blurred with what was presented in the commercial (e.g. Holden & Vanhuele, 1999; Skurnik, Yoon, Park, & Schwarz, 2005).

Even though the multi-modal model has been criticized as providing an overly simplified framework for understanding the complexity of our memory system, it still functions as a good foundation for understanding how human memory plays a part in consumer behaviour.

Remembering and forgetting

Techniques that help individuals remember previously encountered marketing information and why they forget some of it clearly have an impact upon consumer behaviour. Psychologists have come up with a number of different reasons for why people remember and forget and there are two theories that are particularly applicable to Consumer Psychology: (1) *Encoding specificity* (which functions as a memory aid); and (2) *interference* (which typically impairs memory).

Encoding specificity
Research has found that our ability to recall information is influenced by the level of similarity between encoding and retrieval conditions (i.e., our ability to recall previously experienced information will be sensitive to any environmental changes which occur between learning and recalling that information). In 1973, Tulving and Thomson found that people remember events much better if they are in the same environment as the one where the information was first learned. This observation was explored further when Godden and Baddeley (1975) set out to test whether long-term memory is context dependent. In their study they asked scuba divers to learn a list of words, either while they were 20 feet under water or were above water. Their findings supported the encoding specificity hypothesis in that memory performance was best when encoding and retrieval took place in the same environment.

The encoding specificity principle lends support to the importance of effective in-store advertising. If the context of an advert can be created at the point of sale, it can aid recognition and recall of product information (Bettman, 1979; Lynch & Srull, 1982). However, it is important that the same type of stimulus is used as it will otherwise fail to produce better recall. For example, if a consumer was originally exposed to a visual stimulus, exposure to a visual element at a later point in time is more likely to trigger recall than an auditory one (Costley, Das, & Brucks, 1997).

Interference

For a long time the theory of interference was one of the most common explanations for why people forget. Interference occurs when memory performance is reduced due to having learned additional information that is preventing a consumer from remembering another particular piece of information (Tulving & Psotka, 1971). There are two types of interference: proactive and retroactive. **Proactive interference** is when new learning is disrupted by old information and **retroactive interference** is when the forgetting of previously learnt information is caused by the learning of new information. The greater the similarity between memory traces, the greater the degree of interference (Wickens, 1972). For example, let's say that an individual is exposed to two commercials of a similar nature in a row. When they are later trying to remember the second commercial, they may actually remember the first one (proactive interference). The more similar advertisements or commercials are (e.g. same product category or products made by the same manufacturer), the more likely consumers are to experience interference (Burke & Srull, 1988). However, the interference effect ceases when consumers are exposed to brand names that they are already highly familiar with (Kent & Allen, 1994).

It is worth pointing out that interference does not have the same effect when the consumers intentionally try to forget information. In such situations it has been found that old information can be temporarily blocked out, meaning that new product information can be more easily retrieved (Shapiro, Lindsey, & Krishnan, 2006).

Implicit memory

Previously, consumer-related research has mainly focused on the effects of explicit memory ('when performance on a task requires conscious recollection of previous experiences', Graf & Schachter, 1985, p. 501) upon consumer behaviour. However, this gradually changed, especially during the past 15 years, when researchers realized that implicit memory ('when performance on a task is facilitated in the absence of conscious recollection', Graf & Schachter, 1985, p. 501) can play an equally important role.

Implicit memory tasks are commonly used in decision-making processes, meaning that consumers are often unaware of what influenced their product choice. The assumption that there is a clear distinction between explicit and implicit memory is becoming more apparent in research focused upon consumer memory and it has been suggested that implicit tasks are more effective when it comes to measuring the impact of advertising (e.g. Lee, 2002) and that it may be more long-lasting than explicit memory (Finlay, Marmurek, & Morton, 2005).

One study that demonstrates the difference between implicit and explicit memory was conducted by Jacoby, Kelley, Brown and Jasechko (1989). They found that new unfamiliar names presented to participants can be mistakenly identified as famous names 24 hours later. The most likely reason for this finding is that the names would later be familiar to the participant, and this familiarity would be confused with fame. However, if subjects were told at the outset that all the names were newly constructed, they later judged the names as non-famous. This effect has also been found to work with brand names (Holden & Vanheule, 1999).

How can marketers aid consumer memory?

Marketers can use a number of different techniques to ensure that their products and services are more likely to be remembered than all the other competitors' stimuli that consumers encounter. Such techniques involve continuously repeating marketing messages, and use of pictures.

Repetition

Repeatedly exposing consumers to marketing stimuli can increase the likelihood of recalling them (e.g. Unnava & Burnkrant, 1991) as well as strengthen associations between specific attributes and brand names (Burke & Srull, 1988). Consumers do not have to be frequently exposed to the exact same marketing message, and it has been found that using different ads to advertise the same brand can be even more effective when it comes to increasing the likelihood of recall (Unnava & Burnkrant, 1991).

Repeated exposure works best when consumers have little or no involvement with the stimuli they are exposed to, as repetition then increases the likelihood of moving information from STM to LTM (Krugman, 1965). Consumers are also much more likely to believe the messages they are repeatedly exposed to when they are not motivated to scrutinize the message content (Hawkins & Hoch, 1992).

Additionally it has also been found that repetition is not as effective in improving memory performance when competitive interference occurs due to the similar nature of other messages that people are exposed to just before or after the intended target stimulus (Burke & Srull, 1988). One way of dealing with interference, in order to make repetition more effective, is to make use of cues that are unique in some way so that consumers cannot confuse them with other marketing stimuli (Keller, 1987).

Pictorial cues

Pictorial stimuli are more likely to capture attention which explains why most consumers tend to look at visual stimuli before they look at the text that often accompanies the picture (Kroeber-Riel, 1986). There is little doubt that pictures are essential when it comes to clearly presenting short messages and stories (e.g. Mandel, Petrova, & Cialdini, 2006) and that they can improve memory and aid recall (Lord, 1980; Swann & Miller, 1982). When information is presented using visual stimuli, it is more likely to be recognized at a later time (Childers &

Houston, 1984). This suggests that when consumers have been exposed to advertising that incorporates pictures, the product advertised will be more easily remembered at the point of purchase, provided that the right cues are in place (such as a point-of-purchase display using similar imagery to an ad) to trigger recall. Additionally making use of pictures that have deeper meaning and are of a slightly complex nature can also ensure that they will be remembered just as well by older consumers (e.g. Park, Royal, Dudley, & Morrell, 1988).

Marketing to older consumers

Because cognitive processes change when people get older, marketers may have to rethink some of the strategies they use when targeting older consumers. The impact of aging upon the memory process is not entirely clear (Kausler, 1994; Schaie, 2005) and it is difficult to know to what extent research findings are applicable to all older people. Nevertheless there are a number of research findings that Consumer Psychologists should be aware of when working with older populations.

One effect of aging is that the speed of processing generally slows down (Cerella, 1985; Salthouse, 1996). In particular, it appears that people's short-term memory is affected (Moscovitch & Wincour, 1992) and consequently older individuals cannot always easily store information about lots of different products and brands, which may in turn explain why they are less likely to spend time searching for and looking at additional product information (Lambert-Pandraud, Laurent, & Lapersonne, 2005; Lin & Lee, 2004).

Older consumers also find it harder to remember pictorial information, and where they heard or saw something (McIntyre & Craik, 1987). Additionally they can also become confused about whether they actually heard or saw information (Light, LaVoie, Valencia-Laver, Albertson Owens, & Mead, 1992) as well as whether the person who told them was a man or a woman (Bayen & Murnane, 1996). The outcome of this is that they often remember things incorrectly (Norman & Schachter, 1997; Tun, Wingfield, Rosen, & Blanchard, 1998). To ensure that older consumers will correctly remember the information they are exposed to, marketing stimuli need to be presented in a way that is meaningful and consequently easily fits into their schema (for definition see page 67) (Park et al., 1988; Smith, Park, Cherry, & Berkovsky, 1990). The reason why putting things into context aids recall is most likely because it facilitates integration within a reduced capacity memory system (Craik, 1986; Park, Smith, Morrell, Puglisi, & Dudley, 1990).

However, if it is necessary to present older consumers with complex information, it may be best to try and do so during the morning. It has been found that they are more easily persuaded during the morning hours when faced with information that is harder to process (Yoon, Lee, & Danziger, 2007) which may be due to the fact that their processing resources have not yet been exhausted.

Learning

From reading the section on memory, you will know that consumers must encode and store information before they can remember it. So by learning about memory, you have also learned some of the cognitive processes involved in learning. However, there is more to learning than memory. Learning can be defined as a relatively permanent change in behaviour which is linked to experience. The experiences that affect learning can be direct ones (using a product) or indirect ones (observing somebody else using a product). Learning in general can be viewed as consisting of five elements: internal drive, cue stimuli, response, reinforcement and retention (as seen in Figure 2.5):

1 *Internal drive*: Encourages an individual to take action to learn. The likelihood that learning will occur may be influenced by an emotional response such as fear or happiness.

2 *Cue stimuli*: This is when a consumer encounters an external stimulus that encourages learning. Such stimulus could be an advertisement, a point-of-purchase display or perhaps a leaflet. Cues are not generally as influential as internal drives in the learning process.

3 *Response*: This is the way in which consumers respond to both the internal drive and cue stimuli. If the internal drive comes together with the cue, then the likelihood of purchase increases. However, future purchases will be determined on the experiences they have after having tested the product and not on the combined drive and cue response.

4 *Reinforcement*: The consumer experiences a positive outcome of some kind as the result of having consumed/purchased a particular product or service. For example, it may be due to affirmative feedback from others or from the product's functionality. If the product purchase is not positively reinforced, the consumer will continue to try different purchases until their needs are satisfied.

5 *Retention*: This is whether or not the learned material reaches long-term memory and can subsequently be remembered.

Most kinds of learning are based upon an association between two mental representations (Dickinson, 1980). For example, we may learn to associate the brand Mercedes-Benz with luxury. Much of what the consumer learns is incidental, even though some learning is intentional. There are three main schools of thought as to how consumers learn: behavioural theories, cognitive theories and social theories. All three will be outlined here in turn.

Behavioural learning

The behaviourist school of learning focuses entirely on the association between an observed stimulus and a response. This approach emphasizes *observable* behaviour and tends to ignore the existence of mental processes involved in

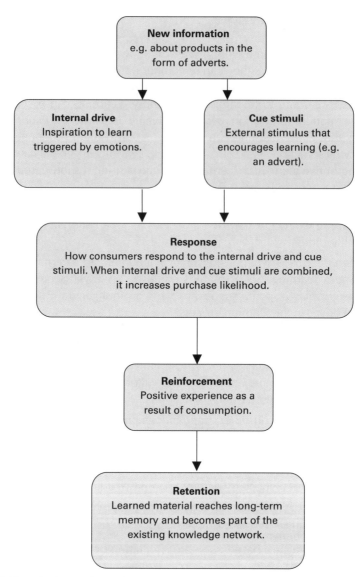

FIGURE 2.5 Five elements of learning.

learning. Behavioural learning techniques have been widely applied to consumption behaviours and two of the most common methods are classical and operant conditioning.

Classical conditioning

Classical conditioning is when a stimulus that elicits a response is learned to be associated with another stimulus that does not originally elicit a response. Ivan Pavlov (1927) was the first to demonstrate the process of classical conditioning. In what was to become one of the most famous experiments in psychology, Pavlov rang a bell every time a hungry dog was fed. On each occasion when the dog realized he was going to be fed, he salivated. After ringing the bell repeatedly every time food was presented to the dog, it was found that the dog salivated upon hearing the bell, even though no food was offered. Hence, the dog had been conditioned into salivating upon hearing the bell.

Prior to the conditioning taking place, the dog had salivated every time it got fed and Pavlov called the food an *unconditioned stimulus* (US) and the dog's response to the food an *unconditioned response* (UR). He also called the bell a *conditioned stimulus* (CS) and when the dog salivated upon hearing the bell, he called it a *conditioned response* (CR). This process is known as first-order conditioning. It is important that the CS is almost immediately preceded by the US. If the timing between the stimuli is changed, the conditioning effect will not be as strong.

The US should preferably be a biologically significant stimulus, meaning that it naturally elicits responses, such as food, sex, or an electric shock. For example, a voluptuous girl in sexy lingerie can make a heterosexual male feel sexually aroused (biological response). The sexual arousal would occur without any prior learning which makes it a US. Sexual imagery is a commonly used marketing technique, ensuring that classical conditioning takes place. See Figure 2.6 for a visual demonstration of the different steps that take place during classical conditioning.

It is important to repeatedly pair the CS with the US, otherwise the conditioning effect may gradually disappear, known as **extinction**. For example, imagine that the CS were to continue to be presented but this time without the US, gradually the likelihood of the CR occurring will decrease. Let's once again use the example of a voluptuous girl in lingerie. The repeated pairing of the girl with a Porsche 911 has led to a number of men feeling aroused upon seeing the 911. However, all of a sudden the advertisements for the 911 change and they no longer contain a sexy-looking woman. The more time that goes by, since having seen the ad with the girl in it, the less likely the men are to feel aroused upon seeing the 911. Hence, extinction has taken place.

Higher-order conditioning

So far what has been outlined is what is known as first-order conditioning, whereby a CS is linked directly with a US. However, there are also other types of classical conditioning such as higher-order conditioning, which is when a CS is not directly linked with the US but instead is paired with an already established CS. For example, a new song by Justin Timberlake that is continuously played in clubs and on the radio will be paired with positive US, such as having fun dancing and nice drinks. After having been repeatedly exposed to the music while enjoying yourself, you will form positive attitudes towards Justin Timberlake's song. His tune is then paired with a new CS such as shampoo in an advertisement. By repeatedly showing the advertisement, positive attitudes will subsequently be formed towards the shampoo.

Music can be a powerful tool in marketing. The impact of music was explored

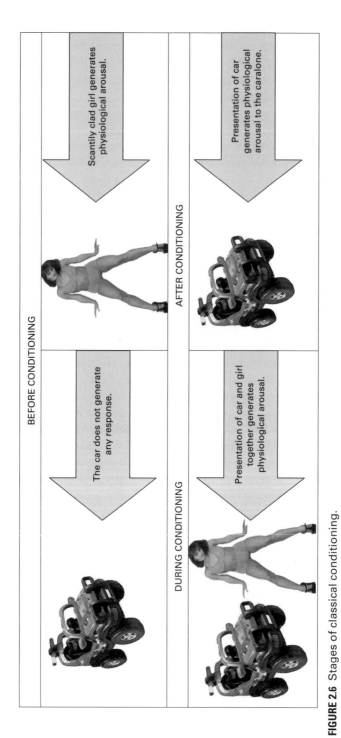

FIGURE 2.6 Stages of classical conditioning.

by Gorn in 1982 when he demonstrated that people tend to prefer products they are exposed to while listening to music that they liked, over other products coupled with music they do not like. However, other researchers have tried to replicate Gorn's findings but with limited success (Allen & Madden, 1985; Kellaris & Cox, 1989), which casts some doubt on whether or not music is always a suitable tool when it comes to enticing consumers. Nevertheless it is generally accepted in the fields of marketing and advertising that the use of music through classical conditioning can create a positive evaluation of a product (Belch & Belch, 1984).

Generally it has been found that most forms of conditioning (apart from first-order conditioning) are rather unstable and that they more easily become extinct. Hence, from a marketing point of view it may be safer to stick to the tried and tested methods of first-order conditioning.

To date, classical conditioning is most commonly applied to advertising, but that is not to say that it cannot be applicable to other consumer-related areas. For example, it has been found that credit cards are closely associated with spending and a positive feeling that arises from purchasing goods and services (Feinberg, 1986). This conclusion was drawn after having found that consumers are willing to pay more for products and donate more money to charity when a credit card logo is present, as well as tip more in restaurants when they paid by credit card. There is little doubt that classical conditioning can be a powerful marketing tool, provided that it is applied correctly. Unfortunately many marketers seem to lack a clear understanding of how classical conditioning should used, resulting in less efficient associative learning (McSweeney & Bierley, 1984).

Operant conditioning

Just like classical conditioning, operant conditioning can also be applied to influence consumer behaviour. Skinner (1953) was the man who introduced the concept of operant conditioning (or instrumental learning as it is sometimes referred to). The word operant refers to a behaviour that has some effect on the world such as asking a shop assistant for help. Depending on the outcome of their actions, the probability may increase or decrease that they will engage in such behaviour again. Naturally, positive outcomes are favoured over negative ones and consequently individuals learn to engage in behaviours that produce positive responses and to avoid those that may result in negative outcomes.

There are two main differences between operant and classical conditioning, the first is the order in which the response appears. In classical conditioning, the response occurs after the stimulus has been presented but in operant conditioning, the response takes place prior to the stimulus being presented. The second difference is that responses in classical conditioning tend to be involuntary while those in operant conditioning are deliberate in that a person is trying to obtain a goal.

Operant conditioning takes place when behaviour is either reinforced or punished. There are two types of reinforcement, positive and negative, and both increase the likelihood of the operant behaviour. *Positive reinforcement* is the use of a reward to demonstrate that a person has engaged in a behaviour that is approved of while *negative reinforcement* is when something unpleasant is removed or terminated, following a desired behaviour. There are also two kinds of punishments, a positive and negative kind, and both decrease the likelihood of the operant behaviour happening again. *Positive punishment* is when an unpleasant stimulus is introduced, and *negative punishment* is when a pleasant stimulus is removed. See Table 2.1 for examples of all four types of conditioning. Generally reinforcement techniques work better than punishment (since people generally prefer it when positive things happen to them), and learning can happen quicker when a reward is given every time a consumer engages in a desired behaviour, which is known

as **continuous reinforcement**. However, **partial reinforcement**, which is when a reward is given infrequently, has been found to make the learning last longer once the reinforcement has been stopped.

How does a stimulus become an effective reinforcer?

Premack (1959) discovered that a good reinforcer is something that individuals like. He conducted a study where children were offered a choice between playing with a pinball machine and eating sweets. When children preferred eating sweets it was found that the rate of playing with the pinball machine could be increased by using sweets as a reinforcer. The same was also found for children who preferred playing with the pinball machine, the number of sweets eaten could be increased by using playing with the pinball machine as a reinforcer. From this, Premack concluded that a person's operant behaviour can be reinforced by offering something as a reward that is perceived as more desirable than the behaviour we wish to reinforce.

Finding something that an individual likes is not difficult, but finding something that a large number of people like can be a bit trickier, and this is a real challenge for marketers wishing to make use of operant conditioning. However, there are

TABLE 2.1 Operant conditioning

Conditioning technique	Stimulus presented as an outcome of behaviour	Effect of stimulus on behaviour
Positive reinforcement	Every time a consumer shops at a Sainsbury's supermarket they can collect points on a store loyalty card that can later be redeemed against their shopping bill.	Increases the likelihood of the consumer returning to a Sainsbury's supermarket.
Negative reinforcement	When a person has a headache they purchase aspirin which relieves it.	Increases the likelihood of purchasing aspirin when having a headache.
Positive punishment	When consumers purchase and drive a 4×4 they have to pay a higher road tax.	Decreases the likelihood of people buying and driving 4×4s.
Negative punishment	A parking lot decides to charge for its parking. Hence removing the privilege of free parking.	Decreases the likelihood of people using the parking lot again.

For a given operant behaviour, reinforcement increases the likelihood of future recurrence, whereas punishment decreases the probability that it will be repeated.

some positive reinforcers that appear to be working well, such as getting points on a reward card every time you buy something in a particular shop, something that has been implemented by a number of shops around the world, for example, Sainsbury's, and Boots in the UK and H&M in Sweden.

Cognitive learning

This type of learning focuses upon internal mental processes. Unlike the behavioural learning approach that focus on behaviours and *what* is learnt, the cognitive approach to learning concentrates on *how* something is learnt. Cognitive learning theorists are interested in how people think about particular products and services, in the hope that they can predict their preferences and choice. It is generally assumed that people are rational in the way that they think and that preferences are created after consumers develop conscious hypotheses that they then act upon.

Most cognitive models for how people learn and remember meaningful information are similar in nature. They generally consist of a number of steps that individuals need to go through in order to be able to store and retrieve encountered materials (e.g. Derry, 1990). The cognitive learning process can be divided into five main aspects: (1) attention; (2) comprehension; (3) learning; (4) recall and reconstruction; and (5) feedback (see Figure 2.7).

1 *Attention*: The first aspect of cognitive learning is that a marketer needs to ensure that they capture consumers' attention. If they fail to do so, their marketing messages simply become part of the clutter that is processed only momentarily and quickly replaced by something else (for further discussion of attention, see Chapter 3).

2 *Comprehension*: New information is entered into STM which is rapidly analysed and the consumer will determine whether or not it interests them. This might be achieved by searching for keywords or symbols to identify what the information is about. For example, an advert for ice cream featuring a football player may be disregarded because the individual has no interest in football and they think the ad is sport related. Generally, whatever cues capture a person's attention will be used to evaluate whether or not to think further about what they have been exposed to.

The new information entered into STM is simultaneously influenced by previous information already stored in LTM. Provided the new information somehow links up with prior knowledge, the individual is likely to think further about the stimulus they have encountered (depending on what other kind of elements may be competing for their attention). If the marketing information is targeting a 'novice' audience, it is imperative that the information is unambiguous and easy to understand. However, if the target audience is mainly those with previous experiences of a particular product or service, then the clarity of the message is not as important. For example, an advert for a new laptop can incorporate technical terminology provided individuals

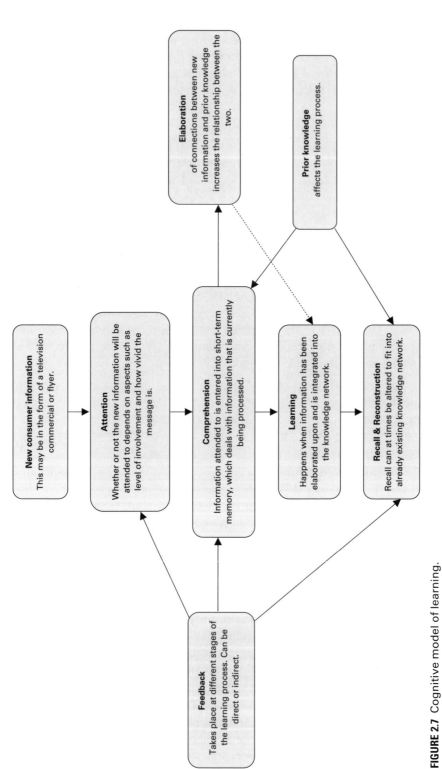

FIGURE 2.7 Cognitive model of learning.

Source: Adapted from Derry (1990).

have good prior knowledge of laptops but if the manufacturer is targeting those who have never previously bought one, the use of 'jargon' should be avoided.

3 *Learning* will take place once the information has been elaborated upon and integrated with the individual's existing store of knowledge. The new details can fit into the existing network of knowledge or they can actually alter it. If consumers do not think further about the message, the information is unlikely to be stored in LTM.

4 *Recall and reconstruction*: Due to the fact that consumers are exposed to so many consumer-related stimuli, it is often difficult for them to remember the exact information presented to them. Instead they will recall the gist of the message rather than the exact wording. However, if the message is ambiguous, they may reconstruct what they have seen or heard so that it fits into already existing **cognitive scripts** (e.g. Bartlett, 1932). This means that sometimes when consumers recall a message, it can be very different from the actual message itself.

5 *Feedback*: Consumers will receive feedback at various stages of the learning process and it is an important determinant in whether or not they will elaborate upon the message, integrate it into already existing information held in memory, whether or not they will receive the information in a positive manner, and so forth. The feedback may be direct or indirect and can come from culture, family, friends, peers, product experience, advertising, and the mass media. The feedback received will be integrated with already existing memories which will in turn affect what kind of information that consumer will focus on and learn in the future.

High and low involvement learning

How involved (or interested) a consumer is will have an impact upon how much they will wish to think about the product information presented to them and to what extent they are keen to learn about new products and services. Significant information processing is unlikely to take place when consumers have little or no interest in the product or service. However, consumers who think extensively about products and marketing messages that they encounter are far more likely to learn about them. In order to ensure that it is not only consumers with high levels of involvement who learn, marketers frequently repeat their messages. Consequently one of the most common forms of consumer learning is through repetition (*rote learning*). Consumers are repeatedly exposed to the same jingles, advertisements and brand names, in hope that rote learning will take place. Rote learning can happen through exposure to both visual (*iconic rote memory*) and auditory (*echoic rote memory*) stimuli. Learning through repetition only generates weakly held beliefs and associations with other pieces of information in LTM and therefore what has been learnt may not be long-lasting. Instead it is better if individuals are allowed to 'discover' information about products by themselves (Lepper, 1985).

It is generally easier for marketers to encourage consumers to learn when they are motivated to do so. If consumers have to make an effort to learn something, they will get more mentally tired and may wish to use their cognitive abilities for other purposes. Hence, consumers keep the information they are exposed to at a minimum, something that has been found to be applicable in situations when the individual has some control over what they are exposed to, such as the Internet. People generally use the same Internet sites repeatedly so that they do not have to learn how to navigate a new one, and are likely to avoid those that are perceived as difficult (Murray & Häubl, 2002; Zauberman, 2002). Consequently, the result is that when individuals conduct online searches for information, they tend to be of a limited nature (Johnson, Moe, Fader, Bellman, & Lohse, 2004).

Consumers' capacity to learn cognitively is also affected by how familiar they are with the products or brands. The less knowledge they have of a product category, the less likely they are to remember the information associated with the product (Lerman, 2003). For example, a person with a keen interest in photography is likely to seek out information in a different way, and learn about different types of digital cameras more rapidly than someone who has no or little experience of photography. Additionally, how easily accessible information is also plays a part in learning process. If the information they require is difficult to come by or unclear, consumer learning is less likely to take place.

Social learning

Social learning is a form of vicarious learning that occurs as a result of observing the behaviour of others as well as the consequences of the behaviour observed. Albert Bandura (1965, 1969) conducted a series of experiments demonstrating how children learn through vicarious social learning. In one of his experiments young children were shown a film of an adult who punched, kicked, and threw things at a Bobo doll (a big plastic doll). The film ended in different ways, depending on which condition the viewers had been assigned to. One group of children saw an adult beating the Bobo doll and at the end they were rewarded for their behaviour. Another group saw a person who was punished for beating the Bobo doll, while a third group saw a person being nasty to the doll but were neither rewarded of punished for their behaviour (this was the control group). Afterwards all children were allowed to play with a Bobo doll while the experimenters were observing them. The children who had seen a film where a person had been rewarded for their cruelty to the Bobo doll, were much more likely to behave aggressively towards the Bobo doll than those in the control group. Conversely, the children who had seen the person punished were less likely than the control group to play in an aggressive manner with the doll.

This shows that observational learning had taken place and that the consequence of the behaviour (being punished or rewarded) acted as a reinforcer for whether or not the children replicated what they had seen. However, in a follow-up study, Bandura, Ross and Ross (1963) found that rewards or punishments are not necessary for social learning to occur. Bandura's research has also been confirmed to be equally applicable to adults, in that adults are often keen to imitate the behaviour of those they admire and respect.

Just as with classical conditioning, social learning is also often used in advertising. For example, if a consumer sees a person that they admire, such as Beyoncé or David Beckham, endorsing a particular product, perhaps Pepsi or Police sunglasses, then they are much more likely to buy the product. Social learning is not only useful for advertising campaigns using celebrities – it can also be effective for product placement in popular TV shows and films.

Expert learners

Those with expertise of particular consumer areas will learn differently from those with little or no knowledge. Research on how experts learn consumer-related information is still relatively new compared to other research areas on learning (e.g. Alba & Hutchinson, 1987). Expertise is achieved when consumers have the capacity to perform product-related tasks in an effective way. This is not the same as being familiar with products and services, even though the experiences from which familiarity is derived can boost an expert's knowledge (Hutchinson & Eisenstein, 2008).

Experts' capacity for learning and adapting information has been found to be considerably greater than novices (Cowley & Mitchell, 2003). For example, consumers with an extensive knowledge of certain products have the capacity to adjust their information to new situations, whereas novice consumers find it difficult to remember products that are suitable for a different usage situation. Consumers with good product knowledge have also been found to remember product experiences better, as well as being less influenced by advertisements aimed at misleading people (Cowley & Janus, 2004).

Key Terms

Chunking
When data is grouped together into meaningful units of information.

Cognitive scripts
Existing knowledge structures that are organized into concepts, e.g. how to behave in a restaurant.

Continuous reinforcement
When a reward is given on each occasion a consumer engages in a desired behaviour.

Encoding
The transformation of sensory input into a form which allows it to be entered into memory.

Episodic memory
Autobiographical memories of events that happened at a particular place and time.

Extinction
When a conditioning effect gradually disappears due to lack of pairing of the conditioned stimulus and the unconditioned stimulus.

Order effect
When information presented at the beginning or at the end is more readily recalled.

Partial reinforcement
When a reward is given infrequently.

Priming effect
When existing information is used to guide people's judgements about other stimuli.

Proactive interference
When new learning is disrupted by old information.

Response-time methods
When people are tested on how rapidly they respond to a stimulus.

Retrieval
When information stored in memory is found when needed.

Retroactive interference
When later learning interferes with the recall of earlier learnt material.

Semantic memory
Our store of general factual knowledge about the world.

Storage
The operation of holding or retaining information in memory.

Summary

For consumers to remember information, they need to encode, store and then retrieve it. Our memory is generally thought to consist of three types: sensory stores, STM and LTM, even though some researchers call for a more complex conceptualization. According to the encoding specificity hypothesis, consumers will recall previously learned information better if the environment in which they are trying to remember resembles the one where they learned it.

Interference can happen when stimuli are similar in nature and this can be combated by repeatedly exposing consumers to a marketing message. Repetition can aid memory, as can the use of good visual stimuli, especially if the message is aimed at older consumers.

Without memory, consumers would not be able to learn about products and services on offer. There are different theoretical frameworks for studying learning, including behavioural, cognitive and social approaches. Behavioural learning emphasizes observable behavioural outcomes, cognitive learning focuses solidly on mental processing and social learning theory puts the spotlight on how people observe others in social settings. All three approaches shed some light on how marketing campaigns might be structured in order to enhance consumer learning.

Class exercise

Show students approximately 20–25 different adverts on a screen (preferably ones that the students may not be too familiar with), one after the other. Let them look at each one of the adverts for around 2–3 seconds. Once they have seen all the adverts, ask them to write down all the adverts that they remember. Discuss which ones they remember and why. Is there a primacy and recency effect? Is their recall limited by the capacity of their STM? Maybe they only remember those that they have previously seen?

CHAPTER

3

Perception and attention

Introduction

Perception and attention are two areas that are integral to understanding consumer processing and choice. The way in which consumer stimuli are evaluated is guided by our perception which is linked to previous experiences. This in turn also affects what kind of stimuli a consumer notices. If consumers do not notice products, they will not be able to purchase them. This chapter outlines the connection between perception and attention, as well as discussing them separately. It seeks to explain why consumers perceive information in the way that they do as well as highlighting aspects that will affect what they pay attention to.

Link between perception and attention

This chapter deals with both perception and attention, since the two are very closely linked. Everything that humans pay attention to will ultimately be affected by the processes involved in perception. Perception starts working as soon as people start scanning for elements to focus upon, something that they do continuously in any environment they find themselves in. How consumers perceive product and services is often influenced by the way in which they are marketed, personal experiences and how they are judged by people's social surroundings.

Perception guides consumers' attention so that they mainly focus on information that they have some sort of interest in. It would be impossible for anybody who lives in a Western society to pay attention to all the marketing stimuli they encounter, as people are constantly bombarded by them. When we go shopping, we are exposed to endless amounts of products packed closely together on shelves, there are billboards on many street corners, a high number of adverts are included in our daily newspapers, and we see and hear commercials on both the television and the radio. Needless to say, consumers do not pay attention to all of them. The fact that we only notice some of the stimuli that we are exposed to, is one of the most obvious parts of attention, as it demonstrates that it generally involves selective processing of certain elements while we ignore others.

Perception

Perception is the way in 'which information acquired from the environment via the sense organs is transformed into experiences of objects, events, sounds, tastes, touch, etc.' (Roth, 1986, p. 81). It is a process whereby stimuli are selected, organized and interpreted. This is not to be confused with *sensation*, since a sensation is information that is simply presented to our different senses but is yet to be interpreted; perception, on the other hand, involves meaning that is attached to the sensations experienced. Such meaning is derived from existing beliefs, attitudes, and general disposition, meaning that the way in which objects are perceived is subjective.

The study of perception is the study of largely unconscious processes through which information in the external environment is attended to, and it is biased by previous experiences so that only certain things appeal to our senses (Eibl-Eibesfeldt, 1988). Our perception is an active process that continuously categorizes and interprets the information provided by our senses. It enables people to almost instantly gain an understanding of what the objects and scenes they encounter mean (e.g. VanRullen & Thorpe, 2001). This is done by linking previous experiences to the stimulus they come across, as well as adapting the way in which they are perceived (e.g. Payne, Bettman, & Johnson, 1992). The information is then co-ordinated to form a perceptual pattern which will subsequently be stored in memory.

Gestalt theories

One aspect of perception that has been very well researched is how features are organized into whole figures. The research was originally conducted by a group of German psychologists in the late 1800s and early 1900s, that became known as the Gestalt school of psychology (Gestalt meaning roughly whole). The name came out of their beliefs that humans tend to be biased to see distinct forms even if they encounter design features that are slightly irregular. Gestalt psychology has undeniably had a major impact on our understanding of perceptual processes (e.g. Gordon, 1989; Roth, 1986). However, part of the critique of the Gestalt laws is that they are difficult to apply to how humans perceive 3D objects (Eysenck, 1993). However, they are applicable to two-dimensional objects such as drawings which also make them highly suitable to integrate into marketing stimuli such as advertising and point-of-purchase displays.

Gestalt psychologists proposed a number of laws (**laws of Prägnanz**) and principles with regard to how stimuli are organized into shapes and patterns so that stimuli are perceived as one complete object, even if you see a stimulus for the first time. Such 'rules' give order to how stimuli are perceived. Some of the most commonly used Gestalt ideas to help understand consumer perception include the law of proximity, the law of closure, the law of similarity and the figure–ground principle.

Law of proximity

Stimuli that are near each other tend to be grouped together (see Figure 3.1 a). For example, if two people are standing near each other and a third person stands 20 feet away from the other two, the third person will be perceived as an outsider or stranger to the other two. Retailers often make use of this principle in that they try to place products close together that they think complement one another in some way so that consumers are more likely to purchase them together. For example, next to the pasta sauces they may place pasta or Italian wines.

Law of closure

When people briefly observe geometrical figures that show irregularities, they fail to notice their incompleteness and instead see them as entire shapes, something that is known as law of closure (see Figure 3.1 b). For example, if a triangle is not entirely complete, people still perceive it as a complete figure due to the fact that individuals make use of prior experience to automatically fill in the gap (Hochberg, 1971). This law of perception explains why consumers are able to fill in the missing letters in words used for marketing purposes. At times advertisements deliberately leave a couple of the letters out because they wish to encourage consumers to interact with the stimuli they encounter in hope that they will pay attention to the message and process the information further. One such example includes a Christmas advert that was used to promote J&B scotch. In that particular advertisement the letters 'j' and 'b' were omitted from the words 'jingle bells', 'jingle bells' and at the bottom it said 'The holidays aren't the same without J&B'.

Law of similarity

The idea of the law of similarity is that humans generally group together objects that are physically similar in some way (see Figure 3.1 c). Wertheimer (1923, p. 119) described it as: 'Other things being equal, if several stimuli are presented together, there is a tendency to see the form in such a way that the similar items are grouped together.'

When categorizing products based on their physical features, consumers often make use of the most salient product features such as colour and shape. Since consumers are automatically using similar features to classify the product, it means

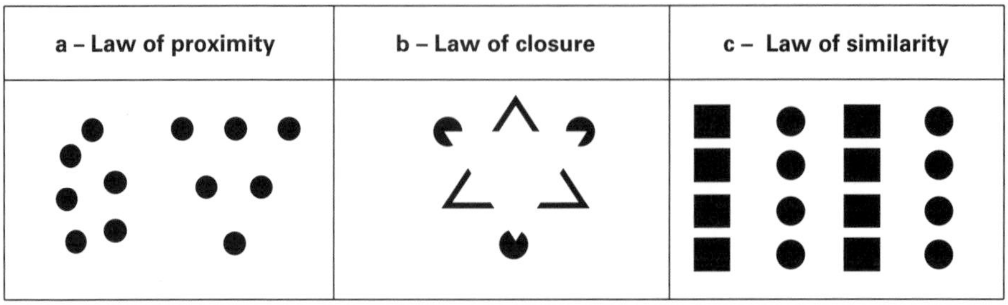

a – Law of proximity	b – Law of closure	c – Law of similarity

FIGURE 3.1 Laws of Prägnanz.

that they perceive them as being essentially the same (Loken, Ross, & Hinkle, 1986). This being why 'own brand products' (such as a supermarket's own cola drinks) are often made to look similar to national brand products (such as Coca-Cola or Pepsi). Additionally, manufacturers also make use of this law if they have an extended product line. They then often try to make the products appear similar in their design so that consumers can easily categorize them as belonging to a particular brand.

Figure–ground principle

The laws of Prägnanz can help explain why humans perceive items as being separate from other surrounding stimuli and as having a distinctive meaningful form. One process that is important in that it enables people to make sense of incoming information, is known as the figure–ground principle. This is a simple concept whereby one part of a stimulus appears to stand out as a solid and well-defined object (the figure), whereas the rest of the stimulus is seen as less prominent (the ground). The more familiar the figure is, the easier it is for individuals to determine whether it ought to be perceived as figure or ground. However, even unfamiliar and non-meaningful shapes can be perceived as figures, as shown in Figure 3.2. Hence familiarity is not necessary for people to perceive form (Carlson, 1987).

There are times when it is unclear which part of a stimulus is the figure and which is the ground, making it possible to perceive a figure in two different ways, something that is known as *figure–ground reversal*. The figure–ground reversal demonstrates how the limited information processing capacity forces people to focus on one stimulus at the time. When you shift between the two patterns in Figure 3.3, you should get a clear idea of figure–ground organization.

Because consumers will only focus on one stimulus at the time, advertisers

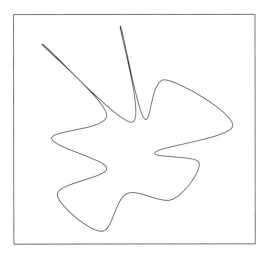

Unfamiliar objects can be perceived as a figure,
provided the outline is closed.

FIGURE 3.2 Example of an unfamiliar object.

What is seen as 'figure' and what is perceived
as 'ground' can vary depending on the viewer.

FIGURE 3.3 Figure–ground reversal.

and marketers often try to make a particular stimulus the focal point. The figure
is typically the information that they wish to stand out and the ground is the information that supports the figure. When using the figure–ground principle, marketers
typically eliminate some of the information that consumers immediately notice and
hence reduce their demands on short-term memory. This means that it can be
easier to process the information and recall it later on.

Use of different senses

The Gestalt theories previously outlined focus mainly on the way in which human
perception is affected by visual input. Of all the senses used, vision is the one that
is most commonly researched and discussed. This is not surprising considering
that visual attention is a vital way to acquire information in consumer (and other)
environments and it does account for approximately 80 per cent of human perception (Levine, 2000). Visual perception enables people to experience the existence
of objects as well as their colour, form and position (Padgham & Saunders, 1975),
and it is said to be a key element in understanding the interaction that consumers
have with point-of-sale displays (Phillips & Bradshaw, 1993). Naturally, this is
partially due to the fact that vision is often the only way to gather information about
products and brands in consumer choice environments.

The first thing that consumers do in consumer environments is to conduct
a visual search in order to locate a target they can focus upon, something that
neuro-anatomic studies have suggested is a key aspect of perception (e.g. Held,
1970). Such visual searches can be guided by underlying motivational factors.
What motivates people also influences the way in which they process visual stimuli

(Balcetis & Dunning, 2006). This was found when participants in a study were presented with an ambiguous figure that could be interpreted as either the letter 'B' or the number '13'. They were told that based on which letter or number they were exposed to they would be assigned to one of two tasks: (1) drinking freshly squeezed orange juice or (2) drinking a nasty smelling and highly unappetizing-looking health drink. The outcome showed that the participants interpreted the ambiguous figure accordingly to which task they wished to be assigned to, hence demonstrating that motivational processes can influence perception.

Even though our vision plays an important part in how consumer stimuli are perceived, it needs to be remembered that most of our knowledge is obtained from more than one sense (Heller, 1982). People's sensory modalities function together in that touch, for example, can influence visual perception of different types of surfaces (e.g. Heller, 1982; Ernst, Banks, & Bulthoff, 2000). Hence, it makes sense that retailers and marketers make use of stimuli that try to influence our perception through the use of other senses and not only through vision.

Hearing

Sounds of different types are frequently used to communicate with consumers. Often noises are simply used to capture their attention but they also have the capacity to alter people's perception. For example, as you walk down a high street, you often hear music that is played in stores, loud and clear from outside the shop. This is partially in hope of capturing people's attention but it is also used to influence the way in which consumers will perceive the shop.

Sounds have the capacity to influence many different aspects of consumer perception, e.g. they can create a favourable mood (Tom, 1990), increase the likeability of products (Gorn, 1982), and affect perception of time (Hui, Dubé, & Chebat, 1997; Yalch & Spangenberg, 2000). The majority of marketing research involves music, which is hardly surprising bearing in mind that consumers are frequently exposed to music in shops, on television, through the radio, and so on. Researchers have found that when music that is clearly perceived to be from a particular country is played within a retail environment, it has the capacity to increase sales figures of products that are manufactured in the country that the music is from (North, Hargreaves, & McKendrick, 1999).

Other sounds that can play a part in how products are perceived are the pitch of the voice used in television commercials. Chattopadhyay, Dahl, Ritchie, and Shahin (2003) found that a low pitched voice that spoke at a faster pace produced an overall more favourable perception of the ad and the brand than other type of voices.

Smell

Different types of odours can make people perceive environments and products in a particular way. Changing the fragrance of a product when it is an integral part of it (such as soap or shampoo) is highly likely to affect the way in which the product is perceived. This is bound to happen even if the quality and overall function of the brand remain the same (Milotic, 2003).

Odours (or scent) can be classified into two distinctive types depending on where it originates from. If the origin is from a particular product, it is generally referred to as *non-ambient scent*, and if it is a general presence such as in a retail environment, it is known as *ambient scent*. Non-ambient scents can be further divided into scents that are either congruent (a product that smells the way it ought to, e.g. a jar of coffee that smells like coffee) or non-congruent (a product that smells inconsistently with expectations, e.g. coffee that smells like strawberries).

Odours in general (includes both ambient and non-ambient scents) have the ability to trigger memories and associations that will make us view certain things in a positive or negative manner. This is why supermarkets make use of the smell of freshly baked bread in hope to make their consumers think that all produce is fresh as well as triggering nice memories of traditional values, which may make us think of experiences such as how our mother used to bake bread and cakes when we were younger. Other types of shops such as those that sell soaps or coffee ensure that potential customers can smell their merchandise long before they are any-where near the front door. This is because 'pleasant' smells have been found to increase the likelihood of the shop and its merchandise being perceived in a positive way (Spangenberg, Crowley, & Henderson, 1996).

Pleasant smells have also been found to impact upon the perception of products, even when there is no immediate link between the two. For example, Nike found that when consumers tried their trainers in a floral scented environ-ment, they showed a clear preference for them than when they tried them in a non-scented room (Lindstrom, 2005).

However, even if the odour is perceived in a favourable manner the strength of the odour used should be controlled as it can otherwise trigger an unfavourable perception of products and retail environments. Researchers have found an inverted u-shape between odour strength and positive reactions (Bone & Ellen, 1999; Chebat & Michon, 2003), meaning that moderate levels of odour will have the most positive influence upon people's perception. This is even applicable to odours that are positively perceived when presented in low concentrations as they can have a negative impact when used in highly concentrated measures.

Just as with auditory stimuli, olfactory cues can also affect consumers' percep-tion of other consumer-related factors, such as the amount of time spent in retail environments. When no scent is present, people have been found to think that they spent longer in a store than they actually did as opposed to when a scent is present (Spangenberg, et al., 1996). Even though there is plenty of research demonstrating that scents can impact upon perception, it is worth noting that it may not always be as straightforward as that, as scent has been found to interact with other factors such as the number of people visiting a retail environment. For example, Michon, Chebat and Turley (2005) found that there is a u-shaped relationship between ambient scent and density of shoppers. Basically a favourable perception of the mall in the presence of a pleasant scent was only found when the density level was moderate. This in turn was also found to generate a favourable perception of product quality.

Touch

Research on how tactile sensations affect the consumer perception of products is still relatively limited, even though in recent years there has been a higher level of interest in the area. Existing studies clearly suggest that touch has the capacity to alter the way in which consumers view objects. This is not surprising bearing in mind that the skin is extremely sensitive to pressure (Montagu, 1986) and the human perceptual system can be just as influenced by the visual and tactile systems when discriminating between stimuli (Ernst & Banks, 2002).

Consumers generally touch objects in order to explore stimuli further, after a visual evaluation, so that they can make some form of discrimination. This is particularly noticeable at an early age when children use touch to explore and evaluate their surroundings (Bushnell & Boudreau, 1991), something that is also carried through into adulthood which is evident from situations such as when people go clothes shopping. First, they tend to visually scan the shop for a garment they like the look of and then touch it in order to determine if it feels the way they expect it to. Hornik (1992) suggested that simply touching a product can make consumers evaluate it in a favourable manner. He drew this conclusion after noticing that consumers were 88 per cent more likely to buy a product that they had touched. However, this is unlikely to be the case if the product does not feel the way consumers expect it to as it is then likely to lead to a less favourable perception of the stimulus (Jansson-Boyd & Marlow, 2007).

Nevertheless, it appears advantageous to let consumers touch products, because if people want to do so and are not allowed, they can become frustrated (Peck, 1999). Such frustration is likely to lead to the consumer perceiving the product in a negative manner (Peck & Childers, 2003a, 2003b).

Taste

Ensuring that people have a direct experience of food products is a good idea in that it has been found to generate attitudes that are much more consistent with consumers' purchase intentions (Smith & Swinyard, 1983). Hence, allowing shoppers to sample food products in-store can be a good way of increasing the likelihood of purchase. Furthermore, giving people taste samples has also been found to decrease the likelihood of their product perception being influenced by in-store stimuli such as labelling used on packets of beef (Levin & Gaeth, 1988).

Because taste can affect the way in which products are perceived, it is important for food and drink manufacturers to understand how different flavours will be evaluated. This is why many manufacturers employ taste test panels to find out whether or not their products are perceived in the way they want them to be. At other times companies also make use of 'blind taste tests' (a test whereby a person tastes a product without knowing which one it is) to find out how consumers perceive products and whether or not they can tell the difference between similar products and brands. Taste tests can be very valuable in that they focus solidly on the taste as opposed to the brand or the design of a product. However, what makes them valuable can also be the downfall in that consumers' taste perception is often guided by brands and visual design features that simply make them think a product tastes better or worse.

Aesthetics

A large part of generating a favourable perception is the physical characteristics that will make the consumer think of a product, display or retail environment as more or less attractive. The way in which products and displays are designed will definitively affect how they are perceived, which is why aesthetics is an area that is increasingly gaining recognition by Consumer Psychologists and marketers alike (Hoegg & Alba, 2008). Despite the fact that aesthetic evaluation impacts on design issues, not many empirical studies in relation to consumer behaviour can be found in the marketing literature (Bamossy, Scammon, & Johnston, 1983; Bloch, 1995). The dilemma for marketers is how to present consumers with information that will generate a favourable perception. Berlyne (1971) suggested that different cultures may be homogenous in their responses to stimuli, which suggests that there are some underlying general concepts that determine consumers' preferences of design in general. He also went on to propose that stimuli that are perceived to be complex, novel and surprising have the capacity to generate a more favourable perception.

Berlyne's ideas led a number of environmental researchers to hypothesize that environments should also be favoured when they are perceived in a particular way (e.g. Herzog, 1984; Herzog, Kaplan, & Kaplan, 1982; Kaplan, 1987). They tested this idea and found that environments that were perceived to be '*mysterious*' (the extent to which a stimulus contains hidden information so that individuals are drawn to it in hope of finding out more), '*complex*' (amount and variety of elements), '*coherent*' (how well elements appear to belong together), and '*legible*' (the degree of distinctiveness that helps the viewer to categorize the contents) generated more favourable aesthetic responses. There is no reason why concepts such as those proposed by Berlyne, Herzog and Kaplan cannot also be applied to products and retail environments. However, this is yet to be tested in an empirically sound way. Nevertheless, making use of already existing concepts might help to generate more favourable consumer perceptions.

Attention

Attention refers to the contents of short-term memory, which can be drawn from both internally and externally presented stimuli (Kahneman, 1973). Wachtel (1967) compared attention to a search light, in that it is briefly directed towards a stimulus that we focus on which we temporarily become conscious of until attention is moved on to the next stimulus and then the next, and so forth. From a marketer's point of view, it is important that they manage to capture the consumers' full attention and that attention stays upon that particular desired focal point, as consumers may otherwise refocus their attention towards competitors' marketing stimuli.

What captures consumers' attention is determined by many factors, such as the relevance of the message and the consumer's motivation. For example, if a consumer has a 'particular' interest, it may direct their attention, such as a fashionable colour that the consumer really likes (Klinger, 1975). Other factors that also play a part in whether or not consumers pay attention to a stimulus include how salient (Greenwald & Leavitt, 1984) and how vivid the message is (Rook, 1986). Some aspects of what capture people's attention (i.e. vividness and salience) are discussed in Chapter 7 about advertising and will consequently not be discussed here. However, both factors have the capacity to capture consumers' attention in many different contexts other than advertising.

What most marketers are aiming for is to ensure that consumers focus their entire attention on a particular stimulus, so that it can be perceived as clearly as possible; this is known as **focal attention** (Schachtel, 1959). Due to the fact that the information consumers pick up from the external environment is temporarily stored in the short-term memory, which can only handle a limited amount of information at any one time (approximately seven units of information), consumers will automatically attend to focal information and neglect non-focal information. Consequently, consumers would be expected to more readily recall the elements that had captured their attention.

Arousal

One particular aspect of how well people focus upon different stimuli is how aroused they are at different points in time. Being alert makes consumers more perceptive to stimuli around them as well as impacting upon the amount of information people can attend to (Kahneman, 1973). Arousal can be measured as a continuum, whereby low levels of arousal are when people are drowsy and very tired or nearly asleep, while high levels are generated by exciting events or physiological stimulants (e.g. caffeine).

Researchers have found that there is an inverted U-relationship between arousal and attention (see Figure 3.4). When arousal levels are low, so is attention. This is perhaps not surprising as most individuals experience great difficulty in paying attention to information when they are tired; something that most students experience at some point when they are doing some last minute, late night 'cramming' for their exams. The attention levels then increase in parallel with our arousal levels up to the point whereby we feel moderately aroused. People's cognitive capacity is at its best when they are moderately aroused and can at that point in time attend to more information than when they experience high or low arousal levels. From there on, the attention levels decrease as the arousal levels increase and consequently over-arousal generates similar effects to what humans experience when they are hardly aroused at all. They will then find it difficult to concentrate due to being over stimulated, perhaps on the verge of restless. In such circumstances it is much easier for people to focus on small amounts of information.

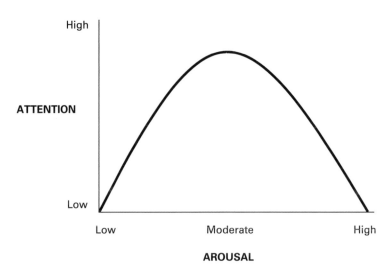

FIGURE 3.4 Relationship between arousal and attention.

Source: Adapted from Kahneman (1973).

The inverted U-relationship demonstrates that it is important for marketers to present information to consumers at a time when they are likely to experience moderate levels of arousal. This is supported by a study whereby viewers of the Super Bowl (the championship of the National Football League in the US) who supported one of the teams playing failed to remember the television commercials shown during the game compared to those who were just watching it for general entertainment purposes. The findings were explained by suggesting that supporters of the two teams playing were highly aroused while watching the game and hence failed to pay attention the commercials (Pavelchak, Antil, & Munch, 1988).

There are many factors that can increase arousal (especially within retail environments), such as noise, smell, flashing lights, temperature and unexpected events. However, all these factors need to be used in moderation as they otherwise may induce too much arousal and subsequently have an undesired affect.

Visual selective attention

The study of visual selective attention is of particular interest to marketers since most consumers initially explore environments visually. Visual selective attention can be defined as the way in which humans select a specific element to focus on and simultaneously manage to ignore all other stimuli that may have the capacity to control an individual's actions (e.g. Tipper & Driver, 2000; Wickens & Hollands, 2000). The element that a person chooses to focus upon is influenced by their perception in that it aids the selection process and continues to direct cognitive processes once the stimulus has been focused upon.

Researchers have found that the first thing humans tend to do in any environment is to conduct a visual search, which is driven by a desire to find specific targets. How consumers conduct visual searches can give retailers and marketers a good insight into where to position products within the retail environment, as well as where to position the most important information on displays, in hope of capturing their attention. In western societies it has been found that most people search environments in a similar fashion to the way they read. Most of the time the search starts at the top left corner of the visual field and the search process is then con-tinued towards the right, across to the left bottom corner and once more towards the right (Megaw & Richardson, 1979). Since search strategies are something that is learnt, they are likely to be culture-specific in that not all cultures read from left to right (e.g. Arabic cultures read from right to left). It has also been suggested that humans also have a tendency to focus their attention towards the centre of any environment or display (Parasuraman, 1986), prior to starting the visual search from top left. However, since much of the visual search is driven by cognitive factors, it is possible that there are no exact consistent patterns of how humans conduct visual searches (Wickens, 1992).

What attracts consumers' attention?

All the senses have the ability to capture consumers' attention, but, just as with perception, most of the attention-based research has investigated vision. That is not to say that stimuli geared towards other senses cannot be equally (and at times even more) efficient than visual stimuli. For example, Morrin and Ratneshwar (2000) found that pleasant ambient scents can increase attention to brand names that are unfamiliar, and in turn also improve recall.

Many different methods can be used to ensure that particular products and marketing stimuli manage to 'break through the clutter' so that consumers will pay attention to them.

Some commonly used methods include buying large blocks of advertising or shelf space in retail environments. That way it will virtually be impossible for consumers not to notice the product marketed and it practically forces them to pay attention to it. Other methods include printing ads upside down as well as putting advertisements in more unusual places where consumers would not normally expect to see them. Undoubtedly, it is getting harder and harder to find such spaces but in recent years putting ads on the back of tube and bus tickets as well as on the back of supermarket trolleys made consumers look twice.

In addition, it is also relatively common to make used of fast paced commercials as they capture audience attention involuntarily (Bolls & Muehling, 2003), as well as making use of unusual stimuli features that can help reduce visual search times in cluttered settings (Roggeveen, Kingstone, & Enns, 2003). It is beyond the scope of this chapter to outline all the possible methods that can be employed to ensure that consumers pay attention to product related information. Hence, what follows is an outline of some of the areas that can impact upon consumers' attention.

Colour

There is little doubt that colour can help attract consumers' attention (Mikellides, 1990) and that humans often spot particularly colourful items (Wickens, 1992). This is because colour is easily detected by our pre-attentive system (Bundesen & Pedersen, 1983), which is readily used to select items for subsequent attentional processing (Kaptein, Theeuwes, & Van der Heijden, 1994). However, using colour to capture consumers' attention can be difficult in that it depends largely on the surroundings in which a colourful item is placed. For example, making use of a bright green display (x) in a retail environment where there are a large number of other displays and items that are also bright green, means that it is unlikely that the display (x) will be noticed. Consequently it can be difficult for marketers to make use of colour as a persuasive or attention-grabbing element (Garber & Hyatt, 2003). Nevertheless there are some research findings that can guide the marketer in regards to how colour may be used to capture consumers' attention. For example it has been suggested that 'basic colours' (i.e. green, red, grey, white, black, blue, orange, yellow, pink, purple and brown) can be more easily identified in highly cluttered retail environments (Jansson, Bristow, & Marlow, 2004). However, this has not been found to be applicable for settings containing fewer stimuli (Boynton & Smallman, 1990).

Using colour to reduce search times and increase the likelihood of consumers paying attention to products is also advantageous in that it is believed to produce favourable product attitudes (in comparison to black and white). This is especially applicable if consumers' processing motivation is low as they then tend to rely on heuristics (a mental shortcut that is a rule of thumb) associated with physical attributes to make judgements (Myers-Levy & Peracchio, 1995).

Novelty

One way of breaking through the clutter and protective selective perception filter is by using novel elements (Berlyne & Parham, 1968). The use of novel elements can be a very powerful tool, as researchers have found that specific areas of our brain respond to such stimuli without awareness (Berns, Cohen, & Mintun, 1997).

Novel products often sell very well in their first year on the market, which can be noted by how well products such as Miller's clear beer did (Lavinsky, 1993). One of the reasons as to why 'novel' products do well is because they can easily capture consumers' attention since they are distinctively different from other products. However, it is worth noting that just as the novelty tends to wear off for new products on the market (hence the decrease in sales after a while), they also capture consumers' attention less as the stimulus is no longer perceived to be novel. This means that marketers can only rely on unique product features for a short while to capture consumers' attention.

It is not just the products that can be made novel, but also the type of marketing techniques used. It may be that an advert looks outstandingly different to all the others and hence consumers will notice it. Other examples include unusual and unique promotional offers that capture an audience attention as well as imagination. For example, at one point a jeweller in the US promised all their customers that if it snowed more than three inches on New Year's Eve they would refund all the purchases made during the Christmas season. Consequently their sales increased over 30 per cent (Ortega, 1993).

Personal relevance and preferences

It can at times be difficult to capture consumers' attention, as they subconsciously may be searching for information that confirms already existing beliefs about products and services. If a consumer has specific goals to start off with, that will affect the types of cues the consumer will pay attention to (Shavitt, Swan, Lowrey & Wänke, 1994). For example, it has been found that people who have an initial preference for a product pay more attention to information that confirmed their preferences than they do to information that disproves their beliefs (Chernev, 2001). Some additional support for this has also been produced by Yeung & Wyer (2004). In a study where they showed participants pictures of products, they found that those who had formed an initial impression of it based upon the visual stimulus later on remembered product information that was consistent with the impression. Hence, the study demonstrates that specific beliefs about products are likely to guide attention towards belief that is consistent information rather than information that is inconsistent with those values or beliefs.

Different people find different types of things interesting. It is therefore hardly surprising that those with a particular interest will spend time seeking out information directly related to them (Goldsmith & Flynn, 1995). Individuals simply cannot be interested in everything. Some may have a passion for handbags, while others may find gardening particularly exciting. Those who are not interested in either handbags or gardening are consequently highly unlikely to pay attention to marketing information about products related to them. Because consumers are so selective when it comes to what they choose to focus their attention upon, marketers do their outmost to get a message across that their particular products are superior to other competitive brands.

If consumers are not interested in a particular product category, it will not matter if the commercial about gardening tools is fast paced, or whether the advertisement for handbags is vivid or salient, as consumers with no interest in the products marketed will still not pay attention to them. Nevertheless, it is worthwhile making use of 'attention-grabbing' factors as not all consumers engage in goal-directed searches and will therefore be open to the influence of other factors (Shavitt et al., 1994).

Brand identity

Since our selective perception filters out information that is incompatible with our interests, creating a clear visual brand identity can be helpful when it comes to making consumers notice products. Ensuring that different types of products that are manufactured by the same brand have visual similarities means that they will be easier to spot and recognize. For example, Apple and Nike are both good examples of what can be deemed prominent visual brand identities. Because such brands are highly recognizable, they easily attract our pre-attentive system, so consumers therefore use little capacity to process the information. Even though consumers may pay little conscious attention to such stimuli, it has been suggested that just the mere repeated exposure to them can produce heightened recognition for them (Zajonc & Markus, 1982).

Key Terms

Focal attention
When consumers focus their entire attention on one stimulus.

Laws of Prägnanz
Laws of how stimuli are organized so that they are perceived as a complete object.

Summary

What humans pay attention to is affected by perception, as it guides our senses as well as interpreting what the stimulus encountered means. The way in which consumers perceive consumer-related information often happens subconsciously and is linked to previous knowledge and experiences. One important part of perception is the way humans use to categorize stimuli in order to make sense of them. Research has found that there are guidelines for how this is done and that whether or not elements are perceived to be connected can depend on their proximity, people's capacity to make use of previous experience to perceive incomplete stimuli as complete, as well as how similar they are. Even though numerous consumer studies have focused on the visual aspects of perception, it is important to acknowledge that all the senses contribute to the way in which products and services are perceived. The different senses can also be used to capture people's attention. What captures consumers' attention depends on numerous factors such as how aroused they are at a particular point in time, how colourful a product is, whether a stimulus is novel and whether or not the information encountered is personally relevant to them.

Class exercise

Briefly show students a PowerPoint slide with several different types of advertisements (or point-of-purchase displays). Once they have seen it, ask them to write down what they saw in as much detail as possible. Then discuss why they think they noticed some of the advertisements and not the others, i.e. what was it that captured their attention.

Identity and consumption

Introduction

Research suggests that humans buy products for reasons other than their practical functions. Often goods and services are bought because people believe that they somehow represent who they are. Furthermore, it has been established that we judge others by their material possessions, meaning that consumption is now an important part in the creation and maintenance of identities. Having a clear concept of who you are and how you fit into society is important in that it generates feelings of belongingness and well-being. This chapter will explore the pros and cons of the relationship between consumption and identity.

Identity

Identity is the subjective concept of how an individual views themselves (Vignoles, Regalia, Manzi, Golledge, & Scabini, 2006). Knowing who you are allows people to answer questions such as where they fit in and where they belong, something that is an essential part of being human (Lewis, 1990). Because our identities are subjective, the way in which we see ourselves is influenced by individual experiences, and groups to which we belong or wish to belong to (Sedikides & Brewer, 2001).

A person can have more than one identity (e.g. Brewer, 2001; Brewer & Gardner, 1996; Donahue, Robins, Roberts, & John, 1993), and they are not always anchored in real life as they can even be specific to virtual online environments (Schau & Gilly, 2003). The number of identities an individual has depends on how many different types of social situations they frequently find themselves in. Generally people play many different roles in life, for example, during daytime it may be that a person needs to fit in to the role as a lawyer, while in the morning and evenings the very same person acts as a mother of three children. Some roles are more integral to our identities than others, such as wife, student or being a boss, while others, such as being a voluntary spokesperson for a charitable cause or even a coin collector, might only dominate people's lives in certain circumstances. What all these roles have in common, whether they are primary or secondary ones, is that people can use different types of products to represent them (e.g. Goffman, 1959; Solomon, 1983). Consequently we consume in the hope of reinforcing or establishing the roles in which we find ourselves or that we would like to be in. However, the impact of who we are upon the way in which we behave has been suggested to be largely unconscious (e.g. Bargh, McKenna, & Fitzsimons, 2002; Greenwald & Farnham, 2000), meaning that consumers may not be aware if their self-concept guides their consumption behaviour.

There has been extensive research into the relationship between objects and identity, and in particular how objects have the capacity to help mould and manage people's identities (e.g. Aaker, 1999; Csikszentmihalyi & Rochberg-Halton, 1981; Dittmar, 1992; Kleine, Kleine, & Kernan, 1993; Tietje & Brunel, 2005). The idea that people use their possessions to express who they are is not a new concept. However, since the 1970s this has become prevalent and consequently more recent research has confirmed that possessions play an important role in how people perceive themselves and others (e.g. Belk, 1988, 2008).

William James wrote as early as 1890 about how people's self is reflected by what they own (see Chapter 1). This demonstrates that for a long time people have made use of belongings to express who they are. However, the realization that goods and services can be used to express individuality and group membership has been further underlined by the fact that the last hundred years has seen a continuous increase in the amount of products that people can choose from. This, in combination with the constant mass bombardment of advertising continuously encouraging people to be materialistic in a way that people's self-worth becomes reduced to that of a consumer (Kanner & Gomes, 1995), means that people's identities are linked to what they consume.

How are identities formed?

The formation of identities is complex as they start early on in life and continue to develop throughout. Generally, self-recognition develops around the age of 2 (de Veer, Gallup, Theall, van den Bos, & Povinelli, 2003; Povinelli, 1994) but at that age the concept of who we are is of a basic nature. Babies can then recognize their own mirror image and basic changes to their physical appearance. Thereafter recognition and concept of self gradually become more complex as humans grow older. Human identities are continuously moulded and influenced by parents, siblings, friends, peers, school, societies or sport clubs they belong to, as well as advertising and other cultural influences. Once people have reached adulthood, they tend to incorporate their feelings, what motivates them, political beliefs, religious beliefs, physical appearance, group memberships, age and the material possessions they own to describe themselves (e.g. Dittmar, 1992; Hart & Damon, 1986; Harter, 2003; Montemayor & Eisen, 1977). The incorporation of so many different characteristics to express who we are shows that our identities are multi-dimensional.

People often overlook that others have more than one identity and this is because humans have a 'basic need to simplify and impose order on the world' (Hogg & Abrams, 1988, p. 78). If we manage to 'pigeonhole' others, then we feel that we know where we stand in relation to what they represent and who they are. Consequently humans (often subconsciously) consign others to groups (social categorization) and compare themselves to others (social comparison) in an attempt to impose order on the world as well as distinguishing how people are similar or different to themselves. Both the categorization and comparison processes also enable us to figure out who we are as individuals.

Social categorization

Humans categorize the world around them in relation to themselves. When doing so, people tend to accentuate their perception of others (Hogg & Abrams, 1988) and objects that they come across (Tajfel & Wilkes, 1963), so that it is easier to find similarities or differences between themselves and those they are categorizing. The perception of others (**person perception**) is often affected by people's material possessions (Dittmar, 2004a; Hebl & King, 2004), while classification of objects (**object perception**) can be influenced by marketing and advertising. The process of categorizing individuals can lead to others (and self) becoming depersonalized. Because we tend to focus on the groups people belong to and the type of possessions they own, we view them as a representation of what the groups and possessions stand for rather than as individuals in their own right. Hence, individuals are perceived as prototypes, meaning that we can assign them stereotypical characteristics and treat them (or in the case of self – behave) accordingly.

Bearing in mind that people make use of material possessions in order to categorize others, it naturally raises the question whether or not the categorization will be representative of what the person is really like. Research has repeatedly shown that brands and products can indeed be used to generate accurate opinions about what others are like. This is even possible when a person has never met or even seen the owner of the possessions. For example, Gosling, Ko, Morris, and Thomas (2002) found that people could correctly judge another person's personality just by having a brief look at their office or bedroom. Similarly, this was also found by Alpers and Gerdes (2006) when they asked participants to match cars with their owners and they were able to correctly pair the two. Presumably such matchmaking skills are based upon the fact that people already have a clear stereotypical concept of what kind of person would be using a particular product (e.g. Belk, Mayer, & Bahn, 1982; Davies & Patel, 2005), meaning that we can make use of those concepts to accurately categorize others.

Social comparison

An important source of understanding oneself is through comparisons with other people. Social comparison is about how people learn about themselves by comparing similarities and differences to others (Festinger, 1954; Suls & Wheeler, 2000).

The continuous comparison to others is driven by a need to maintain and sometimes increase positive self-esteem. Individual self-esteem is linked to feelings of belongingness, which is supported by being a member of groups. 'Just as clothing, accent, grooming, and jewellery can distinguish an individual from others and express an individual sense of being, they can also indicate group identity and express belonging to a group' (Belk, 1988, p. 208).

The social comparison theory can be easily applied to how people compare themselves to the ideals generated by the consumer culture in which we live. From a consumer perspective, purchasing the right kind of products and services can make them feel as if they belong to certain groups as well as genuinely providing group membership. This is often (but not always) driven by different types of marketing techniques. For example, American Eagle Outfitters used the slogan 'Live your life' for quite a while. The slogan was meant to inform consumers that those wearing American Eagle denim outfits were highly individual people who wished to do something unique with their lives. Hence, if people wish to be viewed as belonging to the group of people in society who are living their life to the limit, they would need to wear American Eagle jeans.

Generally people seek out those who appear to do less well in one form or other, as in that way they can make **downward social comparisons**, meaning that when we compare ourselves to those whom do less well, we appear to do better ourselves (Wills, 1981). So if you own a Porsche and most of the people you know drive Volkswagen Beetles, then you are likely to feel superior and consequently increase your self-esteem. Unfortunately there will always be situations when we cannot choose who we compare ourselves with and consequently we may end up comparing ourselves to those who somehow are viewed to be more competent or desirable. This is known as **upward comparison** and it can have a harmful effect upon our self-esteem. Upward comparison often happen when consumers are comparing themselves to 'ideal' media images, something that has been extensively explored in regards to how women rate their own physical attractiveness and the impact upon self-esteem (e.g. Martin & Gentry, 1997; Martin & Kennedy, 1993; Richins, 1991) (Figure 4.1). Most such studies have focused on the impact of 'ideal' images upon women's self-esteem and concluded that it is of a negative nature. It has also been found that younger women are more affected than older ones (Hogg, Bruce, & Hough, 1999; Wood, 1989).

When individuals base their social comparisons on products and brands, it is interesting that there appears to be a general consensus in regards to what they represent and which ones are better than others. Interestingly enough, it has been found that even when people assume that consumer choices ought to be individualistic (meaning that it should not be possible to use them for social comparison), people still think there are right and wrong choices, such as with music (Insko, Drenan, Solomon, Smith, & Wade, 1983). This is due to the fact that they will view some music genres as being more closely associated with the kind of groups that they wish to be seen to belong to. Nevertheless there will always be times when certain choices clearly are subjective.

Covers of magazines often use women who represent what society deems to be the 'ideal' look.

FIGURE 4.1 Use of models in mainstream media.

Source: Courtesy of Cosmos Communications, Photo: Cathrine Jansson.

Symbolic meaning of products

The fact that we categorize and compare ourselves to others based on the possessions they own clearly shows that material goods have meaning. If different goods and services did not clearly represent different values and beliefs, individuals would be unable to use them as the basis of categorization and comparison and in turn establish our own and others' identities.

The concept that brands symbolize different meanings is not a new one (e.g. Gardner & Levy, 1955) but it is only since the late 1980s that psychologists have researched it more extensively and there is now evidence that inanimate objects can even become associated with human characteristics (e.g. Aaker, 1997; Plummer, 1985).

Symbolic interactionism

Brands and products can be transformed into symbols and in turn become ways of communicating with others. The meaning of the product mostly comes from marketing and is subsequently reinforced by the social environment. Inspiration to research how material possessions can be used to manage identities partially stems from a theory of self called symbolic interactionism. The idea of symbolic interactionism is that the self arises out of, and is continually modified by, human interaction. In order to interact effectively with others, people make use of symbols that must have a shared meaning. A lot of the time the symbols are constructed through continuous social activities (Mead, 1934). The social activities are then used by individuals to reconstruct and express who they are, as well as to decide what others are like, all of which happens subconsciously (Greenwald, 1980).

Another aspect of symbolic interactionism is that individuals must be capable of viewing themselves from the perspective of others. Basically the theory suggests that the sense of who we are is shaped by us being able to imagine how we are perceived by others. This has led to speculation that the symbolic meanings of products and brands can act as tools for make-believe identities. For example, a Mercedes car is often seen as a symbol of success and consequently the driver of one may therefore view themselves as being well off and successful (Dittmar, 2008b). The original theory never mentioned material possessions, but as times have moved on it has became apparent to many (e.g. Dittmar, 1992) that they play an important part in how people responded socially to others.

When do we first learn about symbolic meanings?

Individuals learn gradually from a young age that material possessions mean certain things, something that is done through direct and indirect learning methods. Indirect learning such as observation of others may be through the media or immediate social surroundings, while direct learning will be through interaction with others and objects. One example of indirect learning through the mass media is that children repeatedly see on television (advertisements or children's programmes) that only those kids who have certain toys have a lot of friends. Consequently they will start to believe that in order to be popular, they need to own specific types of possessions.

Children also learn early on that others respond to them in a certain way depending on the objects they own, such as clothes and toys. Therefore, their own possessions may teach a child about their values, which may in turn be internalized through play (Rochberg-Halton, 1984). Humans continue to learn about the symbolic value of products and services through the media and by social interaction from childhood to late adulthood. Hence, how we learn the symbolic meaning of consumer products is an ongoing process.

Avoiding products with undesired meaning

The majority of products and services represent something symbolically and at times what they stand for may be perceived by some as highly undesirable. Just as carefully as consumers choose products they think will make them appear more appealing, they also choose what *not* to buy. Opposite to our ideal self is our undesired self, the person people do not wish to become (Ogilvie, 1987). Hence consumers emphasize who they are just as much through what they consume as what they do not consume. A number of studies have lent support to this idea. For example, it has been found that people label products as 'me' or 'not me' and tend to reject those that are viewed as 'not me' (Kleine, Kleine, & Allen, 1995). Consumers have also been found to easily express their dislikes (Wilk, 1997) and to avoid certain brands in order to distance themselves from what they stand for (Englis & Solomon, 1995; Freitas, Kaiser, Chandler, Hall, Jung-Won, & Hammidi, 1997). Sometimes people also try to move away from what they see as an 'old and outdated self' by getting rid of possessions that represent the former self (Belk, Sherry, & Wallendorf, 1988; Myers, 1985).

Use of symbols to signify group memberships

Being a part of a group (or groups) is important to people's identities as it helps them define who they are as well as boosting their self-esteem and general well-being. This was outlined in what is known as the **social identity theory**. Tajfel described social identity as 'that part of the individual's self-concept which derives from their knowledge of their membership of a social group (or groups) together with the value and emotional significance of that memberships (1981, p. 255). It is increasingly common that groups use consumption to signal to others that they somehow belong together. This is done by individuals using brands, products and services to differentiate themselves from others by using them to demonstrate their commonality with the groups to which they belong (Jenkins, 1996). However, this internal identification process must be recognized by non-group members in order for a collective group identity to become apparent, meaning that the products need to have a clear symbolic value. As previously outlined in this chapter, the symbolic meaning often stems from advertising and other marketing techniques. The consumption tools available for the formation or maintenance of a group's social identity are presented through different marketing practices (Molnar & Lamont, 2002), as they categorize and objectify groups to provide clear links to specific groups and sub-groups. Consequently, marketers offer individuals easy solutions as to how they can achieve full group membership or at least how they can signal that they wish to belong to a specific group.

Identifying with products

There is no doubt that individuals make use of goods and services to 'make sense' of those around them, to compare themselves to others, and to signal group membership. All three examples clearly show a strong association between people and material possessions. However, none of these examples takes into consideration whether the number of people who use certain products can play a role in whether or not individuals identify with them. Neither do they consider if certain types of people are more likely than others to make use of products and their symbolic meanings to express who they are. Both are aspects that have been found to be significant in regard to how strongly people identity with products.

Brand identification and minority influence

Some consumers have a stronger relationship with their preferred brand than other users of a similar product category and this has been linked to the number of product users. In a study where Macintosh and PC users were compared, the Macintosh brand was found to be much more likely to be a part of consumer's self-concept (Brunel, Tietje, & Greenwald, 2004). See Figure 4.2 for a hypothetical

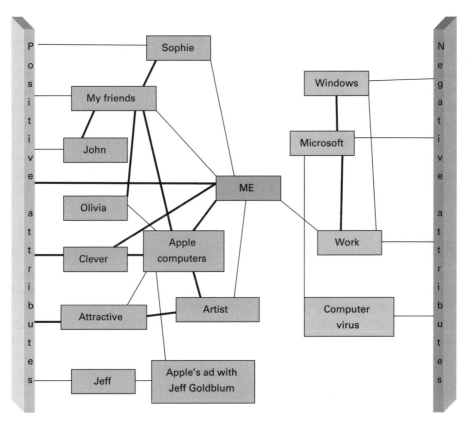

The consumer is at the centre and positive and negative attributes are represented on the sides. The thickness of the links between the attributes demonstrates the strength between the concepts. It can be noted that the consumer perceives themselves as more closely linked to Apple computers and in turn links the computer to other positive attributes.

FIGURE 4.2 Conceptual social knowledge structure for a computer user.

Source: Adapted from Brunel, Tietje, & Greenwald (2004).

construct of how Apple computers can be more strongly linked to self. The stronger self-connection to the product was explained by the fact that Macintosh computers are less commonly used and hence make the user think of themselves as a part of a small closely knit community (Muñiz & O'Guinn, 2001). Because of the small number of people who use Macintosh computers compared to PCs, it may be that it fosters 'a strong social bond and deep-rooted loyalty' (Muñiz & O'Guinn, 2001). Additionally, it is also possible that where people encounter the Macintosh or PC may play a part in whether or not people strongly identify with the product. For example, PC users are most likely to be using them because of work availability and consequently people may not feel strongly connected to them since they did not choose the computer themselves (Brunel et al., 2004).

Some people identify more strongly with products
Research clearly shows that most individuals are likely to identify with different kinds of products, if not frequently, at least on a few occasions in their lives. However, it has been suggested that perhaps there are those who are a bit more likely to make consumer choices in line with how they wish to be perceived by others. One such category of people is those with narcissistic tendencies (Sedikides, Gregg, Cisek, & Hart, 2007). The underlying idea is that narcissists wish others to see them as special and superior and consequently will purchase expensive products that are viewed by most as being highly desirable in some way. Purchasing such products helps them to feel good about themselves since others will admire and envy them because of the possessions that they have. Because narcissists want others to look up to them, they will be much more likely to buy products and services that have a greater symbolic value.

Self-fulfilling prophecy

It is clear that people consume to reinforce who they are. What is less clear is whether or not such consumption genuinely alters people's identity. It is known that people assign attributes to others based upon what they wear, the kind of services they use and the possessions they own, consequently people can alter the way others perceive them by consuming the 'right' kind of products. By doing so they can also change the way in which people treat them and behave towards them, and because they are treated in a particular way they start to act accordingly, something that is known as *self-fulfilling prophecy*.

The most famous study of self-fulfilling prophecy was conducted by Rosenthal and Jacobson in 1968. They asked school children to complete an IQ test and told their teachers that the results would be indicative of rapid intellectual development. After the test teachers were given names of 20 children who were deemed to be 'early bloomers'. Shortly thereafter the teachers rated the 'non-bloomers' as being less curious and interested than the 'bloomers' and student grades were consistent with the teachers' opinions. However, what the teachers did not know was that the names of the 'bloomers' they had been given had been randomly chosen by the researchers, hence there was no difference in terms of IQ scores between the 'non-bloomers' and the 'bloomers'. Interestingly enough, when the children's IQ were tested once more a year later, it was found that the 'bloomers' had a considerably higher IQ score than the 'non-bloomers'. The study clearly showed that assumptions about an individual affect how we interact with them and after some time the individual will also change their behaviour in line with the expectations.

As Rosenthal and Jacobson's study shows, there are three steps to self-fulfilling prophecy: (1) people must have expectations of what another person is like; (2) the person (x) who holds the expectations must be influenced by their beliefs in how they act towards that person (y); and (3) person (y) must subsequently respond by behaving in line with the other person's (x) expectations.

It is easy to see how consumer goods and services fit in to the three steps and how they in turn can help individuals to reinforce or alter their identities (see Figure 4.3). The use of possessions to build identities might happen consciously or subconsciously. If consumers are aware of how the self-fulfilling prophecy works, then they can think about which brand and products are most likely to generate the preferred responses from others. However, most would not be aware of how the process works in full but simply purchase products they think will strengthen group membership or set them apart from others, meaning that their own behavioural

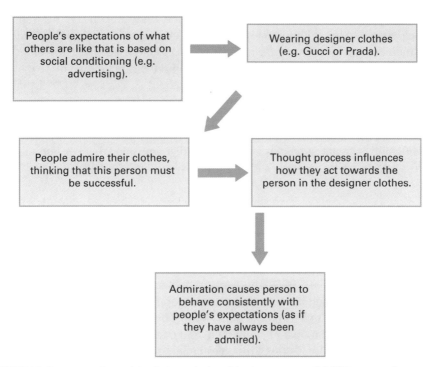

FIGURE 4.3 Conceptual model of the relationship between self-fulfilling prophecy and material goods.

change is often just an added bonus. Nevertheless, the self-fulfilling prophecy shows that consumption can have the capacity to alter people's identity.

Negative aspects of consumption upon self

So far the only mention of any negative consequences of consumption upon the self has been in regards to upwards social comparison. Even though in many cases consumption is simply a part of establishing and preserving our identities, there are instances when it can be detrimental to who we are. At times, possessions are simply used as an extension of the self (Belk, 1988) but they can also be used by individuals to compensate for what is perceived to be flaws in their self-concept (Wicklund & Gollwitzer, 1982). Consequently, the consumer culture is often blamed for physical and psychological problems linked to identity.

Many studies have found that both women and men do not believe that their current body form is attractive, even though men tend to think that their bodies are not too far off what they deem to be the ideal shape (e.g. Fallon & Rozin, 1985; Stunkard, Sorensen, & Schulsinger, 1980). Such negative body perceptions are most likely the consequence of the media promoting 'ideal identities' that have often been digitally altered by using PhotoShop.

It is interesting that people are affected by 'ideal images' of beauty, especially since most people tend to agree that physical beauty is superficial and that it should not be deemed to be as important as a person's intellectual, emotional, and spiritual qualities. However, research has repeatedly found that physically attractive individuals are perceived by most to be socially more desirable than those that are perceived as being unattractive (e.g. Dion, Berscheid, & Walster, 1972; Langlois, 1986), something that is likely to have been reinforced by consumer societies and further fuels the consumption of cosmetic products and procedures. The fact is that never before has the cosmetic industry sold more beauty products (to both men and women), and cosmetic surgery is at an all-time high, meaning that it is important to address how this affects people's identity and psychological well-being.

Body image

Because of the constant exposure to media messages telling consumers that physical appearance is important, it has been suggested that body image should be considered part of our identities as it is part of an individual's self-representation (e.g. Halliwell & Dittmar, 2006). The pressures to become 'picture perfect' start at a very young age and then it is often inadvertently applied through products used by children to play with such as Barbie dolls. Many young girls who play with Barbie dolls have been found to identify with them and think of them as role models (e.g. Dittmar, Halliwell, & Ive, 2006). This gives children a skewed picture of what the female ideal should be like as Barbie is not in any way representative of what real-life women are like. Moser (1989) pointed out that the average American woman weights approximately 124 pounds, so in order to look like Barbie they would have to increase their bust by 12 inches, reduce their waist by another 10 and be 7 ft 2 in. tall. That would make an interesting-looking woman indeed!

In the light of unrealistic ideals of physical attractiveness, it is also common for teenagers to conclude that their physical appearance falls short of what society deems to be attractive. Consequently they embark upon the task of changing their physical appearance, but because it is impossible to achieve their set targets, they get on a 'treadmill of destruction' leading to poor physical and mental health (e.g. Friedman & Brownell, 1995). This is unfortunate since adolescents should emerge into adulthood with a sense of self that includes being comfortable with their own bodies (Erikson, 1968) in order to achieve an identity they are comfortable with. When they fail to be comfortable with their physical appearance, they will continue to buy beauty products and services in the hope that it will make them feel better. This can naturally also be applicable to adults as well as teenagers.

Self-discrepancy theory

One theory that offers a clear explanation as to why people become unhappy with their physical appearance is the self-discrepancy theory (Higgins, 1987). This theory proposes that people have three types of self-**schema** (schema being organized sets of expectations and associations about an object):

1 *Actual self* – the way people are at the present point in time.
2 *Ideal self* – the self that we aspire to be.
3 *Ought self* – they way we think we should be.

The 'ideal self' helps us to strive to be in a way that we think is perfect while the 'ought self' prevents us from doing things that are not in line with what we should be like. For example, the 'ideal self' may help us to strive to be like Brad Pitt, while the 'ought self' might make us strive not to be like the most obese person we know.

It is important that there are no discrepancies between the actual and 'ideal self' or the 'actual' and 'ought self'. If there are discrepancies, it can motivate a person to try and reduce it. However, if they fail to do so, a discrepancy between the actual and 'ideal self' can produce feelings of dissatisfaction and disappointment while a discrepancy between actual and 'ought self' can lead to agitated types of emotions such as anxiety or fear.

Those with high discrepancies are much more likely to suffer from low self-esteem (e.g. Dittmar, 2004b) and it has been suggested that they are also likely to 'engage in identity-seeking buying behaviour' (Dittmar, 2008a, p. 104). Such findings explains why repeated exposure to 'ideal images' that are unattainable for most will have a negative impact upon their self. For example, a young girl who thinks her 'ideal self' should be the equivalent of 'Kate Moss' but who in reality is actually overweight and not incredibly attractive, might very well find that she feels highly discontented with her physical appearance. Consequently she may start to buy beauty products in hope of achieving the 'Kate Moss look'.

How the media can help to boost people's identities and self-esteem

Provided that individuals are comparing themselves to people portrayed in the media, they are just as likely to compare themselves to people who are of average, chubby or slim build. Thus there is nothing to say that a picture of a 'normal-sized' person cannot help boost people's self-esteem. Using realistic images to promote products has indeed been found to make people feel better about themselves, as people have been found to be more likely to compare themselves with those who are similar rather than dissimilar (Wood, 1989) and at times it is even possible that they will disregard the beauty of the models if they are perceived to be 'too' ideal (Hogg & Fragou, 2003). Self-esteem can also be increased when advertisements make use of individuals who are perceived to be less attractive than ourselves in some way (Martin & Gentry, 1997).

The fact that we like to compare ourselves to those similar to us helps explain the success of advertising campaigns such as Dove's 'real beauty' that made use of ordinary women to promote products such as firming lotions and body wash (Figure 4.4). Just in the first month alone of using 'real women' in their advertising campaigns, Dove reportedly increased their sales figures by over 3 per cent (Lee, 2005).

A successful advertising campaign making use of 'real' women rather than 'perfect' models.

FIGURE 4.4 Use of real women in advertising.

Source: Courtesy of Ogilvy & Mather. Photo: John Akehurs.

Key Terms

Downward social comparison
When people compare themselves to others who are seen as inferior. Also sometimes referred to as frames or scripts.

Object perception
The way in which objects are classified and perceived.

Person perception
They way in which people perceive others.

Schema
Organized sets of expectations and associations about an object.

Social identity theory
Individuals' identities stem from the groups to which they belong.

Upward comparison
When people compare themselves to those who are seen as superior.

Summary

Consumers often purchase products and services in order to establish and maintain identities and to signify group memberships. People are taught gradually from an early age that products and brands have meaning which means that they can be used to categorize self and others. Meaningful products also allow us to easily compare ourselves to others so that we can judge whether or not they are inferior or superior to us. This is a great advantage in that humans can rapidly assess others without having to spend a lot of time and energy trying to figure out what people are like.

The meaning of different products stems from marketing and tends to be continuously reinforced by our social environment. Generally consumers strive to own those products that are perceived to be highly desirable and to avoid those that are seen as undesirable. One of the advantages of consuming certain products is that they can make others perceive us in a more favourable way and consequently they will behave accordingly towards us. However, there are also disadvantages in that certain types of consumption can make us feel inadequate in various way and subsequently affect our mental and physical health.

Discussion questions

1 Is it possible for individuals who do not have a strong sense of who they are to 'shop for an identity'?

2 How do material possessions affect how we perceive others?

3 What are the positive aspects of using consumption to create or maintain an identity?

4 How is it possible for people to have more than one identity? Can having multiple identities lead to confusion about who you are?

5 Try to think of 'consumer aspects' that teach us about the meanings of products. If possible, give specific examples.

5

The emotional consumer

Introduction

Since the 1990s many researchers have acknowledged that consumers are not always rational because they are driven by their emotions. The impact of emotions upon consumer behaviour is evident through many different aspects of research. It is impossible to cover all aspects of affect that have been researched so far as there have been a vast number of papers published. However, there are aspects of affect that clearly indicate that it is an important part of understanding consumer behaviour fully such as attention, recall, decision-making, atmospherics and persuasion, all of which will be discussed in this chapter.

Emotions

Consumers are sometimes described as being rational in the decisions that they make and the ways in which they interact with different types of consumption. The rational theories used to explain 'rational consumer behaviour' mostly assume that emotions are something that can be controlled and at times even completely disregarded so that humans are capable of acting in a rational manner. Some researchers argue that emotions do not really fill a function (e.g. Ledoux, 1998) and from such a perspective there is no reason why the impact of emotions upon consumption should not be ignored. However, there are many more scientists who argue that emotions do indeed play a role in human functioning (e.g. Damasio, 1994; Frijda, 1986) and there is no reason why this would not also be applicable to consumer behaviour. Consequently, it would be rash to assume that emotions can be controlled and that consumers always act in a rational manner. Since the 1990s this has been recognized by many consumer researchers, so that it now is one of the most popular lines of investigation within consumption-related studies.

So what is emotion? *Emotion* can generally be defined as intense affect. The word affect is commonly used in the research literature to describe an internal feeling state that can incorporate both emotions and mood. An emotion is a feeling that comprises physiological, behavioural and cognitive reactions to internal and external events (Carlson & Hatfield, 1992) and they tend to be intentional in that they represent something in particular (Frijda, 1993), such as when a consumer is especially pleased with the effectiveness of a product. Mood, on the other hand, is a bit more difficult to clearly distinguish from emotion. Generally, moods are more pervasive, longer lasting and less intense than emotions. To date, it appears that a high number of consumer researchers that have investigated affect have chosen to focus on mood (e.g. Barone, Miniard, & Romeo, 2000). Perhaps this is partially due to the fact that moods have been found to be easily manipulated by the use of stimuli such as music and pictures (Cohen & Andrade, 2004).

Researching affect

There is no 'standard' way to investigate the impact of emotions and mood upon consumer behaviour and thought processes. Since the 1990s there has been a surge in the amount of research conducted within this area, but even so there are those who think that the research does not link emotion to a wide enough range of consumption experiences (Richins, 1997). With an increase in the quantity of consumer studies investigating affect, the research world has naturally also seen a wider range of methods used. What the high number of research studies conducted have in common is that the researchers have had to make use of some sort of method to ensure that their participants are somehow experiencing the emotions that they wish to measure.

Inducing emotions and mood

Making people experience certain feelings can be difficult at times, which is often why researchers instead opt for mood induction. Even when researchers are successful in inducing the emotions that they wish to test, it is important that the dependent variable is measured shortly afterwards as induced emotions tend not to last long (Isen, Clark, & Schwartz, 1976).

The research literature shows that the methods used to induce certain types of feelings and moods vary. Some of the methods used include using films or film clips to try and make people feel happy or sad (e.g. Adaval, 2001; Andrade, 2005), music that has previously been established to be disagreeable or agreeable (Gorn, Goldberg, & Basu, 1993), as well as providing people with positive or negative feedback on performance (Barone, Miniard, & Romeo, 2000). None of the methods used have been identified as being superior in the induction of emotions and mood. However, some of the methods used have been criticized in that, depending on how the research is conducted, an experimenter may generate more than just the feelings they wish to measure. Put simply, some methodologies may impact on participants in other ways that may also in turn influence the research results. For example, providing people with negative feedback may decrease their self-esteem as well as changing the way they are feeling (Hill & Ward, 1989) and consequently it can be difficult to determine which of the two factors have generated the research results. Such examples demonstrate that researchers need to be alert when it comes to considering any confounding variables in their research studies.

Measuring emotional responses to stimuli

One common way to measure consumers' responses to a particular stimulus is by the use of self-reports (most commonly questionnaires). Typically participants are then presented with a number of questions that are directly linked to both positive and negative types of emotions that measure how they may feel about a stimulus. A lot of the time the questionnaires are analysed by using factor or cluster analysis in the hope of establishing specific underlying emotional factors that can explain how people feel about certain products and services. Using self-report techniques such as questionnaires has its drawbacks as participants are often prone to provide answers that they think are socially desirable or that they think the researcher wants, which can lead to incorrect research outcomes. Even so, questionnaires (in combination with factor analysis) have been very helpful when it comes to establishing scales that explore people's emotional responses. In particular, a number of useful scales have been developed that tap into how people feel about different types of advertisements (e.g. Edell & Burke, 1987).

Many of the scales developed incorporate a high number of different items, some as many as 90 or more (e.g. Holbrook & Batra, 1987). Regardless of how many items the scales consist of, most have been found to have only a few underlying emotional factors (e.g. Edell & Burke, 1987; Holbrook & Batra, 1987). There are even some that have been narrowed down to consist of only two factors that can be neatly described as positive and negative affect (e.g. Oliver, 1994). Categorizing emotional responses into positive and negative may be far from ideal, as not all positive (and negative) emotions generate the same kind of response in consumers. Consequently it can be wiser to divide positive (and negative) emotions into sub-categories or treat them as single entities (as will be discussed further in this chapter).

Emotions, attention and recall

Emotions impact upon people's cognitive processes, as they can affect the ability to encode, store and retrieve information (Blaney, 1986). Two particular areas that clearly demonstrate how emotions play an important part in how consumer-related information is processed are selective attention and recall. Both areas show that emotions are an integral part when it comes to understanding how people function and why they are more likely to focus on certain factors than others.

Selective attention

Most marketers want to know what it is that makes consumers focus more on some products than on others and whether specific product attributes are more likely to capture their attention. It appears that how people are feeling at a particular point in time may (at least partially) offer an explanation.

In a study conducted by Bower, Gilligan and Montiero (1981), it was discovered that mood can make people engage in selective learning. Participants were made to feel happy or sad through hypnosis and were afterwards asked to read drafts of psychiatric interviews. Interestingly enough they found that happy participants focused on and remembered a higher number of happy facts than did the sad ones, while sad participants remembered more sad facts. Hence the study shows that emotions activated by subconscious experiences can bias the information they focus on and encode into memory. One explanation as to why this happens is because material that is congruent with the way people feel is more likely to be semantically elaborated upon (Bower & Cohen, 1982).

Another piece of research that also supports the idea that mood can make people biased in what they pay attention to was conducted by Adaval (2001). She showed that Bower et al.'s research findings are also applicable to the product domain. Adaval's participants were given a mood-induction task so that they felt either happy or sad. Afterwards they were asked to evaluate a piece of clothing that was described by an attribute which was likely to be judged on subjective or non-subjective criteria. The results demonstrated that participants were more likely to pay attention to information that matched the feelings they were experiencing at the time, even though the feelings had no relationship to the piece of clothing. Hence, the research provides evidence that emotion can play a part in how much attention people pay to certain types of product information, provided the information is similar in valence to the evaluator's mood.

Impact on recall

Similar to selective attention, recall is also impacted upon by mood-congruent information. In particular, it has been suggested that a positive mood is more likely to generate recall of positive events than a negative mood (Bower & Forgas, 2000). One explanation as to why negative moods are different may be because people are generally motivated to make themselves feel better (something known as **affect regulation**) and consequently negative feelings can at times encourage recall of positive events (Isen, 1984). There are also some who suggest that not only are individuals in a positive mood more likely to recall positive information, they are also more likely to recall information of a negative nature. This may have something to do with the relevance of the information encountered. When highly relevant information is presented to people that are in a good mood it is just as likely to be recalled regardless of whether the information is positive or negative (e.g. Trope & Pomerantz, 1998). For example, in a study conducted by Raghunathan and Trope

(2002), it was found that high caffeine consumers had an enhanced recall about negative aspects of caffeine consumption when they were in a good mood. However, this was not found to be the case for low caffeine consumers. Hence, it would appear that how relevant the information is to the consumer will play an important part in whether or not a 'happy' consumer remembers the information encountered.

An additional factor that plays a part in understanding emotional impact upon recall is the actual strength of the emotions that people are experiencing. Highly intense emotions have been found to increase immediate and long-term memory. In a study by Bradley, Greenwald, Petry, & Lang (1992), pictures were used to generate different levels of arousal in their participants; some made the participants feel highly aroused while others produced low arousal levels. When participants felt highly aroused, they were better at recalling the pictures they had seen. The findings were the same whether the recall was conducted immediately after seeing the pictures or a year later. It should be noted though, that highly arousing stimuli may not necessarily generate accurate recall since highly affective experiences are just as prone to reconstruction as any other kind of memories (Levine, 2000).

Impact of emotions upon decision-making

Emotional reactions have been suggested to precede and be fairly independent of cognitive judgements (Zajonc, 2000). When confronted with products and services which consumers can choose from, it appears that they search their feelings in an attempt to establish how they feel about the stimuli they are exposed to (e.g. Schwarz, 1990). This may be done without the individual being aware of it (Peters & Slovic, 2000), something that is recognized as a 'how-do-I-feel-about it' heuristic (e.g. Finucane, Peters, & Slovic, 2003). This heuristic is used as a basis for making a judgement (Schwarz & Clore, 1983) and consequently consumers' moods inform their decisions even if how they are feeling is unrelated to the decisions they are about to make. This is why it is important to try and ensure (when possible) that consumers are in a good mood when deciding upon what to consume as otherwise they may end up associating a particular product with their negative mood and subsequently evaluate the product in a disapproving way. Individuals who are in a good mood have repeatedly been found to evaluate stimuli more positively whether it is consumer goods (Isen, Shalker, Clark, & Karp, 1978; Srull, 1983) or something else such as other people (Forgas & Bower, 1987) or past life events (Clark & Teasdale, 1982). However, positive emotions are unlikely to influence the evaluation of a highly familiar stimulus (e.g. Srull, 1984; Salovey & Birnbaum, 1989) as consumers are then more likely to be guided by past evaluations that are already an integral part of their schema.

Controlling feelings through consumption

At times, consumption-related decisions are linked to the consumer's desire to control the way they feel. When consumers experience negative emotions of some sort, they tend to be eager to engage in consumption behaviours that will lighten their mood (Cohen, Tuan Pham, & Andrade, 2008). Examples of consumption-related behaviour that they might make use of in such instances include buying presents for themselves, watching funny television programmes, eating chocolate and listening to uplifting music (Andrade, 2005; Cohen & Andrade, 2004; Luomala & Laaksonen, 1997; Weaver & Laird, 1995). It does not really matter what kind of consumption activities a person with negative emotions engages in as long as they genuinely believe that they will enhance their mood. This means that if marketers can create associations between products and the belief that they will make people feel happy, consumers in a bad mood are much more likely to purchase them.

Additionally, the type of feelings that consumers are hoping to change also plays a part in what kind of mood changing activities they take part in. For example, if an individual is experiencing anxiety, they are less likely to take part in something that is perceived as risky (Raghunathan & Pham, 1999), and consequently will purchase something that they feel certain will have guaranteed benefits.

The Appraisal-Tendency Framework (ATF)

The Appraisal-Tendency Framework (ATF) is a general theory that can be applied to explain consumer choices (Han, Lerner, & Keltner, 2007). The framework was proposed by Lerner and Keltner (2000; 2001) and is based upon the idea that explicit emotions generate specific cognitive and motivational processes, which in turn also influence consumers' evaluations of objects and events that they come across when experiencing the emotion. This means that people appraise situations and objects based upon how they are feeling at a particular point in time – a process known as *appraisal*. It is worth noting that the appraisal can impact upon both the content and depth of processing (Lerner & Tiedens, 2006) during the decision-making process.

Prior to the ATF, most theories of emotional influences on choice have made use of a *valence-based approach*, basically looking at the impact of positive versus negative emotions (e.g. Bower, 1991; Mayer, Gaschke, Braverman, & Evans, 1992). However, what they failed to take into account was whether or not specific emotions of the same valence could impact differently on the choice process. Consequently the ATF was structured to find out if emotions of the same valence that differ in appraisal generate different judgements.

The idea was first tested by Lerner and Keltner in 2000 when they investigated two types of emotions of the same valence: anger and fear. They found that those who experienced fear generally made more pessimistic judgements of future events, while angry people tended to make optimistic ones, hence, demonstrating that judgement and choice can be affected differently by the same type of valence-based mood. This was also reinforced by a later study conducted by Lerner and

Keltner (2001) when they found that angry individuals perceive risk in a similar manner to happy individuals, rather than those who experience emotions of fear which is valence-congruent with anger. Consequently, if marketers and retailers try to make use of stimuli to induce positive or negative moods in consumers they should not assume that all positive or negative emotions will influence evaluations and choice in the same way.

Risk taking

When it comes to the likelihood of engaging in risk taking behaviour, it is good to categorize mood into only two categories. People have been found to be more likely to take risks when they are in a good mood, provided that the chances of loss are low. However, if the chances of risk are high, they are less likely to take risks (Arkes, Herren, & Isen, 1988). This is most likely because they wish to maintain their good mood which may be negatively influenced if they experience some sort of loss.

Unfortunately, researchers who have investigated the impact of negative affective states on people's willingness to take risks have not managed to come up with evidence that is as clear-cut as those for positive affective states. Some have suggested that negative moods can increase the likelihood of individuals taking risks (e.g. Leith & Baumeister, 1996), while others have found that negative emotions make people risk averse (e.g. Fessler, Pillsworth, & Flamson, 2004). The explanation for this may be found in Lerner & Keltner's (2001) Appraisal-Tendency Framework. It may simply be that one should not assume that all 'negative emotions' generate the same kind of results. Instead it may be better to distinguish between different types of negative emotions.

Atmospherics

Another way to influence the decisions people make in store is by using the environment to create a certain atmosphere that can produce emotional responses that in turn impact upon people's in-store behaviour, something know as **atmospherics**. The term 'atmospherics' was first used by Kotler (1973) when he suggested that consumers do not just buy the product itself, but that they are influenced by other additional elements such as the packaging, advertising, image, as well as the atmosphere in the place where they bought it. It is important to get the atmosphere right within a shop as it can be the difference between a business being a success or failure (Bitner, 1990) as it may determine whether or not a consumer chooses to approach or avoid that particular environment (Mehrabian & Russell, 1974).

Four categories of atmospheric stimuli

It has been proposed that atmospheric stimuli can be divided into four different types of categories (Berman & Evans, 1995). The four categories are as follows:

1 *External variables* (include all exterior aspects of the shop).

Examples of variables include: signs, building size and colour, parking availability, surrounding stores and general area, and the entrance.

2 *Interior variables* (all general aspects of a shop interior).

Examples of variables include: lighting, music, flooring, colour schemes, scents, width of aisles, temperature and cleanliness.

3 *Layout and design variables.*

Examples of variables include: space design, placement of equipment and work stations, waiting areas, furniture, and dead areas.

4 *Point-of-purchase (POP) and decoration variables.*

Examples of variables include: POP displays, pictures, price displays, wall decorations, and permanent product displays.

In addition to the four categories outlined by Berman and Evans, a fifth category has been proposed by Turley and Milliman (2000): the human variables. This category proposes that factors such as how crowded the shop is, what kind of people work there and what they wear (e.g. uniform) can also play an important role in the generating the right kind of ambiance and consequently affect the way the consumer is feeling.

To date, only a limited amount of research has been produced in regard to external variables and store atmospherics. Nevertheless, there are some interesting ones, such as the impact of window displays (Edwards & Shackley, 1992), and parking (Pinto & Leonidas, 1994) upon consumer behaviour. Nor has much research been conducted on how layout and design affect consumer behaviour, but the existing research has demonstrated some interesting and significant results. For example, Iyer (1989) found that when consumers have plenty of time to stroll around a shop and little prior knowledge of the shop itself, they are more likely to make unplanned purchases. Unlike external and layout and design variables, POP variables have generated a lot of research studies, most of which seem to agree that a well-designed and well-placed display can increase sales, sometimes dramatically (e.g. Gagnon & Osterhaus, 1985; Wilkinson, Mason, & Paksoy, 1982). Perhaps the most well-researched category out of the four proposed by Berman and Evans is the one focusing on general interior variable and in particular how music affects retail consumers.

Use of music

Music is often used to create a certain image and atmosphere in retail environments and it appears to have the ability to influence a wide range of cognitive and behavioural responses in consumers, even when they are not consciously aware of it (Gulas & Schewe, 1994; Milliman, 1982). In supermarket settings it has been found that the pace of classical music can change the speed of the in-store traffic (Milliman, 1982). Slower music decreased the speed of the traffic and increased sales volume. Similarly, this was also found when fast and slow-paced music was tested in a restaurant. It was then found that slower music made the customers eat at a slower pace and that they spent more on alcoholic drinks (Milliman, 1986).

The impact of background music in travel agents has also been investigated (Chebat, Chebat, & Vaillant, 2001). In particular, the authors were interested in whether or not music may be a contributing factor to how consumers process in-store information. They showed their participants four different videos of a couple visiting a travel agent so that they could get information about trips abroad. Each video had different classical background music that varied in the arousal quality through changes in tempo. The music used had been pre-tested so that the music was perceived to be equally pleasurable. Their findings showed that soothing music that created low arousal in the participants increased cognitive activity, while highly arousing music hindered cognitive activity. However, it is questionable if retailers ought to encourage heightened cognitive activity as the study showed that it went hand in hand with less desirable attitudes. The authors proposed that the underlying reason for this may be that the 'fit' between the highly arousing music and the context of their message from the travel agency was low.

It has been found that when shoppers like the background music played in a store, it influences their desire to affiliate in buyer–seller interactions (Dube, Chebat, & Morin, 1995). Research has also demonstrated that it is important to choose music that 'fits' with the type of store. This was suggested when Grewal, Baker, Levy, & Voss (2003) used classical music as a variable to test if it impacted upon the atmosphere in a jewellery shop and people's intention to shop there.

Unfortunately, music is often tested in combination with other factors such as lighting, which makes it difficult to determine to what extent music is an influential factor. For example, in a study where music and lighting were combined to create either high or low ambience, ambience was found to interact with the number and friendliness of the staff (Baker, Levy, & Grewal, 1992).

Shopping satisfaction

All retailers want all of their customers to be satisfied ones, as it increases the likelihood of repeated custom. This is particularly important in the current shopping climate where many consumers are increasingly turning away from traditional shopping trips to stores and malls and are instead favouring online shopping. The question is, can retailers make use of store atmospherics to make their consumers feel more satisfied?

For some time it has been known that emotions impact upon how satisfied people feel (e.g. Mano & Oliver, 1993; Oliver, 1996; Westbrook & Oliver, 1991), and such emotions can possibly be generated by the in-store environment. However, only recently was it actually explored whether or not the feeling of satisfaction may be stronger at certain times depending on the source responsible for the feelings (Machleit & Powell Mantel, 2001). In a field study, 738 students and 153 non-students were asked to answer a questionnaire after a shopping trip.

Three types of questions were incorporated into the questionnaire: (1) shopping satisfaction: (2) emotions; and (3) what they attributed their feelings to. The results indicated that emotions have a stronger impact on whether or not the consumer is satisfied if their feelings are believed to be related to the store. Consequently, it appears as if retailers should pull out all the stops available to create an 'emotionally pleasant' shopping experience for their consumers as they are more likely to feel satisfied which ought to mean repeat business for them.

Persuasive theories of emotion

In addition to looking at how emotions influence aspects such as cognitive processes and decision-making, researchers have also investigated how emotion can be used to persuade people to consume certain products and services. Two theories of emotion that are particularly useful when it comes to explaining whether or not consumers may be persuaded are Mandler's and Zillman's theories of emotion.

Mandler's theory of emotion

Mandler (1975, 1982, 1984) suggested that emotional arousal is produced by *discrepancies* or unexpected events. Discrepancies often require people's immediate attention so it is good that they increase arousal so that we are alerted to them. As a general rule the greater the discrepancy, the greater the increase in arousal levels. Small discrepancies tend to produce enjoyable feelings as small arousal levels tend to be experienced as interesting, while greater discrepancies produce negative feelings due to their high inconsistency with our schemas. The reason why greater inconsistencies with our schema produce negative emotions is because if events clash with our existing knowledge structures, we tend to think that something is wrong.

Just like discrepancies, unexpected interruptions also produce arousal and can generate positive and negative emotions. The more a person thinks that what they are doing is important, the more the arousal increases when they get interrupted. Negative emotions occur when the interruptions are preventing people from achieving a goal; for example, you are about to purchase a new laptop when you are told that the shop is about to close and consequently you have to wait until another time to get it. However, interruptions that assist us in achieving a desired goal will produce positive arousal. For instance, you feel under pressure to decide which laptop to buy because you know that the shop is about to close, when a friend calls you on your mobile who wants to offer to drive you to another shop with a bigger laptop selection that is open longer.

Meyers-Levy and Tybout (1989) argued that Mandler's theory can be applied to explain why brands that are moderately different from other brands in the same product category are viewed more favourably than brands that are highly typical or not at all typical of the product category. Basically when consumers are trying to figure out why and how one product differs from another they are happy to do so, provided that the differences are not too great as it would then be cognitively too straining for them. If the products are very similar, consumers are less likely to think in more depth about the products and as a result they would not be evaluated as positively.

It is also worth noting that it has been suggested that prior knowledge of a product also plays a part in whether or not moderate incongruity will generate positive feelings about a product (Peracchio & Tybout, 1996). If people have low prior knowledge of a product category, a moderate incongruity effect is likely to happen. However, individuals with high prior knowledge of a product category are more likely to rely on what they already know and consequently ignore category-inconsistent information.

In line with Meyers-Levy and Tybout's research it has also been suggested that Mandler's theory might offer some insight as to why trying 'own brand' products may increase likeability of that product (Sprott & Shimp, 2004). Several studies have supported the idea that certain products are favoured over others based purely on the brand and stores' 'own brand' products are generally thought of as inferior to national brands (e.g. Allison & Uhl, 1964; Bellizzi & Martin, 1982). However, such perceptions can be combated by making people take part in taste tests. This was found by Sprott and Shimp (2004) when they asked people to taste and judge the quality of juice. The results demonstrated that provided the 'own brand' juice was of good quality, those who actually tasted it generally evaluated it favourably compared to those who had not tried it. One underlying explanation for this is that once the participants had tasted the 'own brand' juice and realized that the quality was just as good as national brands, their 'own brand' schema and their actual experience were moderately incongruent. Consequently, the moderate incongruity resulted in positive emotions for the 'own brand' product.

Zillmann's theory of emotion

Zillmann's theory is based upon the idea that emotional excitement can be trans-ferred from one stimulus to another, something that is known as **excitation transfer** (Zillmann, 1978). He suggested that there are four key aspects of emotions:

1 Arousal can make both positive and negative emotions stronger.
2 People tend not to notice small changes in arousal.
3 Individuals normally assume that there is one single cause for arousal.
4 Perceived arousal tends to disappear more quickly than physiological arousal.

The third and fourth aspects of emotions seem to indicate that there is a very small window of opportunity when emotions can be transferred from one stimulus to another. That individuals assume that there is something in particular that is making them feel aroused suggests that they would focus so much on it that very little transference would take place, and once arousal starts to decrease, it will not be long before there is nothing left to be transferred. Hence, arousal transference is most likely to happen between the two stages when focus on a single factor and arousal decline is at moderate levels.

Having an understanding of Zillmann's theory can be particularly useful for those working in media planning as it may have implications for which TV programmes the commercials are integrated into. Watching television can cause people to become physiologically aroused (Klebber, 1985) and it is possible that evaluations of commercials can be more extreme when they have become highly aroused by what they have watched. This seems perfectly feasible since research has found that evaluations of objects are normally more intense and focused when consumers happen to be highly aroused due to other factors non-related to the object being evaluated (e.g. Gorn, Pham, & Sin, 2001; Mattes & Cantor, 1982; Zillmann, 1971).

Zillmann himself suggested that sport-related programmes are highly likely to generate strong emotional responses which subsequently may be transferred over to the adverts seen during a commercial break. Researchers have also found that the type of emotion experienced can be easily confused with another kind of emotion. For example, in a study where participants had to walk either over a scary and unstable or a stable concrete bridge while being interviewed by an attractive female it was found that fear can be transferred into feelings of attraction (Dutton & Aron, 1974). Participants who had walked across the scary bridge were later much more likely to call the attractive female experimenter to find out what the results of the study were. Hence it is possible for marketers to make use of the excitation transfer even in situations where the emotion generated is not of a positive nature.

Key Terms

Affect regulation
People generally strive to make themselves feel better.

Atmospherics
Creation of a certain atmosphere that has the ability to generate emotional responses.

Excitation transfer
When emotional excitement can be passed on from one stimulus to another.

Summary

Affect-based research is often focused on people's mood rather than emotions. At times it can be difficult to research how emotions and mood impact upon consumers. Nevertheless, it has been established that affect has the capacity to guide attention and increase recall, provided the information encountered is congruent with how people feel. Affect has also been found to contribute to how consumers make decisions. The decisions made are often influenced subconsciously by the way consumers feel at the time, even though it may have no relevance to the decision-making task. It is important not to assume that positive and negative feelings will impact in the same way on the decision-making process, which is evident from the Appraisal-Tendency Framework. Atmospherics have also been found to influence whether or not consumers will shop in a particular store, as well as the decisions made when there.

Mandler's and Zillman's theories of emotions offer some insight into how the way people feel can be used to persuade consumers to see products in a more favourable light. Mandler suggest that positive emotions can be generated through small discrepancies between a stimulus and our expectations of the stimulus, while Zillman suggests that emotional excitement can be transferred from one stimulus to another.

Discussion questions

1 Is it possible to distinguish between emotions and mood?

2 How can emotions be used to persuade consumers to purchase specific products and services?

3 What are the potential pitfalls a researcher needs to consider when investigating emotions?

4 Are consumers rational? Explain your answer by providing research examples that support your argument.

5 What does the Appraisal-Tendency Framework teach us about emotions?

Attitudes

6

Introduction

This chapter outlines the answer to questions such as what attitudes are, why people have them, what functions they fill, how attitudes are formed, as well as how they can be altered. In relation to the aforementioned, the chapter introduces you to different models that seek to further the understanding of attitudes such as the expectancy-value model and the cognitive dissonance theory. Additionally, it is also briefly explored whether or not attitudes can predict behaviour, as well as how the media can play a direct part in the formation and guidance of attitudes.

How are attitudes generated?

Attitudes are evaluations of people, objects and ideas. Such evaluations are something that we learn over time and can therefore vary drastically from one person to another (e.g. Fishbein & Ajzen, 1975; Oskamp, 1977). There is almost an infinite amount of sources that can help shape and establish a person's attitudes, such as parents, siblings, peers, television, advertising and politicians.

To date, there have been many suggestions in regard to why attitudes exist. It has been suggested that they are means to goals, and that they can protect people's self-esteem (Katz, 1960). Also, they are simply object appraisals (Fazio, 1989) and they help to save on cognitive energy (Smith, Bruner, & White, 1956). Regardless of whose theory one wishes to apply, attitudes are clearly useful in that they have the capacity to steer us towards consumer products and services that we view in a favourable way, without putting too much mental effort into analysing the pros and cons of them.

Attitudes can be cognitively based, affectively based or behaviourally based. All attitudes have affective, cognitive, and behavioural components. However, some are more heavily weighted towards one of the three (Zanna & Rempel, 1988). When attitudes are *cognitively based,* it means that they are mainly based on facts. For example, if a consumer decides to evaluate the efficiency of a Ford Focus car, they may base their evaluation of it on how much petrol it consumes, how fast it can go, and whether or not it has it has side-impact air bags. Cognitively based attitudes simply classify the pros and cons of any given object so that it rapidly can be categorized into products that we wish to use and be associated with or into those that we do not wish to use or be associated with. Consequently, it can be said that attitudes can be generated as a result of putting some thought into different aspects of a product or service.

Affectively based attitudes are based on how we feel about elements (e.g. Breckler & Wiggins, 1989). Often consumers find it hard to rationalize why they like a particular product for the simple reason that it is their emotions guiding them. Affectively based attitudes can be the result of a number of different sources such as people's values, religious beliefs, and moral beliefs. They are merely a way to express (and at times validate) an individual's basic value system (e.g. Maio & Olson, 1995; Schwartz, 1992; Snyder & DeBono, 1989). For example, in the case of moral beliefs, a consumer who strongly believes that it is wrong to conduct animal testing is unlikely to purchase cosmetic products that have been tested on animals. Hence, their attitudes towards shampoos that have not been tested on animals tend to be positive while they are negative towards shampoos that have been tested on animals. Some research has suggested that affectively based attitudes come to mind more rapidly than cognitive ones, which might mean that they are more accessible in memory (Verplanken & Aarts, 1999; Verplanken, Hofstee, & Janssen, 1998) and in turn more likely to be more readily acted upon.

Just as cognitively based attitudes are the result of more extensive processing, affectively based attitudes are generated as the result of having strong values and beliefs.

Behaviourally based attitudes come from people's observations of how they behave toward a person or stimulus. This is notable from Bem's **self-perception theory** that proposes that in some situations, individuals are unaware of how they feel until they see how they behave (Bem, 1972). For example, if you asked someone you know what they think of Nike trainers and they reply that they must really like them as they have repeatedly purchased them every time they need a new pair of trainers, then your friend's attitude is behaviourally based since it is based more on an observation than on their cognitions or affect. However, it is worth noting that people only infer their attitudes from their behaviour under certain conditions, such as when a person's initial attitude is vague or weak and when there are no other plausible explanations for their behaviour.

The expectancy-value model

Another way to look at how attitudes are developed is through what is known as the expectancy-value model. This emerged in the 1960s and 1970s and proposes that a person's behaviour is a function of their expectations and the value of the goal towards which they are working (e.g. Feather, 1959; Fishbein, 1963, 1967). If more than one kind of behaviour is possible, the behaviour chosen will be the one with the greatest combination of expected success and value. For example, if a consumer has to choose a particular brand of trainers, they will evaluate the alternative brands in order to decide which brand will be most closely linked with the image they wish others to have of them. This means that people's attitudes towards a particular brand of trainers are determined by their beliefs about the object, where a belief is a subjective probability that the brand has a certain attribute (Fishbein & Ajzen, 1975). In the case of the trainers, a brand such as Adidas would be the attitude object, while their belief that they are popular with 'sporty' types would be an attribute. Consequently, Adidas may therefore be the brand that the consumer chooses to buy based on the fact that it will make them appear to be 'sporty'. In the light of this, it appears that people's chosen behaviours can be interpreted as if humans are goal-oriented beings in that they only engage in behaviours that they think will achieve a particular outcome.

However, in order to determine which behavioural outcome will be the most beneficial, the expectancy-value model suggests that there are several subjective evaluations of the attributes associated with the product that will influence the outcome, as well as the strength of these associations. Those that are the most accessible (i.e. those that can be recalled from memory more easily and are expressed more quickly) at the time of making a consumer decision will be the ones that will influence the consumer's attitude towards a product the most (Fishbein, 1963; Kaplan & Fishbein, 1969).

Explicit and implicit attitudes

Existing attitudes can either be explicit or implicit. **Explicit attitudes** are easy to report as people are consciously aware of them. They are evaluations of products when we are asked questions such as 'What do you think of a Ford Focus?' **Implicit attitudes**, on the other hand, are involuntary, uncontrollable, and often unconscious (e.g. Fazio & Olson, 2003; Wilson, Lindsey, & Schooler, 2000). Implicit attitudes can be automatically activated without a person being consciously aware of it (Bargh, 1997; Johnson & Weisz, 1994), and can therefore influence consumers even though they are unaware of it. For example, in one study, participants read a magazine with text on one page and an advertisement on the other. Information from the ad was found to influence their attitudes about the brand and ad, even though they had focused solidly on the page with the text and had no explicit memory of the ad (Janiszewski, 1988, 1990).

Testing implicit attitudes can be difficult but increasingly it has been found that using the Implicit Association Test (IAT) can predict consumer brand preferences and behaviour (Maison, Greenwald, & Bruin, 2004). The IAT is a computerized test whereby participants have to sort stimuli into different categories. For example, participants may be exposed to images of various products at the same time as the words good and bad. They then have to then decide on whether or not to classify the product as good or bad. An example of how the test works can be found on https://implicit.harvard.edu/implicit/. The use of IAT should be treated with some caution as it does not necessarily represent absolute attitudes but rather relative preferences (Maison, Greenwald, & Bruin, 2004) but nonetheless can be an effective way to try and tap into people's subconscious.

What motivates people to change their attitudes?

There are many different ideas in regard to why people change their attitudes. Here we will take a look at three theories (functional theories, cognitive dissonance theory, and the heuristic-systematic model) as to why attitude change may take place. The three theories present an array of ideas that incorporate cognitive, behavioural and emotional aspects.

Functional theories

Functional theories are based upon the idea that attitudes serve specific functions (Eagly & Chaiken, 1998). Katz (1960) proposed early on that attitudes may in particular fulfil four different types of functions:

1 *Knowledge function* – This function helps people to understand the world around them and to organize and categorize information they encounter. Attitudes have the ability to guide our information processing, but only once they are well established (Fazio, 1989; Shavitt, 1990). Because people are continually categorizing the products and services they encounter, it helps to steer them towards those that they favour and to stay away from those that they do not like.

2 *Utilitarian function* – This is the idea that attitudes assist us in achieving goals and to avoid punishment. Consequently people tend to hold positive attitudes towards products that are consistent with their goals and hold negative attitudes towards products that are likely to be a hindrance to their goals and needs. For example, a consumer is likely to have a positive attitude towards a product that they think is going to make them be perceived more favourably by their peers and in turn make them more popular; while the same person is likely to hold a negative attitude towards products that their peers will disapprove of.

3 *Value-expressive function* – The value-expressive function suggests that attitudes themselves make a statement of who we are. By expressing our attitudes towards products and services (as well as issues and people) that we feel strongly about, we validate our own self-concept. This may be evident when consumers shy away from products that can be viewed as ethically unsound, perhaps due to environmental reasons or because of animal testing. Or consumers may express favourable attitudes toward products such as Dom Perignon champagne and Rolls Royce cars in the hope that it will reflect their expensive taste, in turn making others perceive them as being sophisticated.

4 *Ego-defensive function* – Katz (1967) proposed that at times people may hold

attitudes towards certain objects in the hope of hiding their feelings and therefore in turn protecting their own self-esteem. For example, an individual may truly like to eat Pop Tarts™ for breakfast but is aware that they are not perceived to be the 'right' thing to eat by their health-conscious friends. So when discussing what they eat for breakfast with their friends they say that they would never eat pop tarts for breakfast as they are not nutritious enough for their liking.

Katz's four types of functions can easily be used to explain how attitudes can serve different types of functions in a consumer society. They may not necessarily explain all types of attitudes, but can at least be used to demonstrate that attitudes can clearly be functional in nature. However, when the attitudes are no longer fulfilling a particular function, individuals are likely to change them in order to ensure that they do.

One aspect of functional theories is that in order for them to be effective, the method used to change consumers' attitudes must match the attitude function (Katz, 1960; Smith et al., 1956). Persuasive messages that are factual have been found to work for knowledge-based attitudes; rewards and punishments work on utilitarian-based attitudes; social-image appeals are effective for value-expressive attitudes; and fear appeals have been found to be useful for ego–defensive-based attitudes.

Different kinds of people tend to have attitudes that serve different attitude functions (Snyder & DeBono, 1985). High self-monitoring people are often very concerned about their self-image, while low self-monitoring individuals are more concerned about utility (Snyder, 1974, 1979). Consequently, image-oriented persuasive messages should be effective for those high in self-monitoring, and focus on quality should be more persuasive for low self-monitors. This was confirmed when Snyder and DeBono (1985) showed participants image-oriented and quality-oriented advertisements for products such as Barclay cigarettes and Irish Mocha Mint coffee. The advertisements for each product were identical but differed in terms of the captions. For example, the Irish Mocha Mint coffee ad in the image-oriented condition showed a couple in a romantic setting with a caption that said 'Make a chilly night become a cozy evening with Irish Mocha Mint'. However, in the quality-oriented condition the emphasis of the caption was on taste rather than the appearance (see Figure 6.1).

Cognitive dissonance theory

This theory proposes that people strive for *consonance* (consistency between target behaviour and a target attitude) (Festinger, 1957). Not only does this theory explain why people may change their attitudes, it also sheds some light on the problem of attitude-behaviour discrepancy. The theory is similar to the balance theory discussed in Chapter 8.

The main underlying idea of the cognitive dissonance theory is that people will be motivated to engage in certain activities in order to maintain consonance. That

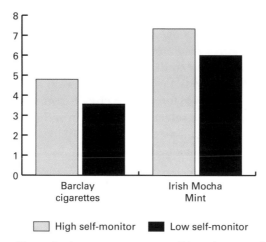

Individuals high in self-monitoring are more susceptible to image-oriented appeals.

FIGURE 6.1 Susceptibility to image-oriented advertising.

Source: Adapted from Snyder and DeBono (1985)

is, attitudes are changed in order to reduce feelings of unease that arise when an attitude is inconsistent with some information they encounter such as the contents of a persuasive advertising message (Festinger, 1957; Festinger & Carlsmith, 1959). For example, a chain smoker sees an advert about how smoking causes cancer. They may then think that it is important to give up smoking. However, the problem is that they are still smoking 20 cigarettes a day. Consequently they need to either change the way they are thinking or the way they are behaving as they otherwise will suffer from feelings of unease. Since cognitive dissonance always causes discomfort, it is in an individual's interest to try and reduce it. There are a number of ways through which it can be done (for examples, see Table 6.1).

TABLE 6.1 Reduction of cognitive dissonance

Cognitive dissonance can be reduced by	Example of action taken
● Changing their attitude to a more extreme position.	● I am too busy to come up with suitable ways to give up smoking, and it is unlikely it will kill me.
● Adding consistent cognitions to eliminate the inconsistency.	● Emphasize the negative aspects of giving up smoking, how they may suffer from terrible withdrawal symptoms.
● Rationalizing how important the cognitions are.	● If I go to the gym, it will leave less time for work.
● Changing behaviour so that it is consistent with cognition.	● Actually going to the gym.
● Denying that a contradiction exists.	● Rather than admitting that they never exercise a person may claim to do it: i.e. I walk from the train to work every day.

Cognitive dissonance is most powerful when people's self-image is threatened (e.g. Aronson, 1992, 1998; Greenwald & Ronis, 1978). The reason for this is that it makes people realize that they are not who they think they are due to the fact that they have not behaved accordingly. Realizing that you may be a different person can be very upsetting. Generally people tend to try to avoid exposure to information that might arouse dissonance, in order to avoid feelings of discomfort, something that is known as the **selective exposure hypothesis**. However, there are individuals who are not particularly choosy in regard to what kind of information they are exposed to. Such individuals either tend to have very strongly held attitudes or very weak cognitive systems. If people have strongly held attitudes, they tend to have the ability to easily argue against the dissonant information they come across and therefore do not have to try to avoid it. If their attitudes are weak, it can seem better to try to discover what the 'truth' is immediately in order to avoid potential long-term suffering. This would then be done by making the appropriate adjustments to attitudes after having encountered the dissonant information (Frey, 1986; Frey & Rosch, 1984).

The heuristic-systematic model

The heuristic-systematic model (HSM) was proposed by Chaiken and is an alternative to the Elaboration Likelihood Model (ELM) that is discussed in Chapter 7 (Chaiken, 1980, 1987; Chaiken, Liberman, & Eagly, 1989; Chaiken & Maheswaran, 1994). This model proposes that attitudes are likely to change when people are persuaded by a convincing message. The message itself has to be processed either systematically or heuristically. Systematically processed messages are likely to be scrutinized while heuristically processed messages are likely to be taken at face value. *Systematic processing* occurs when people consider the available arguments, while *heuristic processing* come about when we do not wish to think much about the information presented. When heuristic processing takes place, cognitive heuristics are employed in order for people to simplify the handling of information encountered. You may recall from Chapter 3 that a heuristic is a mental shortcut that is a form of rule of thumb (see also Chapter 8). Consequently, when a consumer is judging a persuasive marketing message while using heuristic processing, they may conclude that 'statistics don't lie' or that 'longer arguments are generally stronger'. Put simply, they are effectively judging the book by its cover!

The fact that a high number of consumers resort to heuristic processing when it comes to persuasive messages means that many advertising campaigns make use of 'superficial cues' to communicate with their audiences (see ELM discussed in Chapter 7). For example, advertisements for health-related products often contain authoritative-looking people dressed in white coats. This is done in the hope that the consumer will automatically draw the conclusion that the health product is endorsed by a scientist who clearly knows what they are talking about. The heuristic processing is generally used as long as consumers feel confident about the attitudes they have adopted. When they start to lack confidence, they tend to resort to systematic processing so that they can think more extensively about the messages they encounter (Petty & Wegener, 1998).

It has been found that emotions can play a role in which type of processing people engage in. When persuasive messages contain high levels of emotions, people are more likely to process the information through heuristic processing, while if the message contains low levels of emotions, they are more likely to process the information through systematic processing (Hale, Lemieux, & Mongeau, 1995).

The mood of the consumer can also influence the processing route. A happy consumer is likely to pay more attention to a message and hence use systematic processing (Wegener, Petty, & Smith, 1995), most likely because they associate their own happy mood with the message content.

Do attitudes predict behaviour?

It is often assumed that consumers' attitudes will ultimately influence consumer decisions (Ajzen, 2008). However, if the two don't go hand in hand, marketers may simply be wasting their money, since they tend to rely on the fact that their campaigns will change people's attitudes and in turn their consumption behaviour.

The link between attitudes and behaviour has been frequently researched and unfortunately it is not a clear-cut relationship. At times it has been found that attitudes are a poor predictor of behaviour (e.g. Balderjahn, 1988; Hines, Hungerford, & Tomera, 1987; LaPiere, 1934), which may partially be due to using less rigorous research methods as well as failing to measure specific attitudes that are likely to be directly linked to the behaviour one wishes to measure.

Researching consumers' attitudes and using them as predictors of behaviour is particularly difficult since it is impossible to take the situational influences into account that consumers may be subjected to while out shopping. Bearing in mind that many attitude studies are lab based, it therefore means that many studies lack ecological validity. Nevertheless, some aspects of attitudes have been rigorously researched and are established factors (e.g. attitude strength, attitude accessibility and direct experience) when it comes to predicting behaviour.

Attitude strength

Strong attitudes (i.e. when people are confident of their attitudes) are more likely to predict behaviours (Fazio & Zanna, 1978), make people less susceptible to persuasive messages (Bassili, 1996; Krosnick & Abelson, 1992; Petty & Krosnick, 1995), and are more readily accessible (Fazio, 1995). Fazio argued that this is because they are evaluative associations with objects. The associations can vary in strength from having no links (i.e. no attitude), weak links, or strong links (see Figure 6.2). Only strong associations automatically come to mind from memory (Fazio, 1995; Fazio, Blaschovich, & Driscoll, 1992; Fazio, Sanbonmatsu, Powell, & Kardes, 1986). *Automatic activation is important* since only activated attitudes have

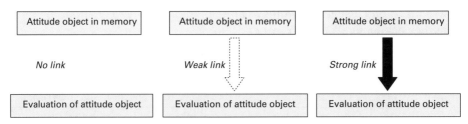

The associations can vary in strength. Only strong associations automatically come to mind from memory and are likely to predict behaviour.

FIGURE 6.2 Fazio's evaluative associations.

the ability to guide an individual's behaviour. Strong associations often stem from direct experiences and/or something that we are specifically interested in. For example, a person who has been driving a Saab for years will have stronger attitudes in regard to the car's performance and how other people perceive them. Provided both the performance and others' perception of the car have generated favourable attitudes, the Saab driver is likely to buy yet another Saab when the car is due to be replaced.

Attitude accessibility

Attitudes that can be recalled from memory easily and that can be expressed more rapidly (Eagly & Chaiken, 1998), can more readily guide behaviour (Fazio, 1986; Doll & Ajzen, 1992). Additionally, accessible attitudes are also more stable over time and are resistant to change (Fazio, 1995). Just as research in attitude strength did, research on attitude accessibility has also made use of Fazio's (1995) model of attitudes. The underlying idea is that the functionality of an attitude depends on the extent of automatic activation and that the likelihood of activation depends on the strength of the object-evaluation association (Bargh, Chaiken, Govender, & Pratto, 1992). Strong object-evaluation associations are useful in that they facilitate decision-making and guide visual attention and categorization (when a stimulus is assigned to belong to a particular group) (e.g. Roskos-Ewoldsen & Fazio, 1992; Smith, Fazio, & Cejka, 1996). To demonstrate how accessible attitudes influence categorization of objects that could be put into several categories, Smith, Fazio and Cejka (1996) experimentally enhanced either health foods or dairy products. Participants were then asked to choose from a number of categories to describe an object. Hence, when participants had rehearsed their attitudes towards dairy products, yoghurt was more likely to be categorized as a dairy product. However, when participants had rehearsed their attitudes towards health products, yoghurt was more likely to be categorized as a health product (Eagly & Chaiken, 1998).

It is worth noting that Fazio's theoretical model has been criticized because object-evaluation associations have been found to correlate weakly with self-reports (Karpinski & Hilton, 2001), meaning that people's thoughts are not necessarily the same as what they say.

Direct experience

Direct experiences will not only affect the strength of an attitude (as previously mentioned) but also the accessibility. Attitudes that are formed as a result of a direct experience have been found to correlate more strongly with behaviour than those that are the result of indirect experiences (Doll & Ajzen, 1992; Fazio & Zanna, 1978; Regan & Fazio, 1977). For example, tasting a food product is more likely to predict future likelihood of purchase than just reading about it. However, the link between attitudes generated from direct experience and behaviour is not always a strong one. This can be evident from those who are caught drink driving or taking drugs; there is no certainty that they will not engage in such behaviour in the future.

The influence of the mass media

As previously mentioned, our attitudes can be learnt through many different sources and it is always difficult to say for certain that one particular attitude stems from a particular source. Even so, there is research evidence that has clearly demonstrated that there are some sources that definitely help shape people's attitudes. If they don't create them, then at least they reinforce and maintain them. The mass media in particular is such a source. It has been found that the influence of mass media upon attitude formation is most influential when attitudes are weak (Goldberg & Gorn, 1974). This most likely explains why television plays an important role in attitude formation in children (e.g. Atkin, 1977; Chaffee, Jackson-Beeck, Durall, & Wilson, 1977; Rubin, 1978) since children are continuously involved in the process of developing attitudes about elements that they may have no or limited experience of. Basically, they are using the mass media to learn about the society in which they live, something that is known as the **cultivation hypothesis** (Gerbner, Gross, Morgan, & Signorielli, 1994). Because the media often show a skewed picture of reality, people may develop one of two distinct images of the world: a social reality, or a TV reality. The cultivation hypothesis suggests that those who spend a lot of time watching television will develop a 'TV reality', meaning that their view of life is more in line with television's portrayal than with actual reality. This hypothesis predicts that a person who is continuously exposed to mass media that is not representative of real life will therefore adopt attitudes in line with the skewed life portrayal. However, it is possible that the relationship between media consumption and attitudes is not always a linear one, as proposed by the cultivation hypothesis (e.g. Durkin, 1985a; Potter, 1991). Nevertheless, this hypothesis appears to be supported by several research studies exploring areas such as stereotypical sex roles and violent pornography. From such research it can be noted that consumption of certain films, television programmes, newspapers, etc. can play a part in the formation and maintenance of people's attitudes.

Stereotypical sex roles

It has been suggested that the media is the most influential factor in creating stereo-typically gender-related attitudes (Durkin, 1985b). The media's influence starts from the moment we are born. Cards and gifts that are used to congratulate parents on the birth of their son or daughter make use of stereotypical cues (Bridges, 1993). For example, typically a blue colour is used for boys and pink for girls and children are dressed in a way that sets them apart from the opposite sex (see Figure 6.3). Television programmes and books for young children continue to build on the idea that men and women should be portrayed in a specific way. Programmes often depict women as weak and passive, with men and boys doing most of the action (Durkin, 1985b) while books often portray females as being dependent on male characters (Kortenhaus & Demarest, 1993). The constant exposure to stereotypical sex roles seems to affect children in their views of men and women. This was found

Children are typically dressed in a way that clearly shows the sex of the baby. Likewise, toys that will reinforce their gender are also bought for babies.

FIGURE 6.3 The use of stereotypical cues to reinforce sex roles.

Source: Courtesy of Cathrine Jansson ©

by Signorelli and Lears (1992) in a study where children in Grades 1, 3, 5 and 7 who spent a lot of time watching television had more stereotypical beliefs about what type of household chores men and women should do.

Stereotypical sex roles are not only used in programmes and books targeted at children but also in media aimed at adult audiences. In a study where 1,750 visual images from newspapers and magazines of men and women were analyzed, it was found that depictions of men give greater importance to the head, while depictions of women give greater importance to the body (Archer, Iritani, Kimes, & Barrios, 1983). This difference has been termed *face-ism*. Face-ism can influence people to think that women are only important for their physical appearance while the male facial prominence signifies ambition and intelligence (Schwartz & Kurz, 1989). Consequently, the focal point of imagery in the media can affect the attitudes that people have towards men and women.

Violent pornography

Violent pornography has been found to affect men's attitudes towards the treatment of women. This was notable in a study conducted by Donnerstein and Berkowitz (1981). In their study, participating males were angered by a female accomplice prior to watching a film. They were assigned to see either a violent pornographic, a non-violent pornographic or a neutral (containing no violence or porn) film. Afterwards the participants were given the opportunity to act aggressively toward the woman who had angered them by deciding on the level of electric shock (unbeknown to the participants they were not real) she would receive in an unrelated learning experiment. The findings showed that those who had watched the violent pornographic film were much more likely to administer higher levels of electric shocks. This suggests that it is the combination of violence and pornography that leads to aggressive behaviour towards women (Mussweiler & Förster, 2000). Similar results have also been found by other researchers. For example, men who watch violent pornography in which women are shown to enjoy it are more willing to aggress against women (e.g. Linz, Donnerstein & Penrod, 1988). When violent pornographic films portray women as enjoying the violence, they have also been found to reinforce rape myths and weaken social restraints against violence towards women (Malamuth & Donnerstein, 1982).

That violent pornography plays a role in males' attitudes toward rape and how rapists should be punished was outlined in a study conducted by Zillman and Bryant (1984). Participants were either exposed to a high amount of violent pornography or no pornography at all. It was found that those who had been subjected to a large dose of pornographic violence were generally unsympathetic about what they had seen, became more tolerant of rape and were less likely to give harsh prison sentences for rape cases (see Figure 6.4).

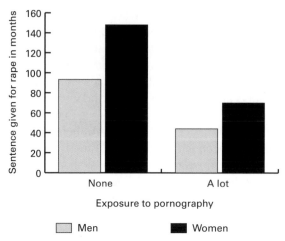

FIGURE 6.4 Effect of number of pornographic films watched by juries on sentencing of rape defendants.

Source: Adapted from Zillmann & Bryant (1984)

Key Terms

Cultivation hypothesis
Sometimes individuals use the mass media to learn about the society that they live in.

Explicit attitudes
Attitudes that people are consciously aware of.

Implicit attitudes
Attitudes that are involuntary and unconscious.

Selective exposure hypothesis
People try to avoid exposure to information that can cause them feelings of discomfort.

Self-perception theory
People can at times discover how they feel as a result of behaving in a particular way.

Summary

Attitudes are evaluations of people, objects and ideas and can be generated through cognition, emotions or behaviour. The expectancy-value model also proposes that they can be generated as the result of trying to reach a particular goal. Attitudes are either explicit (conscious) or implicit (subconscious) and both types have the ability to affect the way consumers view products. There are many theories in regard to why people change their attitudes. Functional theories propose that they are changed so that they serve a specific purpose. Cognitive dissonance theory states that attitude change takes place as a result of trying to maintain consistency between actual behaviour and attitudes. The heuristic-systematic model looks at how persuasive messages are the underlying factor to attitude change.

Not all attitudes predict behaviour, but they are more likely to do so when they are strong, easily accessible and are the result of a direct experience. One source that has the ability to influence people's attitudes is the media. Research on stereotypical sex roles and violent pornography clearly demonstrates such an influence.

Discussion questions

1 How can marketers try to generate positive attitudes towards a product?
2 Can the cognitive dissonance theory truly explain why people are motivated to change their attitudes?
3 Under what circumstances are attitudes unlikely to predict behaviour?
4 What *types* of media may impact upon people's attitudes?
5 Why are marketers interested in attitude formation?

Advertising psychology

Introduction

These days there is no way of escaping advertising messages as they are incorporated into a multiple of settings. Every year billions are spent on advertising and it affects consumers' attitudes towards products and services as well as what they buy. However, not all ad campaigns are successful when it comes to increasing sales figures. There are a number of methods that can be applied to help distinguish an advertisement from those of its competitors. This chapter outlines and discuss some factors that are well known to influence audiences and how some variables also help generate more thorough processing of the information provided.

Advertising

In most societies people are bombarded with advertising messages through the television, radio, direct mail, the Internet, billboards, newspapers, magazines, on buses, via telephone, and so forth. It was not that long ago when advertisers were mainly using leaflets, newspapers/magazine advertisements, billboards and TV commercials as their main outlets. But as times have moved on the pressure for advertisers to be more creative has meant new ways of reaching consumers. Partially such creativity will have naturally grown alongside new technology. For example, when Virgin re-launched in Australia in 2004 a high proportion of their campaign relied upon text messaging (*Effective Advertising 8*, 2006). However, the need for innovative resourcefulness is mostly due to fierce competition, the result being that advertising can be seen pretty much everywhere you turn. It is difficult to determine exactly how many adverts consumers see on a daily basis, but estimates suggest that it may be between 500 and 3,000 (e.g. Lasn, 1999; Wilson & Wilson, 1998).

Many consumers think that adverts affect others but not them (Wilson & Brekke, 1994), and they often try to avoid paying attention to them (Wilson, Houston, & Meyers, 1998). However, there is little doubt that advertising does influence people and it is impossible to avoid each and every advert that they are exposed to (e.g.

Abraham & Lodish, 1990; Ryan, 1991; Wells, 1997). Naturally it is impossible for consumers to pay attention to and fully process all the advertising messages they encounter. If they did they would be mentally exhausted. When adverts are noticed and remembered, they can at times help increase sales of products and services by as much as 20 times (Feldwick, 1990). However, such large increases are rather uncommon (Green, 2007).

It is particularly difficult for new brands to compete with already established brands. Brands that consumers are familiar with are less susceptible to competitive advertising campaigns (Kardes, 1994; Kent & Allen, 1993) in that established brands are more easily recalled (Kent & Allen, 1994). Whether or not it is a new brand that is being marketed, advertising is fiercely competitive, and hence it is imperative for new as well as established brands to make use of whatever techniques may give them the competitive edge they need.

So what makes some advertising campaigns successful while others seem to have very little (if any) impact upon their audience? Unfortunately, there is not one single answer to that question and because the psychology of advertising is a well-researched area, it is not possible to cover all aspects in this chapter. Readers with a particular interest in this area should conduct further reading. Nonetheless, there are certain psychological aspects that are particularly worth familiarizing yourself with when trying to create a successful ad campaign, such as what captures consumers' attention and what kind of elements are more likely to increase elaboration, which will be discussed here.

The role of attention

Advertising relies upon capturing consumers' attention (see Chapter 3 for information about how attention works). Hence, advertising researchers have been busy trying to figure out methods that can be applied so that viewers will automatically notice advertising messages (MacInnis, Moorman, & Jaworski, 1991). In a competitive market where advertising stimuli are constantly competing with numerous other marketing elements, it is imperative that consumers notice the ads or they are unlikely to have any impact upon the consumer.

There are specific factors that can increase the likelihood of advertisements being noticed such as vivid and salient stimuli, both commonly used in advertisements and commercials. **Vivid stimuli** are something that 'stands out' from the rest of the advertisements. Such advertisements have been found to be noticed more frequently as they attract consumers' attention in an automatic and involuntary way (e.g. Kisielius & Sternthal, 1986; Rock, 1986; Taylor & Thompson, 1982). A vivid stimulus stand out regardless of what other stimuli are present and should be 'a) emotionally interesting, b) concrete and image-provoking, and c) proximate in a temporal, spatial or sensory way' (Nisbett & Ross, 1980, p. 45).

Examples of vivid stimulus use in advertising can often be found in Benetton ads and those campaigns are often discussed by people on the streets as well as in the media. A memorable example is the use of a picture portraying a newborn baby that had not yet had their umbilical cord cut in an ad for Benetton (Figure 7.1).

When using vivid imagery in a persuasive context, it needs to be treated with some caution. To ensure that vividness works for a persuasive message, the vivid message itself has to be congruent with the message conclusions (Smith & Shaffer, 2000), otherwise it is possible that it may distract the viewer away from the core of the message itself. The likelihood of the audience being distracted by the vividness increases if they do not have to pay attention to the message. In such situations it has been found that individuals are less likely to remember the message and not to be persuaded by it. However, when people are told to pay attention to a message containing vivid elements, such elements appear to have no negative impact upon memory and persuasiveness (Frey & Eagly, 1993).

Just like vivid stimuli, **salient stimuli** have also been found to have the capacity to capture consumers' attention. However, these differ in that they are context dependent, so they may not 'grab' people's attention in all settings. Nonetheless, provided the advertisement stands out from the environment in which it is placed, it can capture consumers' attention involuntarily (e.g. Greenwald & Leavitt, 1984; Nisbett & Ross, 1980). Some salient auditory stimuli have even been found to have the ability to increase recall (Olsen, 2002). Examples of salient stimuli may include

UNITED COLORS
OF BENETTON.

Example of how vivid imagery can be used to capture consumers' attention.

FIGURE 7.1 Vivid imagery.

Source: Courtesy of United Colors of Benetton. © Copyright 1991 Benetton Group S.p.A. – Photo: Oliver Toscani

increase in volume (commonly used in television commercials), use of bright irregular shapes, and shift in brightness between two scenes.

Elaborating on advertising messages

One important aspect of advertising is to change consumers' attitudes towards products and brands. Much has been written about how persuasive messages can be used to change attitudes and it is imperative to understand such methods when trying to create effective advertisements. Attitudes that are changed as a result of advertising exposure will vary in strength depending on how extensively the information in the ad was processed. Different techniques can be employed to guide consumers to superficially or extensively elaborate upon a persuasive message and the chosen method depends on what is being advertised and how long the advertiser is hoping the attitude will last.

One model that seeks to explain how different types of processing of persuasive messages can lead to stronger/weaker and long-lasting/short attitudes is the Elaboration Likelihood Model (ELM) by Petty and Cacioppo (1986a). The model supports the concept of a dual route perspective whereby one route will generate relatively strong and long-lasting attitude changes (Central Route) while the other generates relatively weak and temporary attitude changes (Peripheral Route). Generally the idea is that the more a person elaborates upon a message, the more likely they are to be persuaded by the message, provided they like what they hear or see. How personally relevant the message is generally determines which one of the two routes that will be followed. Additionally, the likelihood of using the Central Route also depends on the consumers' motivation and ability to engage in processing. When the motivation and ability are high, the individual will make use of the Central Route (Figure 7.2). The Peripheral Route is a default option. Hence, when the message is not really personally relevant, and motivation and ability are low, individuals will automatically make use of the Peripheral Route. It is essential for advertisers to understand which route consumers are the most likely to make use of, as consumers use different types of information depending on which path to persuasion they use.

Central route to persuasion

As can be seen from Figure 7.2, an individual starts off by evaluating whether or not they are motivated to elaborate upon the persuasive advertising message encountered. This is done by addressing whether it is personally relevant to them, if the message is important, should they feel some level of personal responsibility and whether or not they need to think more extensively about it. All the questions are dealt with in an instant and often subconsciously. Should the answer turn out to be yes to any of the questions, they will go on to assess if they have the ability to elaborate on the message. In order to be able to elaborate on the message, the

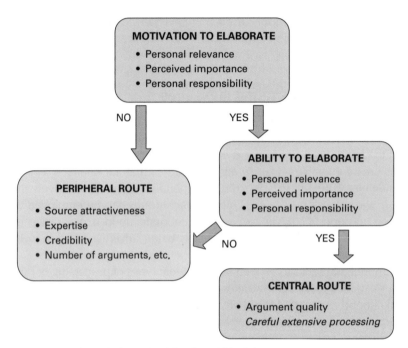

FIGURE 7.2 Outline of the Elaboration Likelihood Model.

Source: Adapted from Petty & Cacioppo (1986a)

individual needs to have enough time to think further about it, not being distracted by other stimuli; they must be able to understand it and have some previous know-ledge of the subject area. Provided these criteria are satisfied, the individual will then carefully process the message and look at the argument quality. However, if there are obstacles in the way for being able to elaborate upon the message they will automatically switch to the Peripheral Route instead.

Attitudes that are the result of being processed through the Central Route are stronger in that they are more resistant to change, are persistent, and increase the likelihood of predicting behaviour (Petty & Cacioppo, 1981, 1986b). The main reason why they are stronger is because the information encountered is integrated more thoroughly into an already existing schema. By making adverts directly rele-vant to a particular consumer group, the chance of encouraging them to elaborate on the contents of the ad increases. It is also advisable to carefully consider the type of language used as it can be the determining factor in whether or not consumers are persuaded by a message when they are motivated to process the information further (Levin & Gaeth, 1988).

Peripheral route to persuasion

As previously mentioned, people can shift to the peripheral route of processing if they lack the ability to elaborate upon a persuasive advertising message. However, that is not the only path towards peripheral processing. Consumers may also decide to use the peripheral route just after realizing that they are not motivated to elaborate upon the message (see Figure 7.2). Once they reach the peripheral route, instead of thinking extensively about the message itself, they will make use of superficial cues (e.g. how attractive the source is or the number of arguments used) to determine whether or not they like the advert.

Factors known to increase persuasiveness of communication when using the peripheral route can be divided into three categories: (1) the source; (2) the message; and (3) the audience.

Source factors

Who is presenting the information about a product or service can affect whether or not consumers will be persuaded by the message. *Credibility* and *trustworthiness* are two aspects that determine if the source will be deemed in a favourable way, and the two often go hand in hand (Priester & Petty, 2003). Experts are generally found to be more credible than the average member of the public. However, how credible they may seem depends upon trustworthiness.

That experts are more persuasive was found early on in a study conducted by Hovland and Weiss (1951). Participants were asked to read a persuasive message about the utility of atomic submarines that they thought were either written by a famous American physicist or a Russian newspaper. A higher number of the participants found the message to be convincing when written by the American physicist.

Trustworthiness has also been linked to how likeable individuals are. This in particular is applicable to celebrities (Friedman, Santeramo & Traina, 1978), which is why advertisers commonly use famous, well liked people to endorse products, such as David Beckham (e.g. Giorgio Armani and Pepsi), Pierce Brosnan (e.g. Omega and Aquascutum) and Liz Hurley (e.g. Magnum ice-cream and Estee Lauder). However, market research has suggested that consumers do not find celebrities who endorse a high number of products to be credible, rather they assume they are only in it for the money (King, 1989). Instead the use of multiple unpaid sources in advertising campaigns can generate more positive perceptions (Moore, Mowen, & Reardon, 1994), as people assume they are endorsing the product for its genuine qualities.

Other influential source factors include the *gender of the speaker*, (men are generally more persuasive than women), and *how similar the person presenting the message is to ourselves*, (the more similar they are, the more persuasive they tend to be). Similarity may include physical appearance, what kind of job the person presenting the message has and social status. It has even been found that the similarity of another individual's name to the message recipient can increase the likelihood of the recipient complying with a request as well as increasing likeability of the presenter (Garner, 2005). However, dissimilar sources tend to do better when things that are a matter of fact are presented (Goethals & Nelson, 1973), as opposed to when it is about taste or judgement when a similar source tends to be more persuasive.

Additionally, how fast a person is presenting the information in the ad can also affect if the audience is persuaded. Fast speech has been found to inhibit processing of the arguments presented and simultaneously increase the likelihood of persuasion (Smith & Shaffer, 1991, 1995).

Personal characteristics of the presenter are also important, as unpopular and unattractive individuals tend to be less persuasive. There is little doubt that beautiful people are more persuasive, which explains why models and attractive celebrities are commonly featured in ads. People are more likely to believe that a cream can reduce their wrinkles when advertised by Jane Fonda than they would be if the advert showed an unattractive celebrity.

The impact of a beautiful woman can be the greatest when she expresses a desire to influence the audience (Mills & Aronson, 1965). This may be because people tend to want to please those they find attractive just as they expect attractive people to support opinions they think are desirable (Eagly & Chaiken, 1975). However, in order to ensure that physical attractiveness has the desired impact upon the audience, it is best to ensure that the physical attributes are clearly linked to the product category advertised (e.g. Baker & Churchill, 1977; Caballero & Pride, 1984; Kahle & Homer, 1985).

Getting the message right the first time around is preferential. However, sometimes it may not be the end of the world if people are not initially persuaded by it. This can be the case when a good argument is at first rejected due to low credibility and often such credibility is linked to the actual source presenting it (Pratkanis, Greenwald, Leippe, & Baumgardner, 1988). In such situations the message may later on be remembered but the reasons for disregarding it may have been forgotten and hence the persuasive message still impacts upon the audience. This is known as the '**sleeper effect**'. Hovland and Weiss (1951) tested the sleeper effect in a study whereby participants were presented with a message containing either a high or a low credibility source. All participants were asked about their attitudes immediately afterwards and it was found that those presented with a high credibility source were much more likely to have changed their attitudes. However, when the participants were asked once more about their attitudes, four weeks later, it was found that the change in attitudes were almost the same for both groups. Hence, those who had been presented with a low credibility source had been affected by the sleeper effect.

More recently it has also been proposed that the sleeper effect is more likely to take place when the message argument as well as the reasons for discounting the message had originally made a strong impact (Kumkale & Albarracín, 2004).

Message factors

How the persuasive message itself is presented also helps determine whether or not the audience will perceive it favourably. In terms of *content* it is better to present a two-sided argument rather than just present a biased view but only when the brand advertised is unfamiliar to consumers. That way, consumers are likely to think that you are being truthful as opposed to just painting a very rosy picture. On the other hand, a one-sided argument has been found to work better when consumers are familiar with the products advertised (e.g. Lumsdaine & Janis, 1953).

Try to avoid designing a message that appears to be deliberately persuading consumers. Using a *strategic communication* technique tends to be much more effective than when the message is clearly designed to persuade people. Make sure the message is also repeated. *Repetition* increases the likelihood of believing that what is advertised is correct, regardless of whether or not the claims in the advert are inaccurate (Hawkins & Hoch, 1992). It also aids recall while out shopping.

Audience factors

The *receiver's initial position* affects how consumers respond to persuasive advertising messages. If the audience hold beliefs that are more closely related to the message itself, they are much more likely to be persuaded than they would be if there were a huge discrepancy between the message and their initial position.

Another variable that impacts on the likelihood of being persuaded is *self-esteem*. Research has found that there is an inverted U-curve relationship between how easily persuaded people are and self-esteem. Those with either high or low self-esteem are less easily persuaded than those with moderate self-esteem (e.g. McGuire, 1968; Rhodes & Wood, 1992). Women are also more easily persuaded than men. Hence it matters *whether the audience is female or male*. This was found by Schuller, Smith, and Olson (1994) when they set up a mock court case where a woman had killed her husband. Participants had to imagine that they were part of the members of the jury. One set of jurors heard an expert witness testify that the woman had been repeatedly beaten by her husband and that had eventually led to the killing, while another set of jurors did not get to hear the expert witness testimony. Male jurors in this study were found to be almost as likely to convict the woman of murder regardless of whether or not they had heard the expert witness. However, the percentage of female jurors convicting the woman of murder was much lower if they had heard the expert witness testify.

Intricacies of the elaboration likelihood model

The fact that the ELM is a complex model means that the structure is not always black and white. There are aspects of the model that may cast a shadow of doubt on how religiously it ought to be applied to the world of advertising, such as how fluid the factor fit is and to what extent it can be used to predict whether or not consumers will act upon the persuasive messages that they have been exposed to.

Factor fit

The above discussion about how different factors fit into the ELM is not written in stone (e.g. Haugtvedt & Kasmer, 2008; Petty & Cacioppo, 1986b). For example, 'brand name' has been found to be a factor that fits nicely into the peripheral route (Maheswaran, Mackie, & Chaiken, 1992), while others have suggested that they can be used to trigger more thorough elaboration of persuasive messages

(Haugtvedt & Rucker, 2003, as cited in Haugtvedt & Kasmer, 2008). The latter may perhaps be more likely in circumstances such as when consumers have a particular interest in the brand advertised.

Other examples that show certain factors don't always just fit into the one route of persuasion include research by Priester and Petty (1995). They found that people's expectations of source trustworthiness can produce either more or less elaboration. Others have found that personal characteristics such as attractiveness are used as a peripheral cue when it is unrelated to the product, but that it can serve as a cue for further processing when it is clearly linked to the product category advertised (Kang & Herr, 2006).

Due to the aforementioned, it is worth treating persuasive factors with some caution and look at their individual merits and how they may fit with the product advertised and the type of advertisement used.

The link between attitudes and behaviour

The ELM is designed to look at how persuasive messages impact upon attitudes, meaning that it also needs to be considered to what extent attitudes actually predict behaviours. As discussed in the previous chapter, research investigating how well attitudes predict behaviour is not clear-cut. However, when attitudes are altered as a result of careful elaboration consumers are more likely to act upon attitudes formed (Cacioppo, Petty, Kao, & Rodriguez, 1986). This was confirmed by Priester, Nayakankuppam, Fleming, and Godek (2001) when they investigated the effect of elaboration upon choice. They showed participants an advertisement for a candy bar they had invented that contained strong arguments as well as positive super-ficial elements that could function as peripheral cues. The incorporation of strong arguments as well as peripheral cues was to ensure that positive attitudes were formed irrespective of whether a central or peripheral route of processing was used. Half of the participants were instructed to pay attention to the thoughts and emo-tions experienced while reading the ad (central route) while the other half was asked to count words within the ad that contained more than one syllable (per-ipheral route). Afterwards when they were asked about their attitude towards the candy bar, all reported a positive one. However, when they were later asked to choose a candy bar it was found that those who had elaborated upon the message were much more likely to choose the one that had been advertised, demonstrating that extensive elaboration is more likely to impact upon behaviour.

Other factors that make advertisements successful

The ELM explains how many factors can make a difference when it comes to changing consumers' attitudes towards an advertisement. In addition to the ELM, a vast amount of research has been conducted that investigates variables that also impact upon how advertisements are perceived and whether or not they are easily remembered and noticed. Variables such as humour, sex, music, fear and shock in advertisements have proved to be effective. Additionally the type of programme in which a commercial is placed near and when certain information is presented have also been found to influence advertisement success.

Role of humour

Somewhere in the region of 10–30 per cent of all TV commercials contain humour (Krishnan & Chakravarti, 2003; Rossiter & Percy, 1997) meaning that humour is commonly used in the advertising industry. Funny ads can be a good way of getting consumers to pay attention to them (e.g. Weinberger, Spotts, Campbell, & Parsons, 1995) as well as engaging the audience (e.g. Spotts, Weinberger, & Parsons, 1997), and enhance ad responses (Scott, Klein, & Bryant, 1990; Weinberger & Campbell, 1991). Research has suggested that humorous advertisements generally work better under low involvement conditions and hence humour is more likely to function as a peripheral cue (Zhang & Zinkhan, 2006).

There have been a string of successful ad campaigns that have made good use of humour. One example of a funny campaign is for 'Egg money' where guinea pigs were using credit cards for different shopping purposes (Figure 7.3).

Many have discussed the effectiveness of funny advertisements but it is not as well researched empirically as it perhaps should be. Even though there appears to be clear advantages in using 'funny' ads, research in the field has thrown up some doubts on its effectiveness (Weinberger & Gulas, 1992). One obstacle is that humour can generate mixed feelings (Gelb & Zinkhan, 1986; Nelson, 1987), while another is that there are cultural variations in what is perceived to be funny (Francis, 1994). In a world where advertising campaigns are used in multi-cultural societies and in several countries, this can be a problem.

It has also been found that it is important not to make ads 'too funny' as humour can usurp the attention and consequently the observer may not notice what is being advertised (Belch & Belch, 1984). To avoid this happening, it is important that the brand/product is very visible and that it is clearly integrated into the story (Cline & Kellaris, 2007). The key is to ensure that the type of humour used is perceived to be clearly linked to the product advertised. But which type of humour is the most appropriate for each product will depend on the actual product category (Speck, 1991; Spotts et al., 1997), and to date there are no hard and fast rules.

Does sex sell?

Since the 1970s the advertising industry has increasingly made use of sexy images and sexual innuendos. For example, during the 1980s a Calvin Klein jeans commercial featured a 15-year-old Brooke Shields, asking 'You want to know what comes between me and my Calvins? Nothing' (Bello, Pitts, & Etzel, 1983) as the camera shot focused on the length of her leg, slowly moving up to her inseam before filming the whole body. Such images are used because research has found that 'sex sells'. One such piece of research was conducted by Smith and Engle in

FIGURE 7.3 An example of a humorous advertisement.

Source: Courtesy of the Citigroup. Image and all usage rights owned by Citi.

1968. They showed two groups of male participants a car advert that either contained a 'sexy-looking' female or no female at all. Interestingly the mere presence of the sexy-looking woman made the participants rate the car as being faster, more expensive and better designed.

Not only do 'sexy ads' generate a more favourable perception, they also have the capacity to attract attention (e.g. Dudley, 1999; Reichert, Heckler, & Jackson, 2001), as well as being engaging and viewed as more interesting than those that contain no sexual aspects (e.g. Judd & Alexander, 1983; Reichert & Alvaro, 2001). In a study using the earlier described Calvin Klein commercial, two versions (one sexual and one non-sexual) were used to test if sexual adverts are seen as more interesting. The results showed that both the male and female participants thought that the sexual version was more interesting (Bello et al., 1983).

In a high number of cases, 'sexy' advertisements make use of classical conditioning (see Chapter 2 for a more detailed account of classical conditioning). Through repeated pairing of a product with (let's say) a sexy-looking female, the consumer learns to associate the product with the aroused feeling they experience upon seeing the woman. In the scenario just mentioned, the unconditioned stimulus would be the sexy-looking female, and the unconditioned response is the arousal felt upon seeing her. The conditioned stimulus would be the product advertised and the conditioned response the arousal felt upon seeing the product once the connection between the sexy lady and the product has been made (see Figure 2.6 in Chapter 2). Classical conditioning tends to work best when something triggers a physiological response and hence sexual images can be a pretty powerful tool.

Use of music in advertising

Many commercials contain music and music is often used to draw and hold audience attention. However, research is lacking that clearly explains the effect of music upon attention (Hecker, 1984). That is not to say that music does not impact upon the audience. A string of studies have shown that there are links between music and recall (e.g. Roehm, 2001; Yalch, 1991), persuasion (Muehling & Bozman, 1990) as well as purchase probability (North & Hargreaves, 1998). It has also been debated what kind of music impacts upon cognitive responses and it appears that it depends upon the type of music used and how it is related to the information featured in the advertisement (Baker, Parasuraman, Grewal, & Voss, 2002). Provided an appropriate music choice is featured in an advert, it has the ability to generate pleasurable feelings (Sweeney & Wyber, 2002) and to communicate meaning (Zhu & Meyers-Levy, 2005), which can further strengthen the message.

Just as with sex, classical conditioning can also be applied when it comes to the use of music. This was demonstrated by Gorn (1982) when he wanted to test if music could be matched with a particular product so that individuals thought of the product when later only hearing the music. Participants saw an advertisement for either a beige or blue coloured pen. When seeing the ads for the beige pen they simultaneously heard music that had been previously judged in a favourable manner and while watching the ad for the blue pen they heard what had previously been rated as unfavourable music. Afterwards the participants were asked to choose either beige or a blue pen and 79 per cent chose the beige one. Most participants claimed to have chosen the beige pen due to colour preferences and only one mentioned the music that they had heard. Hence it was concluded that the music had acted as a conditioned stimulus that elicited pleasant emotions that increased the likelihood of the participants selecting the beige pen. It is probably worth pointing out that some have tried to replicate the results using different experimental methodologies, but with no success (e.g. Allen & Madden, 1985).

Fear appeals

Using fear in advertising is particularly common when trying to change what may be deemed reckless behaviour such as driving too fast and drinking. Such ads put a lot of emphasis upon what may happen if the behaviour in question is not altered, the idea being that advertisements can frighten people into changing their attitudes (e.g. Bennett, 1996; King & Reid, 1990) and hopefully behaviour.

So do fear appeals work? The answer is yes they do work, but to create a strong response it is best to use a moderate amount of fear as well as presenting audiences with a solution to the problem that is presented in the ad (e.g. Leventhal, Watts & Pagano, 1967; Ray & Wilkie, 1970; Ruiter, Abraham, & Kok, 2001). So in the case of campaigns hoping to reduce the number of drivers who drink and drive, you should not scare them too much, i.e. it is perhaps best not to include dead, bloody bodies in the ad, and provide them with a number for a taxi firm so that they can get home.

Provided a moderate amount of fear is used and consumers think that listening to the message will teach them how to engage in appropriate behaviour, they are likely to carefully elaborate upon the message and in turn change their attitudes (Petty, 1995; Rogers, 1983). If the audience feels too threatened by what they have seen, they are more likely to ignore the message (LaTour & Zahra, 1989). On the other hand if too little fear is being used, the audience may still choose to ignore the ad. Hence the relationship between fear and attitude change is like an inverted U-shape (see Figure 7.4) and it is imperative to get the amount of fear used right.

Advertisements containing threats generally belong to one of two categories: (1) social threats; and (2) physical threats. Physical threats are directly linked to a person's body, health and sometimes life while those of a social nature are more concerned with people being socially excluded (e.g. Laroche, Toffoli, Zhang, & Pons, 2001; Schoenbachler & Whittler 1996). Physical threats are more commonly used in advertisements even though some researchers have suggested that the use of social threats can be just as and sometimes more persuasive than physical ones (e.g. Dickinson & Holmes, 2008; Smith & Stutts, 2003). However, this is likely to depend upon what is advertised and to whom. For example, a study conducted on UK adolescents found that anti-smoking information emphasizing short-term

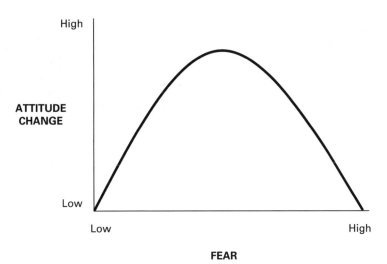

FIGURE 7.4 Relationship between fear and attitude change.

cosmetic effects of smoking that may make them seem socially undesirable had more of an impact than long-term health-based information (Michaelidou, Dibb, & Ali, 2008). Older audiences seem to respond well to information containing physical long-term health-based threats (Leventhal et al., 1967).

Use of shock tactics

The use of shocking contents in advertising is relatively common, similar to fear appeals, and on occasion the two methods are used simultaneously in adverts. A 'shock advertising appeal' deliberately shocks and offends the audience (Gustafson & Yssel, 1994). Offence is generally caused by violation of norms created by the legal system, the culture or the custom that people have become accustomed to through socialization procedures. Some examples of norm violations used in advertising include adverts by Benetton featuring a black woman breastfeeding a white child, Barnardos showing a baby being fed toxic spirit and PeTA using skinned animals in their adverts (Figure 7.5). Some say this simply heightens social awareness while others are clearly outraged by such images, but nevertheless they tend to be noticed and discussed.

In a study where participants were shown five different advertisements of which one of them made use of shock, fear or information, it was found that the ad containing a shocking element captured the participants' attention and aided recall and recognition much better than the other ads. The ad containing fear was found to be the second best for the three aspects measured (Dahl, Frankenberger, & Manchanda, 2003), showing that even though it may not have the same impact as shock, it still makes an impression on the audience. However, to effectively capitalize on attention, it may be better to incorporate a shocking element into an advertisement.

The text reads 'She's got her father's eyes'.

FIGURE 7.5 Example of adverts making use of shock tactics to heighten awareness of the advertised stimuli.

Source: Courtesy of PeTA

Source: Courtesy of NBC Universal

When to present the key aspects of a message

Research has found that information presented at the beginning (primacy effect) or at the end (recency effect) of a message tends to be noticed and remembered more (e.g. Jones & Goethals, 1971; Kruglanski & Freund, 1983; Miller, 1956). However, such order effects are mainly applicable to messages that tend to be lengthy and the consumer gets tired of processing all the information encountered. The primacy and recency effect is greatly reduced when individuals are exposed to shorter messages or when the message is compatible with their interests and hence they are motivated to elaborate upon the entire message (e.g. Haugtvedt & Wegener, 1994; Kruglanski & Freund, 1983).

The importance of where television commercials are placed

Another factor that can also determine the effectiveness of an advertisement is where a television commercial is placed. Just as with all other kinds of advertising, a television commercial needs to be seen and remembered by the audience. Hence, advertisers try to make them as memorable as they can (Harris, 1999). However, what is often forgotten is that even if the ad when tested on its own is easily recalled and liked, that is not to say that it will be once it is viewed between other commercials and TV programmes. Consumers have a limited amount of attention to direct towards what they see on TV (Lang, Newhagen, & Reeves, 1996) and the more they focus on TV programmes the less attention they will have for TV commercials (Bushman & Bonacci, 2002). A large amount of an individual's attention has also been found to be directed to television programmes that are of a violent or sexual nature (e.g. Geer, Judice, & Jackson 1994; Geer & Melton, 1997; Lang et al., 1996). Such findings led Bushman and Bonacci (2002) to test whether memory for commercials shown in between violent and sexually explicit programmes were less likely to be recalled afterwards. In their study, three groups of participants were assigned to watch either a neutral, violent or sexually explicit programme, all containing the same nine commercials. After watching the programmes they were asked to recall the brand names they had seen during the commercials. Additionally, the participants also had to take part in a recognition test whereby they were shown slides of supermarket shelves containing four brands. One of the brands was one they had seen earlier during the commercials. This was then repeated so that all the nine brands featured in the ads were included in the recognition test. The following day all participants were phoned and asked to recall the names of the nine brands they had seen in the commercials. It was found that the three types of memory measures produced similar results. Participants who had seen the violent or sexual programmes remembered fewer of the brands featured in the commercials than those who had seen a neutral programme. Hence, this suggests that advertisers ought to think carefully about what types of programmes they choose to advertise within. Recently Fried and Johanson (2008) criticized Bushman and Bonacci's research, claiming that they failed to control all aspects of the programmes used in the study. Fried and Johanson propose that if programme content is held constant, sex and violence will not affect recall, but that instead the plot and how funny the programme is may play a part. Since research in this area is still in its early stages, it may be a little premature to make exact recommendations for what programmes to avoid. Nonetheless it is something that advertisers and media buyers may wish to bear in mind.

Subliminal advertising – fact or fiction?

It is interesting that a high number of consumer-related text books are still covering subliminal perception when they discuss advertising, bearing in mind that no real substantial evidence has ever been produced in favour of it. Nonetheless the interest in the subject area seems to be a real 'die hard' and hence it will also be a mentioned in this book. Subliminal messages refer to stimuli that cannot be consciously perceived but still supposedly affect people's judgements, attitudes and behaviours.

It all started when in the late 1950s James Vicary decided to trick the world into believing that subliminal advertising works. He claimed to have flashed the messages 'Eat popcorn' and 'Drink Coca-Cola' so quickly that they could not consciously have been perceived by the audience, during a movie shown in a cinema. During the interval the sales of popcorn and Coke reportedly increased manifold. However, Vicary had not told the truth (Weir, 1984). Ever since Vicary's claims, the idea that subliminal messages may work has continued to fascinate many and consequently a string of studies have been conducted in the hope of proving or disproving that it works.

Research investigating subliminal perception has not managed to find that hidden messages that we cannot see or hear consciously are likely to make us buy any larger quantities of popcorn any more than subliminal messages on self-help tapes can help people reduce their eating or stop smoking (e.g. Brannon & Brock, 1994; Merikle, 1988; Moore, 1992; Pratkanis, 1992; Theus, 1994; Trappey, 1996). Even though the research is overwhelmingly against the idea of subliminal perception, there are a few controlled lab-based studies that suggest it still may work (e.g. Bornstein & D'Agostino, 1992; Strahan, Spencer, & Zanna, 2002). In one such study, participants were shown a series of Chinese ideographs and then had to rate how much they liked the look of each of them (Murphy & Zajonc, 1993). Prior to seeing each ideograph they were also shown either a happy or angry-looking face or a polygon showing no emotion. None of the participants were aware of seeing the pictures that preceded the ideograph as they were only flashed for 4 milliseconds, which is too fast for individuals to perceive on a conscious level. The results showed that the Chinese ideographs were liked the least when it had been preceded by an angry face, the most liked when it was preceded by a happy face, and the second most liked when it had been preceded by an unemotional polygon. These are doubtless interesting findings. However, it needs to be remembered that lab-based studies often lack ecological validity as factors that cannot be controlled in real life are controlled for in lab settings. In real-life consumer settings, where and how people are seated, noise and those surrounding us are likely to be factors that will interfere with whether or not we are affected by sub-conscious variables. Hence, it seems unlikely that consumers can be affected by subliminal messages.

Cultural differences

Advertising campaigns are often conducted on a global scale and it can be an expensive mistake to assume that an advert will be perceived in a similar manner in different countries, even within western cultures. Numerous studies have found that people respond differently to advertising depending on cultural and subcultural variations. Hence, when thinking about advertising in different cultures, it is worth test piloting adverts to check whether or not they generate the desired response.

Advertising for charity

One area of advertising where cultural differences are important is when charities appeal for money or help. It has been suggested that people's attitudes towards charities are determined by whether or not their values are congruent with the appeal (Supphellen & Nelson, 2001). Advertising messages are much more likely to be seen in a positive light if the charity appeal is in line with the audience cultural values (Han & Shavitt, 1994; Zhang & Gelb, 1996).

Cultural differences are often compared between individualistic and collectivist cultures. However, evidence for whether or not the two types respond differently to charity advertising is not consistent (e.g. Aaker & Williams, 1998; Han & Shavitt, 1994). Perhaps such inconsistencies can be explained by additional cultural aspects such as whether they are masculine or feminine. This was proposed and investigated by Nelson, Brunel, Supphellen, & Manchanda in 2006. They conducted a study in four different countries, all individualistic, that differed in masculinity (America and Canada) and femininity (Denmark & Norway). Participants were subjected to two types of charity advertising that either made use of altruistic or egoistic motives to encourage them to give money. The outcome demonstrated that in masculine cultures men preferred the egoistic appeal while women preferred the altruistic one, while in feminine cultures the opposite was found. Nelson et al.'s research clearly demonstrated that when researching cultures it may be misguided to look at broad concepts such as collectivism and individualism since these may not be representative for the entire population in the country investigated.

Key Terms

Salient stimuli
Prominent stimuli that are context dependent.

Sleeper effect
Persuasive messages that are not initially perceived as believable can alter people's opinions later on.

Vivid stimuli
Stimuli that are of a prominent nature.

Summary

The psychology of advertising is a complex topic, whereby many variables need to be considered in order to understand what it is that can make an advert more or less successful. First and foremost it is important to capture an audience's attention, which can be done by the use of vivid and salient stimuli. Once this has been accomplished, the level of involvement will help determine if consumers will think extensively about the message they encountered, as proposed in the ELM. The likelihood of consumers elaborating upon a message should direct what types of variables are included in the ad. If possible, it is worth encouraging individuals to make use of the central route of processing as it tends to generate long-lasting attitudes which are more likely to affect behavioural outcomes. Humour, sex, music and fear are all examples of variables that can be used in advertising to generate desirable responses. Generally it appears that it is best to ensure that the variables are presented on a conscious level rather than subliminally. Whichever methods are used to increase the effectiveness of advertising, it is essential to consider how the culture in which it will be shown may perceive them.

Class exercise

Select four adverts from a magazine or newspaper. Choose two that you think will encourage individuals to make use of the peripheral route of processing, and two that are aimed towards the central processing route. Explain why you think the adverts would encourage a particular processing route by giving specific examples of what is being featured in the ad and what kind of audience that it is aimed at. Additionally, you may also discuss how successful you think the ad may be at achieving minimal or extensive elaboration.

CHAPTER

8

Motivational determinants of consumer behaviour

Introduction

Why are we motivated to consume products and services? This chapter seeks to address this question by looking at what motivation is and how it consists of three features: direction, effort and persistence. It will then go on to look at several specific motivational theories including Maslow's hierarchy of needs, drive reduction theory, expectancy value theories, balance theory and arousal theory. The chapter ends with a brief outline of methods (i.e. the importance of knowing your target audience, use of positive reinforcement, and involvement encouragement) that can be applied to encourage consumer motivation.

Motivation

What motivates humans is a question that psychologists have pondered for a long time and consequently there are many different theories in regard to why consumers become motivated to purchase goods and services. *Motivation* can be described as the processes that lead people to behave in a particular way. The original Latin meaning is 'to move' and hence it is natural that research involving motivation focuses on how beliefs, values, and goals affect consumer behaviours.

Motivation can be said to involve three features (Arnold, Robertson, & Cooper, 1995):

1 *Direction*: What a person is aiming to do.
2 *Effort*: How much effort a person is willing to make in order to achieve the desired goal.
3 *Persistence*: How long a person is prepared to try and achieve a goal.

The three features suggest that there should be an underlying *need* to engage in a particular behaviour that then has to be pursued (*drive*) until the need has been fulfilled (*goal*). Needs are the triggering factor, a drive is what makes a person put a certain amount of effort in and goals are what one is trying to be achieved. Both needs and goals are continuously changing in response to factors such as the environment, interactions with others and life experiences. Hence, there is a strong relationship between needs, drives and goals (see Figure 8.1).

Needs

Humans become motivated when a need is aroused that they have a desire to satisfy (e.g. Murray, 1951). This is applicable to both behaviour and deliberative (conscious) processing (e.g. Fazio, 1990; Kruglanski, 1989). Needs can be both *innate* (biogenic) and *acquired* (those that are learnt in response to our environment). Innate needs include the need for food, water, sex, and clothes, while acquired needs might include needs for affection, self-esteem or prestige. At times innate and acquired needs can be combined in that being hungry will result in a person wishing to eat and hence will seek out a place where they can obtain food (innate need). However, the kind of place an individual chooses to get food from may be an acquired need. For example, a well-paid city lawyer may choose to go to a very expensive and upmarket restaurant to eat and in such a case it would satisfy both innate and acquired needs.

Innate and acquired needs are also closely related to two other definitions of needs; *utilitarian needs* (a need that has a practical of functional benefit) and *hedonic needs* (experiential needs that involve emotional responses). Utilitarian needs generally occurs as an immediate response to an innate need (e.g. if you are hungry you will try to find something to eat) and hedonic ones are similar to acquired needs in that seeking out an upmarket restaurant might also trigger emotions of feeling satisfied.

It may appear as if it is rather clear-cut whether or not a product fits into the category of being a utilitarian or hedonic need. But as the previous example of food and restaurants demonstrate, food (just as many other consumables) can satisfy both types of needs (Lowe & Butryn, 2007). Due to the fact that well-nourished individuals are consuming food driven by hedonic needs, they are also at risk of over-consuming calories which can lead to obesity (Lundy, 2008), demonstrating that a certain type of need can motivate people to engage in consumer behaviours that are not necessarily good for them. Perhaps this is because it is easy to entice consumers with hedonic alternatives as long as they are not directly compared to utilitarian alternatives (Okada, 2005).

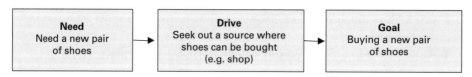

FIGURE 8.1 Relationship between need, drive and goal.

Drives

Regardless of what kind of need a consumer is experiencing, there is likely to be some discrepancy between a person's current state and what they perceive to be an ideal state. For example, there may be a discrepancy between what you currently have and what you would like to have. Such a discrepancy can cause tension and psychological discomfort which in turn will make people experience some level of arousal, and it is the arousal that is known as a drive.

What drives people's wants and what they do are key aspects of motivation since consumers will be striving to reduce the arousal they are experiencing (see also drive reduction theory later in this chapter). Consequently people aim for a suitable goal that can reduce their tension. Once the consumer has reached their goal, tension is reduced and motivation disappears until a new tension occurs. If a person is feeling hungry, the arousal caused by the hunger can be reduced by eating. However, there are many possibilities in regard to what an individual may choose/wish to eat and consequently the drive to reduce the tension of hunger is not only affected by hunger itself but also by other factors such as culture or individual characteristics such as self-esteem maintenance and enhancement, self-improvement, and the need to belong to a group.

Goals

Goals are the results of motivated behaviour, and can be defined as 'what an individual is trying to accomplish; it is the object or aim of an action' (Locke, Shaw, Saari, & Latham 1981, p. 126). Just like needs, goals can also be classified into more than one type, generic and product-specific. *Generic goals* are general categories of goals that consumers see as a way of fulfilling their needs. For example, a woman may state that she needs a new handbag; she has then expressed a need for a new bag but not for a particular type and hence it is a generic goal. However, if the same woman was to say that she needs a new 'D gold' Gucci handbag she has articulated a *product-specific goal*.

For most consumer needs there are many different goals that can all be equally appropriate. What makes consumers focus on a particular goal is affected by several different factors such as internal beliefs, previous experiences, societal norms and values. Perhaps one of the most important factors is that of how individuals perceive themselves and how the goals fit in with their 'consumer identity' (e.g. Emmons, 1996; Kasser & Ryan, 1993; Winell, 1987). As discussed in Chapter 4, consumers tend to purchase products and services that express who they are and subsequently their goals will be heavily influenced by it. Other ways in which individualistic qualities can influence the goals people set can be noted from research that has distinguished between two types of goals: (1) *ideals*, which epitomize wishes, hopes and aspirations; and (2) *oughts*, which stands for duties, responsibilities and obligations (Higgins, 1987; Pham & Avnet, 2004). Both types of goals affect people's self-regulatory systems. Ideals are linked to what is known as the promotion system (which help to regulate nurturance needs) and oughts are linked to the prevention system (which help to regulate security needs). In order to reach a desired goal, such as buying a new expensive plasma screen television, the promotion system relies mainly on approach strategies, saving as much money as possible, while the prevention system relies on avoidance strategies such as refraining from buying extra snacks at lunchtime (Higgins, 1998). So in the broadest possible sense it can be said that goals are either approach-oriented or avoidance-oriented. The type of goal orientation used impacts upon how consumers view products marketed to them. For example, it has been found that it affects how advertisements are evaluated. When consumers are concerned with ideals, they tend to rely more on feelings in evaluating adverts, while those concerned with oughts rely more on the factual content (Pham & Avnet, 2004).

Intrinsic and extrinsic motivation

Goals can also be either intrinsically or extrinsically motivated. Intrinsic motivation is when people have a desire to engage in an activity for its own sake as oppose to extrinsic motivation which is when people expect some sort of reward such as money or a bonus gift. Those who are intrinsically motivated tend to engage in their chosen behaviours for longer time periods than those who are extrinsically motivated (Decci & Ryan, 1985). This was found in studies where participants were rewarded with money for participating in an interesting activity. Under such circumstances they spent less time engaging in the activity than participants who were not paid (Deci, 1971, 1972). Similarly, when Lepper, Greene, and Nisbett (1973) asked nursery school children to take part in an intrinsically motivating task they put the children into three groups: one that expected a reward, another where they did not expect a reward, and in a third where they were unexpectedly given a reward. A week later the researchers observed the children's interest in the same task and found that those who expected rewards showed little interest while the other two groups continued to be interested in the task.

Specific types of consumption such as playing computer games, which tend to offer intrinsic forms of entertainment (Klimmt, 2003) may therefore not appeal to consumers who favour extrinsic gratifications (Hartmann & Klimmt, 2006).

Theories of motivation

Over the years psychologists have produced many different theories of motivation. Some of those theories have similar theoretical foundations while others have no comparable underlying beliefs. Certain theories also set them apart in that they have no empirically based research to support them. It is not simple to establish what motivates people and in that respect the range of existing motivational theories simply reflects the complexity of the subject area. Consequently it is good to familiarize oneself with a range of motivational theories in order to get a broader understanding of motivation.

Maslow's hierarchy of needs

Maslow's hierarchy of needs is commonly included in consumer behaviour textbooks as an example of how human needs can be the underlying factor of consumption. Maslow (1970) proposed that there are five different levels of needs (Figure 8.2) that have to be mastered in the order proposed before an individual can progress on to the next level. The hierarchy can be classified into two broad definitions: physiological and psychological needs. At the bottom are *physiological needs* which are essential to survival (e.g. needs for water and food). This level is pretty self-explanatory in that if applied to consumers they would be consuming food and drink. The next level consists of *safety needs* (e.g. needs for shelter and feeling secure within a particular environment). In order to fulfil their safety needs, a consumer may purchase a flat in a secure block of flats, or pay for health insurance. Above that level comes *belongingness and love needs*, which is followed by *need for esteem* (e.g. respect of others and self-confidence). Consumers might express their need for belongingness through consumption of activities such as attending concerts, going to the pub or to a museum. By doing so they feel that they are part of a certain group of people that indirectly provide them with a sense of belongingness.

The need for self-esteem is something that all humans have from a very early age, and is likely to exist even if the other needs have not been fully met (Csikszentmihalyi, 2000). From a consumer perspective it is likely that people will

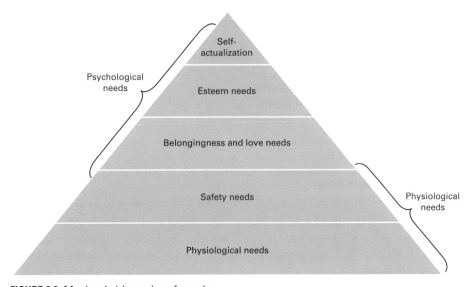

FIGURE 8.2 Maslow's hierarchy of needs.

purchase products that seem to set them apart from others. Generally products used for such a purpose have a clear symbolic value that is easily interpreted by others. Many studies have confirmed that material possessions are extensions of self (Belk, 1988) and consequently using products to express aspects of self (e.g. status and wealth) can theoretically increase people's self-esteem.

The final level in the hierarchy is the need for **self-actualization**, which is when individuals strive to fulfil their own potential. Such a fulfilment happens on a psychological level and it appears that it is almost spiritual in nature. Maslow (1970, p. 46.) himself described self-actualization in the following way: 'A musician must make music, an artist must paint, a poet must write, if he is to be ultimately at peace with himself. What a man can be, he must be.'

When the theory was first proposed, it provided a new and interesting way to look at what motivates human behaviour. However, since he made use of a phenomenological approach to motivation (rejection of scientific methods in favour of descriptions of conscious experience), his theory is very difficult to test. In particular, self-actualization is not clearly defined and is therefore very hard to measure. Nonetheless it appears that some consumer decisions are driven by the need for self-actualization (Csikszentmihalyi, 2000) and consequently might be used to explain certain purchases. Examples may include having a desire to visit the Dalai Lama in order to find inner peace. Unless you live in India this would require you to purchase a plane ticket to go and see him, meaning that purchasing an air fare can be motivated by the desire to self-actualize.

Those who have tried to empirically test his theory have found little or no support for the hierarchy of needs (Arnold, Cooper, & Robertson, 1995). Consequently, there are academics who are prepared to dismiss that people's behaviour is motivated by specific needs. Even if you choose not to believe in the exact theory of needs, it can still be useful in that it distinguishes between physiological and psychological needs, which are similar to utilitarian and hedonic needs. Furthermore, it is also possible to utilize it as a yardstick to measure 'the value of consumer behaviour in terms of how choices satisfy existential needs' (Csikszentmihalyi, 2000, p. 269). However, it needs to be pointed out that even though the theory can have its uses in terms of understanding consumer motivations, it is of limited use. Consumers are not always motivated by a specific type of motivation and not necessarily in the order that Maslow proposed (Hilles & Kahle, 1985; Kahle, Homer, O'Brien, & Boush, 1997).

Drive reduction theory

The drive reduction theory is a behaviourist approach to explain why people are motivated to engage in particular behaviours. Hull (1943, 1952) proposed that humans are driven to action by biological needs that generate unpleasant states of arousal. When unpleasant states of arousal are experienced, people become motivated to reduce the feelings of unpleasantness. Hence, consumers engage in goal-oriented behaviour in order to achieve *homeostasis* (reduction of unpleasant feelings which results in a 'normal' balanced feeling). For example, you may have a slight toothache and consequently you will go to the nearest pharmacist in the hope of purchasing something that can temporarily relieve your pain. Provided you manage to find a product that relieves the pain, you are much more likely to purchase the product again if another toothache occurs. However, if the product does not manage to bring you back to homeostasis, repeat behaviour (purchasing the same product again) is unlikely to occur and instead the consumer is likely to engage in a trial-and-error process (trying several different products) until *equilibrium* is restored.

It is worth noting that the drive reduction theory fails to explain all types of consumer behaviour. For example, consumers may delay purchasing something to eat, even though it is almost lunchtime and they are really hungry, because they have arranged to go out for a big lunch later on that afternoon. In fact, such behaviour is directly contradicting the drive reduction theory in that the individual is avoiding immediate gratification in order to reduce the unpleasant feeling of being hungry.

There is little support for this theory in recent times and a number of experiments conducted were done during the 1950s and 1960s without being applied to consumer behaviour. Many psychologists believe that the theory does not provide a good understanding of what motivates people since a high number of individuals engage in behaviour that increases rather than reduces a drive. For example, when people are hungry, they may decide not to eat because they are trying to lose weight. Such behaviour would then increase their hunger drive which goes against the drive reduction theory.

Theories focused on expectations

Expectancy in regard to motivational theories generally refers to an intervening variable of a cognitive nature that is understood to be knowledge about relationships between objects (products or services) and the real world. Such a relationship can be seen as *if* a certain object is registered, *then* a certain event is expected to follow. For example, *if* a male consumer purchases a Lynx spray, they may *then* expect to be viewed as very attractive by women (just as in the Lynx advertisements). Theories that focus on expectations include the self-efficacy theory, expectancy value theories, expectancy-value model and incentive theories.

Self-efficacy theory

Bandura (1977, 1997) proposed a social cognitive model of motivation that, like other expectancy theories, focus on expectancies for success. He described self-efficacy as being an individual's confidence in their capacity to organize and perform a given course of action to solve a particular problem or accomplish a task. The level of self-efficacy experienced varies from individual to individual. Some people have a strong sense of self-efficacy while others do not. Bandura's theory distinguishes between two types of expectancy beliefs:

1 *Outcome expectations*: When individuals believe that certain behaviours will lead to specific outcomes (e.g. purchasing a Louis Vuitton handbag will make you more popular with your friends).

2 *Efficacy expectations*: Individuals' beliefs about whether or not they can effectively perform the behaviour needed to produce the desired outcome (e.g. believing that they can work enough extra hours in order to save up to buy a Louis Vuitton bag).

With his proposed two types of expectancy beliefs, Bandura wanted to distinguish between expectancies that are related to particular behaviours for desired outcomes and people's higher-order expectancies that individuals can use to execute these critical behaviours. The two types of expectations differ in that a person might think that a certain behaviour will produce a specific outcome (outcome expectation) but they may not think that they have the capacity to perform the behaviour required (efficacy expectations). Consequently consumers' efficacy expectations are major determinants when it comes to goal setting and how persistently the goal is pursued.

Expectancy value theories

Expectancy theories are not only relevant to attitude generation (as discussed in Chapter 6) but also to how expectations can motivate consumers to engage in certain types of behaviours. Since the 1980s the theories have been updated so that they integrate expectancies and value constructs (e.g. Eccles, 1987; Wigfield & Eccles, 2000). There are several expectancy value theories of motivation, some of which were not originally intended to explain why people strive for certain goals (e.g. Ajzen, 1985; Fishbein & Ajzen, 1975; Lewin, Dembo, Festinger, & Sears, 1944; Tolman, 1932), nevertheless the underlying principle remains the same. The main idea is that the more desirable a goal appears to be to a consumer, the more likely it is that they will choose such a goal, provided that they think the goal is attainable. Consumers tend to be motivated to choose one product over another because they expect that what they have chosen will result in the attainment of various outcomes weighted by the desirability of these outcomes to the person.

Heckhausen's expectancy-value model

Heckhausen (1991) wanted to incorporate multiple approaches to motivation into his theory, which resulted in a distinction between four different types of expectancy:

1 *Situation-outcome*: An individual's subjective view of how likely they are to attain an outcome in a particular situation without acting.

2 *Action-outcome*: Subjective probability of attaining an outcome by one's actions.

3 *Action-by-situation-outcome*: Subjective probability that situational factors help or hinder one's action-outcome expectancy.

4 *Outcome-consequence*: An individual's subjective perception of the likelihood that an outcome will be associated with a specific consequence.

The model suggests that the expected outcome is imperative in the building of
expectancies. In Heckhausen's model, outcomes are the direct results of people's
own actions. Some of the results are followed by consequences such as self-
evaluation while others do not generate any consequences at all. However, the
results do not have any incentive value on their own. The value is simply attributed
to the consequences of the person's actions, meaning that the drive to act is
dependent upon the value attached to the consequences of a person's behaviour.
Until Heckhausen (1977) proposed the four types of expectancy most expectancy-
value models focused upon action-outcome expectancies.

Use of incentives

Incentives of some sort can motivate consumers to purchase certain products and
services, as can be noted from the expectancy-value theories. No doubt it is the
environment that brings out behaviours in that it sets out goals that people wish to
reach so that consumers are taught (through marketing stimuli such as advertising
and in-store displays) the meaning of different products and services and what we
come to expect of them. Any stimulus that people have learned to associate with
positive or negative outcomes can serve as an incentive, such as looking young,
being popular, having money, or eating ice cream.

People are clearly attracted to behaviours that offer positive incentives and
equally tend to avoid those that they associate with negative or undesirable outcomes. For example, a person using the Internet may see a banner ad that is using a
stimulus that has previously been conditioned to be associated with gain (money,
food, etc.). Thinking that there will be a positive outcome by clicking on the ad
they therefore become motivated to do so.

Incentives may be tangible or intangible. A *tangible incentive* involves awards
or some form of public recognition while an *intangible incentive* is one that is
intrinsic by nature such as feeling good about oneself.

Balance theory

The balance theory is a cognitive consistency theory that looks at how inconsistent
attitudes can motivate individuals to be persuaded. It was proposed by Heider
(1946, 1958) and also revised by Cartwright and Harary (1956) and suggests that
people have both attitudes toward (*sentiment relations*) and connections to (*unit
relations*) other people, objects, ideas, or events. How the relations are organized
will determine whether or not they are balanced. The balance between them can
be viewed as a triad whereby each of the corners represents something: a person
(p), another person such as a friend or a celebrity (o), and a stimulus such as a
product, event or a service (x). If the triad is not balanced, people can feel tense and
will consequently be motivated to reduce the tension that they are experiencing

(Jordan, 1953). Imbalance occurs when one of the elements in the triad is perceived in the opposite way compared to the other two elements. For example, Lisa likes to go shopping for handbags and Paul does not care very much for handbags. Yet Paul really likes Lisa, and values their relationship. Consequently this structure is now in imbalance. However, if Paul were to change his attitude about handbags, the structure would be in balance. Another way to restore balance to the triad is by denying that there is a relationship between two of the elements. For example, if p is you, o is David Beckham, and x is Police sunglasses, imbalance occurs if you really like David Beckham (p likes o), David Beckham likes Police sunglasses (o likes x), and you do not like Police sunglasses (p dislikes x). The way to deal with this through denial is to justify why David Beckham likes Police sunglasses, e.g. he only says that he likes them because he gets paid to say it. Thus, the imbalance can be restored by you separating the David Beckham you like and the one that gets paid to appear in advertisements.

A balanced triad is one that consists of an odd number of positive relationships, which can occur in various forms. They are generally easier to learn, and are rated as more pleasant (Insko, 1981, 1984). There are four unbalanced and four balanced combinations of relationships between two people and a product (see Figure 8.3).

The balance theory is not commonly discussed but can still make a valuable contribution in explaining how consumers can be persuaded by advertising and marketing messages. In particular, this is applicable to advertisements that feature celebrity endorsements. In such cases the marketer is hoping that you the viewer (p) likes the celebrity featured (o) and that you will believe that they like the product they advertise (o likes x). Such a relationship should then compel the viewer into forming a positive attitude towards x, so that the triad is balanced. However, it is worth remembering that if people have strong feelings against a particular element (as in the example of David Beckham and Police sunglasses), they may still not be persuaded by the use of a 'likeable' person as they then may instead choose to deny that there is a genuine connection between the two elements.

Arousal theory

The arousal theory of motivation is similar to Hull's drive reduction theory in that it proposes that humans are driven to maintain a certain level of arousal in order to feel comfortable. However, it differs from the drive reduction theory because it does not rely on the reduction of tension. Instead it proposes that a balanced amount of arousal is needed for people to become motivated (Zuckerman, 2000). Hence, arousal itself may be seen as an incentive. If people experience levels of arousal that are too low, they become bored and de-motivated and if they experience too high levels, they become stressed. The amount of preferred arousal varies from individual to individual. Motivation to behave is encouraged by positive and negative reinforcers in the hope of maintaining the arousal levels. Some people are much more 'sensation seeking' than others because they prefer a higher level of arousal. Such individuals are prepared to take risks in order to reach their preferred

Balanced triads

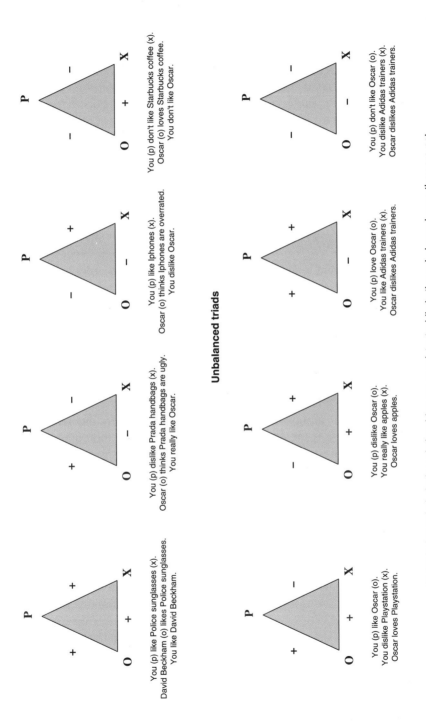

You (p) like Police sunglasses (x).
David Beckham (o) likes Police sunglasses.
You like David Beckham.

You (p) dislike Prada handbags (x).
Oscar (o) thinks Prada handbags are ugly.
You really like Oscar.

You (p) like Iphones (x).
Oscar (o) thinks Iphones are overrated.
You dislike Oscar.

You (p) don't like Starbucks coffee (x).
Oscar (o) loves Starbucks coffee.
You don't like Oscar.

Unbalanced triads

You (p) like Oscar (o).
You dislike Playstation (x).
Oscar loves Playstation.

You (p) dislike Oscar (o).
You really like apples (x).
Oscar loves apples.

You (p) love Oscar (o).
You like Adidas trainers (x).
Oscar dislikes Adidas trainers.

You (p) don't like Oscar (o).
You dislike Adidas trainers (x).
Oscar dislikes Adidas trainers.

In the balanced triads the relationships are consistent while in the unbalanced ones they are not.

FIGURE 8.3 Examples of triads from the balance theory.

arousal levels and it has been suggested that they are more likely to engage in sports such as parachuting, motor cycle racing and downhill skiing (Zuckerman, 1994). Others have lower levels of arousal but in order to avoid experiencing too low levels, which can lead to feelings of boredom, they may have a need to change things around, perhaps by purchasing different types of products.

This biologically based theory of motivation fails to account for all types of motivational behaviour. The way in which people reason is not accounted for and hence it is difficult to explain differences such as why some people (regardless of disposable income) buy all their clothes from charity shops while others only buy highly fashionable and very expensive clothes. Consequently it would appear that there must be other underlying reasons than just biological energy that motivates different consumers.

What can be done to motivate consumers?

There are many different techniques that can be employed in order to encourage consumers to purchase goods and services. There is no simple answer to what motivates consumers; instead it is important that one considers who the consumer is, when they are consuming as well as what they are consuming in order to get a better picture of factors that can be utilized to motivate individuals to consume certain products and services.

Research the target audience

Undoubtedly different groups of people will be motivated by different types of things, which is why it is imperative that as a marketer you thoroughly research what makes a particular audience 'tick'. One way of establishing whether or not certain marketing strategies might work can be established by taking a closer look at the culture in which they exist. The importance of culture is widely appreciated and it has been described as 'the lens through which people view marketing messages' (Shavitt, Lee, & Johnson, 2008, p. 1103). Every culture or subculture has a set of core values that it communicates to its members (Pollay, 1983). It is the shared values that ultimately influence the way in which products and marketing messages are perceived. *Values* can be defined as preconceptions of what is deemed to be important or valuable. Values tend to be general in nature and differ from attitudes in that they are not only applicable to specific situations (Schwartz & Bilsky, 1987).

Every culture has a set of *core values* that it clearly communicates to the members of that particular culture. All values are learnt through socialization agents such as friends, teachers and parents. Some values are shared by most cultures such as the wish to be healthy and wanting world peace. When values are 'universal', what sets the different type of cultures apart is how they rank the values. The set of rankings is the equivalent of a culture's value system (Rokeach, 1973). However, different types of cultures and subcultures also have values that are not of a 'universal' nature. Consequently it is imperative to establish who the target audience is so that one can more closely research the core values of the culture/s targeted. Naturally if the market is aimed at several types of cultures, it is then useful to establish what type of values the different cultures share. Researching or just learning other cultures' value systems is called **acculturation** (Lindridge, Hogg, & Shah, 2004).

Positive reinforcement

Positively reinforcing people's behaviour has repeatedly been found to be an effective way to increase the likelihood of a behaviour happening again (as previously discussed in Chapter 2). This technique is therefore most suitable when consumers are already using products and services that marketers are wishing to promote. To positively reinforce a person's behaviour means that you are rewarding what they have just done (see Table 8.1 for examples). So if you wish a consumer to purchase a specific product again perhaps you will give them a discount, an additional free sample or maybe extra reward points on their store loyalty card.

Rewards can be classified into primary and secondary reinforcers (Rothschild & Gaidis, 2002). Primary ones have intrinsic utility (a product) while secondary ones are not really advantageous but must be transformed into something useful (e.g. tokens and coupons). When using secondary reinforcers consumers experience delayed gratification. For example, when people are given tokens, they naturally must be redeemed at a later date. Because of the time delay between receiving the token and the time that it is redeemed, it reduces the success of the promotion. Secondary reinforcers become valuable over time as the consumer learns that they can be converted into a primary reinforcer (product) but they are still less effective than primary reinforcers. Bearing this in mind it may be better to make use of primary reinforcers that provide instant reinforcement (and gratification) such as two for the price of one offers as they are more likely to motivate consumers to purchase a product which in turn is also more likely to encourage repeat purchases.

TABLE 8.1 Positive reinforcement

Behaviour	Consequence	Behavioural change
A girl eats a chocolate bar.	It tastes great.	The girl is therefore likely to purchase chocolate bar again.
A man purchases a case of wine.	He also gets two bottles for free.	As a result, the man is likely to purchase the wine again.
A mother of two buys two packets of nappies from a supermarket.	She receives an extra 100 points on her reward card as a result of buying the nappies.	Consequently she is likely to purchase the nappies again as well as continuing to shop in that particular supermarket.

Encourage involvement

How involved a consumer feels with a product will also motivate them to purchase it. *Involvement* can be defined as an individual's perception of an object (e.g. product, brand, advertisement or even purchase situation) based on their needs, values and interests (Zaichkowsky, 1985). Involvement is a motivational construct and consequently can be activated by many different antecedents (see Figure 8.4). The level of involvement can vary from indifference to great passion and the more passionate the consumer is the more motivated they are to purchase a product or service. *Involvement persistence* (the duration of the involvement intensity) also affects motivation in that consumers with specialist interests (e.g. wine connoisseurs or ski enthusiasts) are more likely to be motivated to pursue consumption related to their interests than those who show a temporary interest in the same activities (Bloch, 1981; Celsi & Olson, 1988). When consumers show a temporary interest in consumer-related activities, they are likely to change when the situation changes, something that is known as situational involvement (Celsi & Olson, 1988). Consequently it tends to be easier to motivate consumers to take an interest in a particular product if consumers are not highly involved in a product category (Muehling & Laczniak, 1988; Petty & Cacioppo, 1986a).

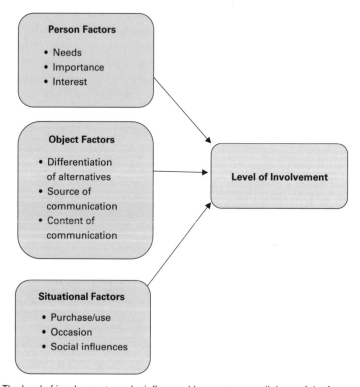

The level of involvement can be influenced by one, two or all three of the factors.

FIGURE 8.4 Conceptual framework of factors that affect involvement.

The Elaboration Likelihood Model (ELM) (discussed in Chapter 7) can be used as a framework for how consumers can be manipulated to become more involved (Petty & Cacioppo, 1986a). The model proposes that personal relevance of an advertised product can be controlled and in turn steer one's involvement toward the product. Additionally, the ELM also outlines factors that have the ability to restrict the level of involvement experienced such as the opportunity to process (e.g. due to distraction) and ability to process (e.g. due to familiarity) (e.g. Andrews 1988; Batra & Ray, 1986a).

Key Terms

Acculturation
Learning about other cultures' value systems.

Self-actualization
When people have fulfilled their own potential.

Summary

Motivation is a process that guides people's behaviour in a particular direction. Consumer *needs* trigger the engagement in specific behaviour, while a *drive* determines the amount of effort they put in, in order to achieve a desired outcome (*goal*). Goals can be both intrinsically and extrinsically motivated.

There are several theories of motivation, including Maslow's hierarchy of needs, drive reduction theory, theories that focus on expectations (e.g. self-efficacy theory and expectancy value theories) and balance theory. Each theory offers a slightly different approach when it comes to explain why consumers engage in particular consumption activities. Such theories can be used to establish what it is that makes a consumer tick. When trying to motivate consumers, it is important to establish what the target audience values in life. Every culture and subculture has a set of core values that they share. Once the values have been established, simple techniques such as positive reinforcement can be applied to motivate purchase behaviours. Another method can be to make use of core values in marketing campaigns in order to encourage product involvement.

Discussion questions

1 Are consumers more likely to be motivated by intrinsic or extrinsic goals?
2 How do toys fit into Maslow's hierarchy of needs?

3 Which motivational theory do you think best explains why consumers become motivated to consume products or services?

4 Is the use of incentives essentially the same thing as positively reinforcing consumer behaviours?

5 Why is it important to have a good understanding of cultural values?

CHAPTER 9

Consumer decision-making and brand loyalty

Introduction

This chapter will explain how consumers make use of different types of heuristics when making decisions about which products and brands they should purchase. In particular, prediction, persuasion and choice heuristics will be outlined. It will also explore whether consumers are capable of making rational decisions (taking heuristics, emotions and level of involvement into account) and how decisions can be based upon specific attributes. The chapter ends with a brief outline of what it means to be brand loyal and why some people choose to repeatedly purchase products from the same brand.

Consumer decision-making

All products and services that consumers use will have been involved in a decision-making process. At times consumers may choose to use a product only once and on other occasions they may decide to use it repeatedly. When products or brands are used repeatedly, it is a sign that customers are loyal to the brand or product. Brand loyalty is something that most manufacturers strive to achieve. In order to achieve brand loyalty, it is imperative to understand how consumers make their decisions and what type of factors can increase the likelihood of continuous repeat purchase.

Most marketers and manufacturers wish that consumers made decisions based solidly upon the information that is presented to them. Unfortunately the consumer decision-making process is rarely so simple. In addition to the information that consumers are faced with, there are many factors that come into play when consumers are deciding what to buy. The context in which products are presented, lifestyle, culture, peer pressure, level of involvement, emotions, social class, amount of choice, in-store stimuli, and attitudes are some aspects that have been suggested can affect consumer decision-making. Even though there are many different factors that can impact upon the decisions consumers make, most decisions are based only on a select few. This is because it would be very time-consuming and laborious for consumers to make use of all the knowledge they have that is in some way associated with the product they are thinking of buying. To avoid wasting time and becoming mentally tired, consumers rely on **heuristics**.

Heuristics

Typically consumers only consider a small part of all the information available to them about a specific product or service and not all the information is attended to and processed. Even though consumers are very rarely presented with all the available information, they are still often faced with more information than they can deal with. Unfortunately consumers often do not have enough time to process even a fraction of that information, and consequently some of the product information encountered will be considered more than others. This is done subconsciously by the use of heuristics.

Heuristics are 'rules of thumb' that individuals subconsciously apply to reduce the effort involved in decision-making (Shah & Oppenheimer, 2008) so that they do not tire themselves mentally. Since humans have limited capacity for mental work, heuristics simply enable us to deal with complex matters by applying simple methods of reasoning. Heuristics are commonly used when consumers lack genuine interest in the products or services they have to choose from or when they are not capable of using complex decision strategies that require a lot of effort.

The trouble with heuristics is that they do not always help consumers to make the right decisions but instead they frequently lead to error and bias. For example, a consumer who happens to have a friend who had problems with a particular product may come to the conclusion that the product is not all that reliable. However, basing their decision upon the information provided by a particular individual means that they overlook the product's generally excellent track record and consequently may be missing out on a product that would have suited their needs perfectly (Solomon, Drenan, & Insko, 1981). Applying heuristics to the decision-making process simplifies it, as it means that consumers often only make use of one particular piece of information.

There are four categories of heuristics that are useful when it comes to understanding consumer decision-making: prediction, persuasion, compliance and choice heuristics. It is important to understand how heuristics impact upon the decision-making process. By understanding how they work, it is possible to change how consumer information is presented, in order to generate a decision in favour of a particular product or service.

Prediction heuristics

Tversky and Kahneman (e.g. 1974, 1983) identified four types of prediction heuristics (see Table 9.1) that have been found to be important for decision-making:

the representativeness, availability, simulation and anchoring-adjustment heuristic. These four heuristics are most commonly applied to decisions whereby the consumer is trying to predict an outcome. The ability to predict an outcome is important when making judgements and decisions about products and services. Hence, the prediction heuristics may be used in situations where consumers are trying to answer questions such as: 'Will I still want to invest my money in the same investment plan in five years from now?' and 'How long will this new sofa last?'

The representativeness heuristic is when individuals make judgements about the probability of an uncertain event in regard to how similar it is to a typical case while ignoring the basic principles of probability (Tversky & Kahneman, 1983). This became evident when Tversky & Kahneman presented their participants with a problem in which they briefly described a lady called Linda mentioning that she had been a philosophy student who used to have a keen interest in social justice. Participants were then asked to rank eight statements in terms of how probable they were. The results showed that Linda was less likely to be a bank teller than both a bank teller and a feminist, something that is incorrect bearing in mind that the category of bank tellers includes all feminist bank tellers. This demonstrates that the participants ranked the statements according to how similar the statement was to the description of Linda and hence overlooked the basic principles of probability.

Consumers apply the same kind of rules when assessing products. For example, a consumer may be faced with information about a new type of music player that can do a lot of things that a traditional CD player cannot do. In such situations the consumer may look at the music player and decide that the new music player's appearance is similar to the traditional CD player and hence classify the new music player as simply being a newer model of an old type of CD player. Such judgements can clearly have an impact on new product launches.

The availability heuristic refers to decision-making that involves probabilities or frequencies that are affected by how easily relevant information can be brought to mind (e.g. Kahneman, Slovic, & Tversky, 1982; Schwarz & Vaughn, 2002; Tversky & Kahneman, 1973). The availability heuristic can be very useful to consumers

TABLE 9.1 Prediction heuristics

Representativeness	Judging one thing on the basis how similar it is to another.
Availability	Assume that events easily retrieved from memory are more likely to occur frequently in the future.
Simulation	Predictions based on the ease with which a sequence of events can be imagined.
Anchoring-adjustment	Forming an initial judgement (the anchor) and then adjusting this judgement in a positive or negative direction depending on further evidence.

and on occasion protect them from making unfavourable decisions. For example, if a person can easily remember several times when they bought ice cream and jam from a shop called 'Bilos', just to find that the same ice cream and jam are cheaper elsewhere, makes them think that the whole selection of products that 'Bilos' sells is probably more expensive than other shops. Hence, the consumer is likely to decide to shop elsewhere in the future.

However, the availability heuristic is not always helpful when it comes to making consumer decisions. This is because consumers will make use of the most readily available information regardless of whether or not it is the most relevant (Wyer, 2004). For example, the media often focus on stories they think are the most sensational and will capture their audience interest. Consequently a plane crash gets a lot of media coverage while a car crash may not be mentioned at all. It is therefore easier for most people to remember plane crashes and consequently a higher number of people are scared of flying even though they are more likely to be involved in an accident when travelling by car.

The fact that people are more easily affected by what springs to mind was proven when participants were asked in a study to think of words beginning with R and then to think of words having R as their third letter (Tversky & Kahneman, 1973). Even though there are more English words with R as the third letter participants could more easily think of words that started with R.

Unfortunately this means that individuals can be misguided by what most easily springs to mind and consequently may not make the decision that is best for them, i.e. they may avoid travelling by plane but happily go by car.

It is difficult to determine exactly what kind of information consumers have readily available and how it may affect the decision-making process, especially if the information is purely based on personal experiences, as it then may not be possible for a marketer or manufacturer to do anything about it. However, if the information that is readily available is linked to general public opinion or media coverage, it should be possible to present consumers with additional information that in turn can influence the decision they make.

Even though heuristic research has found that more accessible information can guide the decision-making process, it is not always as simple as consumers acting directly upon what comes into their mind (Schwarz, 2004). This is supported by research whereby it has been found that consumers view products more favourably after having had several positive attributes brought to mind (Menon & Raghubir, 2003; Wänke, Bohner, & Jurkowitsch, 1997).

The simulation heuristic is similar to the availability heuristic in that, just as information that it is easy to retrieve in memory appears likely to happen, those that are easy to *imagine* (simulate) also appear likely to occur (Kahneman & Tversky, 1982). So if consumers can imagine it happening, they will believe that it is more likely to happen. This was noted in a series of experiments conducted by Gregory, Cialdini and Carpenter (1982). They asked their participants to imagine particular scenarios such as buying cable television service, and winning a contest. After the imagining phase they were tested on whether or not they thought the scenarios were likely to happen to them. It was found that there was an increase in the belief that the event would happen. The authors also conducted a follow-up survey and found that participants who had imagined purchasing cable television had actually done so after the experiment. The idea that events are perceived as more likely to happen after having imagined them has also been found to be applicable to other occurrences such as imagining that the team you support will win (Hirt & Sherman, 1985; Sherman, Zehner, Johnson, & Hirt, 1983). However, this only works if the event is relatively easy to imagine, but if a person fails to imagine the event, it will not be perceived as being more likely to happen in real life (e.g. Anderson & Godfrey, 1987).

The anchoring-adjustment heuristic is another key heuristic whereby decision-makers form an initial judgement (the anchor) and then adjust the judgement up or down. Most of the time consumers' final judgements are close to the original anchor, meaning that it can be very difficult to change their first impressions of a product or service. This was evident from a study where estate agents were shown different price lists for a house prior to seeing the house. The price list was low, medium or high. When the estate agents were allowed to inspect the house so that they could estimate the value of it, the researchers found that most valued the house close to the original list they have been shown (Northcraft & Neale, 1987).

Bearing in mind that estate agents should be more accurate in their evaluations of a property than a 'lay' person, the study demonstrates that experts also make use of the anchoring-adjustment heuristic.

Persuasion heuristics

Research conducted on attitude change and persuasion has shown that individuals either take short cuts in order to process information rapidly or think extensively about the information they process (e.g. Petty & Cacioppo, 1986a). It is from such research that the persuasion heuristics originates (see Table 9.2). (For a full account of processing differences in persuasion, see Chapter 7.)

The kind of short cuts used when processing persuasive messages are often developed from experience and observation (Chaiken, 1980) meaning that when consumers are less motivated to process the information encountered they can draw upon previous experiences in order not to tire themselves mentally (Giner-Sorolla

TABLE 9.2 Persuasion heuristics

Length-implies-strength	Long messages filled with lots of facts and figures indicate that the advertised product is of high quality.
Liking-agreement	People generally agree with people they like.
Consensus-implies-correctness	Majority opinion is usually considered to be valid.

& Chaiken, 1997). This is why consumers may come to the conclusion that advertisements filled with lots of facts and figures are a good sign of the advertised product's high quality. This is known as the *length-implies-strength heuristic.* Similarly, this has also been found for the speech rate used when trying to persuade individuals. Fast speech inhibits processing of the presented argument as well as signalling to the listener that it is a credible message (Smith & Shaffer, 1995).

Superficial cues are also used in the *liking-agreement* and *consensus-implies-correctness* heuristics (Chaiken et al., 1989). The liking-agreement is when consumers are more likely to agree with people that they like. The consensus-implies-correctness is when consumers believe that the majority opinion must be the right one. For example, if an individual hears or reads that a particular brand has been voted the most reliable by the majority of the readers of a particular magazine, they are more likely to be persuaded.

Compliance heuristics

There are six types of heuristics that make it more likely for people to comply with requests (Cialdini, 1993) (Table 9.3). All six are quite different in nature and can be used in different types of consumer scenarios. The *commitment-and-consistency* heuristic states that once people commit to a request, they tend to stick to the agreement (be consistent), even if the nature of the request changes (Cialdini, Cacioppo, Bassett, & Miller, 1978).

The *reciprocity* heuristic convinces people to return favours automatically without being asked (Langer, 1989). For example, if a salesperson gives a consumer a free sample, they are more likely to return the favour by buying something.

Scarcity heuristics can be particularly useful for advertising campaigns. The idea is that consumers want something that most people cannot have. Hence statements such as 'only available for a limited period' can be used.

People also have a tendency to comply when the *social validation* heuristic is used. This heuristic is also known as 'proof in numbers principle'. It is referring to how consumers tend to feel pressurized to comply when they think a high number of people have done something. For example, advertisers may try to create an

TABLE 9.3 Compliance heuristics

Commitment-and-consistency	Once people agree to a request, they tend to stick to the agreement.
Reciprocity	Convinces people to return favours automatically without being asked.
Scarcity	Consumers often want something that others cannot have.
Social validation	When consumers think a high number of people have used a product or service, it exerts implied peer pressure for them to comply as well.
Liking	Find it easier to comply with requests made by people we like.
Authority	People comply with serious requests coming from authority figures.

impression that thousands of people have already bought a particular product and hence exert peer pressure on other consumers to do the same. This is a technique commonly used by fund raisers as it is known that people are more likely to donate to charity when they are exposed to a long list of people who have already contributed (Reingen, 1982).

Liking heuristic refers to the simple fact that people are more likely to comply with requests when they like a person. Additionally people are also more likely to comply to requests from 'authority figures' which is known as the *authority heuristic*. Advertisers commonly make use of cues such as people in white coats to create an image of an 'expert scientist' (Milgram, 1965) in the hope that people will comply.

Choice heuristics

When consumers are particularly unmotivated to process the information they encounter, whether it is due to ability or motivation does not matter, they tend to make use of choice heuristics (see Table 9.4). This is particularly common when purchasing more unexciting and ordinary products such as toothpaste or toilet paper.

Lexicographic heuristics lead consumers to choose a product based on one single attribute that they consider to be the most important (Fishurn, 1974; Payne, Bettman, & Johnson, 1993). For some consumers it may be price, colour or safety, while others may go for the brand that is the cheapest.

However, on occasion the attribute that the consumer perceives to be the most important one may appear in more than one product. In such situations they may use the *elimination-by-aspect* heuristics (Tversky, 1972) to choose which product to purchase. The consumer then employs a cyclical process whereby they eliminate the products that do not have the most favoured attribute and then look for the second most important feature in those that do. If it turns out that also the second most favoured attribute appears in more than one product, the cyclical process is

TABLE 9.4 Choice heuristics

Lexicographic	Make consumers choose a brand based on the most important attribute at the time.
Elimination-by-aspects	When valued attribute appears in more than one alternative – consumers use a cyclical process eliminating the products that do not have the desired features.
Additive-difference	Used when comparing the difference between two brands, weigh the difference by importance, and then add the weighted differences.
Conjunctive and disjunctive	**Conjunctive**: Set minimum acceptable cut-off point for each attribute of the product consumers are looking for. **Disjunctive**: Sets an acceptable, but somewhat higher-than-minimum, cut-off point for each attribute.

simply repeated until a single product is found that has a feature that none of the others have.

If consumers are faced with two different brands they may compare the difference between them. In such situations they make use of the *additive-difference* heuristic which is when they weigh the difference by importance and then add the weighted differences (Payne et al., 1993). For example, if a particular brand of washing-up liquid is expensive but very effective, price is less important than the effectiveness of the product.

When consumers are in a rush they often make use of what is known as *conjunctive and disjunctive* heuristics (Payne et al., 1993). In time-pressured situations the first acceptable brand you see is often deemed to be good enough to purchase. The conjunctive heuristic then guides the consumer so that they make use of a minimum acceptable cut-off point for the features that they are looking for in the brand. The disjunctive heuristic provides a slightly higher than the minimum cut-off point for the desired brand features that are deemed by the consumer to be satisfactory.

Are consumers rational in their decision-making?

Looking at how heuristics impact upon decision-making, it would appear that consumers are not able to be rational. However, research in different areas indicates that it is not as simple as saying that that consumers are or are not rational. For example, becoming more familiar with products may aid their decision-making process in that they will rely less on heuristics (Hutchinson & Eisenstein, 2008) which in turn would make them more rational decision-makers.

Different studies investigating whether or not consumers are or can be rational suggest that at times they are trying to use objective reasoning while at other times they appear to resort to non-logical decision-making. This is evident from two studies conducted by Hsee. In one study he showed that people do not always make rational decisions (Hsee, 1999). Hsee offered his participants a choice of two chocolates, one that was shaped like a cockroach (which was larger in size and worth $2) and the other a heart (it was smaller than the cockroach and worth only 50 cents). The reason for choosing a cockroach-shaped chocolate was to try and induce feelings of disgust in the participants. Most people would be likely to be put off by the sight of the cockroach and therefore choose the chocolate heart instead. However, Hsee's study indicated otherwise. The outcome was that the majority of the participants (64 per cent) chose the chocolate cockroach. So why did most opt for the cockroach when they most likely did not like the look of it? One explanation may be that the participants felt that they had to censor their feelings of disgust towards the cockroach because they felt that acting upon such feelings might be seen as irrational. Being put off by a cockroach shape did not appear to be objective and consequently regardless of how strong those feelings were, the participants could not justify taking the heart-shaped chocolate. Alternatively it may just be that people don't care much about the appearance of the chocolate and are willing to scoff pretty much anything.

In a later study Hsee investigated what has been termed **lay scientism** (Hsee, Zhang, Yu, & Xi, 2003). This time his participants were given a choice between two stereo systems. One system was described as having more power, while the other had a richer sound. Half of the participants had the power described as an objective wattage rating and sound richness as an objective quantitative rating, while the other half was told that power was a subjective experience and sound richness an objective quantitative rating. Participants chose the system with the feature that had been described as 'objective', demonstrating that people are prepared to base their choices on what they consider to be a 'rational' choice as opposed to subjective evaluations.

Role of emotion

The way in which our emotions play a role in making decisions can also help to explain why consumers are not always rational. Research has found that decisions and judgements are affected by inputs that are experimental and phenomenal in nature (Schwarz, 1990, 2004; Schwarz & Clore, 1983, 1996, Schwarz, Bless, Strack, Klumpp, Rittenauerschatka, & Simons, 1991). In particular it has been suggested that emotions can be used as a source of information (e.g. 'I feel happy about it, hence I must like it'); and that they communicate metacognitive information about thinking processes (e.g. 'I find it difficult to retrieve examples: therefore I know little about a subject').

Using feelings as a source of information (Schwarz, 1990, 2001) can be misleading when trying to make a decision (Pham, 1998). Generally pleasant feelings are interpreted as evidence that you like something while unpleasant feelings are viewed as evidence of dislike. Such interpretations would only be correct if a consumer was 100 per cent certain that the mood was the direct consequence of encountering a particular stimulus. However, the actual source of our feelings may not depend on the product or service that we are currently evaluating. It may be other factors that are totally unrelated that are affecting how we are feeling, such as a nice sunny day or hearing your favourite tune, in which case using our feelings as information can lead to inaccurate decision-making.

High involvement

As previously mentioned, consumers tend to make use of heuristics when they are not particularly interested in the products and services, and when they are under time pressure. In such low involvement situations they are more likely to be seduced by 'superficial' attributes such as the brand name (Maheswaran et al., 1992). However, the use of heuristics decreases when a consumer is highly involved with the product category or brand. When they have a high interest in the product or brand, they are much more likely to engage in an in-depth data-driven judgement process, meaning that consumers are making more rational decisions. Consumers will do so provided that they are able and have the opportunity to do so

(Petty & Cacioppo, 1986a). When thinking extensively about the information they encounter, consumers will generate supporting arguments as well as counter-arguments and other plausible cognitive responses (e.g. Batra & Ray, 1986b; Hastak & Olson, 1989). Consequently, if marketers are hoping that their target audience will make rational decisions they should make use of techniques that will encourage elaborative processing.

Attribute-based decisions

Consumer decision-making is often affected by directly comparing particular attributes or features of products. Comparisons of attributes can naturally only be used if they are remembered or the products are present so that a comparison can be conducted (e.g. Biehal & Chakravarti, 1986). One model that can be useful for understanding what kind of information consumers might make use of when making decisions is the accessibility-diagnosticity model.

Accessibility-diagnosticity model

The accessibility-diagnosticity model can help us to understand how certain consumer information that is more accessible from memory and diagnostics can be used to make judgements about products (Feldman & Lynch, 1988). Put simply, the model is proposing that different types of salient stimuli at any given time can affect the type of cues that spring to mind.

This cognitively based model originated from research conducted within the area of social cognition that suggested that temporarily activated cognitions can be more influential when judging a stimulus (e.g. Fazio, Chen, McDonel, & Sherman, 1981; Lichtenstein & Srull, 1985).

The *accessibility* aspect of the model is referring to how easily an input (a piece of information) can be retrieved from memory. It is a direct function of the frequency and recency and activation of information in memory (Higgins, 1989). Accessibility increases when a stimulus is highly salient, vivid or when the consumer engages in elaborative processing. Negative information is generally more easily accessible and so also are recently engaged-in behaviours (Higgins, 1989), demonstrating how the information consumers make use of can be skewed. Not only is negative attribute information salient, it is also diagnostic because it suggests one categorization (such as low quality) over other possibilities (Skowronski & Carlston, 1987). *Diagnosticity* is to do with the perceived relevance and increases as the perceived relevance between two variables increases. Because diagnosticity increases as the perceived correlation between two factors increases, it is very much affected by how knowledgeable a consumer is as well as being contingent upon properties of the situation (Dick, Chakravarti, & Biehal, 1990; Ross & Creyer, 1992). For example, if three brands of tuna fish are being considered by a consumer and they are all the same size, size is irrelevant (non-diagnostic) and will therefore not be a point included in the decision-making. However, if the tuna fish tins differed drastically in size, then size would be relevant (diagnostic) and should be incorporated as a feature to be considered in the decision-making process.

Framing effect

To further demonstrate how complex the decision-making process is in that it is affected by many different factors, it is also worth taking a look at how consumption choices are influenced by contextual variables.

The way in which information is put into context also influences decision-making, known as the **framing effect**. This is because people generate perceptions that are consistent with a frame that is directly influenced by the information specific to a particular environment (Kahneman, 2002). By changing the point of reference one can therefore change consumers' preferences (Kahneman, Knetsch, & Thaler, 1986), something that has been proved from research investigating decisions made under uncertainty (Kahneman & Tversky, 1982; Tversky & Kahneman, 1982). See Table 9.5 for an example.

An example of how the framing effect is applicable to consumers can be noted from how products are described. In a study where beef was described as being 75 per cent lean rather than 25 per cent fat it was found to be more favourably evaluated (Levin & Gaeth, 1988). However, the effect was reduced when consumers were allowed to sample the product.

Older adults have been found to be more susceptible to framing effects when they are using heuristic processing (Kim, Goldstein, Hasher, & Zacks, 2005). Bearing in mind that older adults have limited cognitive resources and therefore tend to make use of a decision-making process known as *affective/experiential* that is intuitive, automatic and fast (Hess, Rosenberg, & Waters, 2001), it is possible that they will rely more on heuristics in general in order to save mental energy for more important tasks. If this is so, then they would also constantly be more susceptible to the framing effect in shopping environments. This seems particularly feasible if one bears in mind that older consumers often fail to engage in conscious

TABLE 9.5 Example of framing effect

Imagine that your country is preparing for an outbreak of an unusual disease that is expected to kill 600 people. Two propositions have been made in regards to how it can be combated and the following are estimates of the consequences of each of the programs.

Positive frame	Negative frame
• If program A is adopted, 200 people will be saved.	• If program C is adopted, 400 people will die.
• If program B is adopted, there is a 1 in 3 probability that 600 people will be saved and a 2 in 3 probability that no people will be saved.	• If program D is adopted, there is a 1 in 3 probability that nobody will die and a 2 in 3 probability that all 600 will die.

Generally negatively framed problems elicit risky responses and positively framed problems elicit less risky responses. Most people choose options A and D, despite the fact that the choices are contradictory as A is actually equivalent to C and B is equivalent to D.

decision-making due to neuropsychological changes that are age-related (Denburg, Tranel & Bechara, 2005).

Framing effects can also influence they way in which the price of a product is perceived. Kimes and Wirtz (2003) demonstrated this when they looked at how fair golfers perceived golf course charges to be. They found that golfers thought it was fair if a golf course charged a regular price for 'prime time' slots and offered a 20 per cent discount for other times. However, they thought it unfair if the course charged a 20 per cent premium for the 'prime time' slots and a regular price at other times. Such research demonstrates that price can play an important role in the decision-making process. Something that is also evident from this is that it can be primed and subsequently become more accessible from memory (Herr, 1989) as well as that it is often used to determine quality (Cronley, Posavac, Meyer, Kardes, & Kellaris, 2005).

Brand loyalty

Knowing that the decision-making process is often complex makes it even more interesting to think that some consumers choose to repeatedly buy a particular product or brand. Buying the same brand due to preference is called *brand loyalty* (Busch & Houston, 1985). It is not unusual that people have a 'preferred' brand that they continue to favour for a long period of time or sometimes even throughout their lives. Manufacturers of a particular brand hope that consumers will favour their brand over others so that they become brand loyal. Having brand loyal customers also means that it is easier for the manufacturer to create new brand extensions, as it has been found that favourable brand associations tend to be transferred onto the extension (Aaker & Keller, 1990; Boush & Loken, 1991).

It is important to note that brand loyalty is different from **inertia**, which is when the same brand is repeatedly purchased merely because less effort is required. However, if another product (for whatever reasons) turns out to be easier to buy, then the consumer will not hesitate to do so. Such a switch would rarely happen when a consumer is genuinely brand loyal as such repeat purchasing would be a conscious decision to repeatedly buy the same brand (Jacoby & Chestnut, 1978).

That brands are important to consumers is evident from research showing that they make consumer experiences more pleasurable, something that is evident from studies conducting taste tests on drinks. For example, Perrier water has been found to be the preferred brand over Old Fashioned Seltzer, but only when consumers know what they are drinking (Nevid, 1981). Other taste tests have shown that Coca-Cola was the favoured brand, but only when drinking out of cups that had the brand logo on (McClure et al., 2004), and liking for a particular beer brand disappeared if the labels were not visible (Allison & Uhl, 1964).

Brand associations

Brand loyal consumers have a strong level of involvement with their preferred brand and they clearly perceive it as being different from other brands (Odin, Odin, & Valette-Florence, 2001). To marketers, it is imperative that the associations consumers have to a particular brand are of a positive nature. The associations formed will determine whether or not consumers will purchase a particular product and affect the likelihood of buying brand extensions (Belen del Rio, Vacquez, & Iglesias, 2001). They also represent individually held beliefs, often based on advertising messages and peer recommendations, of how good the brand is and how it complements their particular lifestyle. If the associations to a brand are particularly strong (e.g. Mercedes-Benz, Figure 9.1), consumers tend to be happy to purchase brand extensions because they believe that the other products by the same brand will be just as good. This appears to be logical provided that the products are of a similar nature. However, it is less understandable when the products sold under the one brand name, but share no manufacturing similarities, such as in the case of Virgin. In theory, there is no reason as to why Virgin flights would comparable to Virgin Cola. Nevertheless there are several products that appear to be successful just because they have a 'valued' brand name attached to them that is perceived to be manufacturing good quality or value for money products.

Why do consumers become brand loyal?

It is difficult to say for certain why some consumers get so attached to a brand that they keep on buying it time and time again. The simple explanation is that they learn that certain brands satisfy their needs. However, it is much more difficult to understand what needs it is that the brands satisfy. The needs may not necessarily be of a practical nature but may instead be connected to psychological fulfilment. One need that most have a desire to fulfil is the need for belongingness. Such need may be established through the culture in which we are raised. Additionally, consumers can also become brand loyal by being given incentives to repeatedly use the same product or service.

Some brand logos function as symbols in that they are instantly recognizable and represent a high number of positive associations.

FIGURE 9.1 Well-known brands generate strong associations.

Source: Courtesy of Mercedez-Benz.

Collectivist cultures

Belonging to certain groups and cultures can impact upon the decisions consumers make. How much a group member's decision-making is influenced by the group to which they belong depends on how strongly connected the individual is to the group. People who are brought up in *collectivist cultures* (where emphasis is on the importance of relationships and roles within the social system) tend to be strongly attached to their social support groups and consequently their choices and decisions tend to be influenced by them. Hence, it is unlikely to come as a surprise that different types of cultures can predict the likelihood of people becoming brand loyal. For example, consumers in collectivist cultures generally like to conform to the groups to which they belong. It is the *need to conform* that increases the likelihood of collectivist cultures being more brand loyal. This is because it is easier to repeatedly buy a product that a group has already approved of rather than take a risk and buy a product that other members have not previously used (Lee, 2000). Buying a product that sets you apart from what is deemed to be the norm by your group is often considered to be an aspect of individualistic cultures as trying a new product involves some amount of risk-taking (Baumgartner & Steenkamp, 1996).

The need for belongingness can also explain why **brand communities** are established (Muñiz & O'Guinn, 2001). This is when need of belongingness can be felt when belonging to a particular group of consumers who all use the same brand. Brand communities have been said to possess specific types of characteristics such as feeling of belongingness to an in-group through shared product consumption, and shared sense of duty and obligation to other members.

Incentives

Providing consumers with an incentive to achieve a goal can make consumers brand loyal. This is evident from a study by Nunes and Dreze (2006) where they gave loyalty cards to customers at a car wash. Customers were either given a loyalty card that required 10 car washes before receiving a free one or a card that required eight car washes before getting a free wash. Those who were given the card that required 10 washes were also given two free stamps so that the two cards essentially required the same amount of effort to achieve the goal of getting a free wash. Some 34 per cent of the customers who got the loyalty card with 10 washes on it filled their card and received their free wash, while only 19 per cent of those who had got the card with eight washes filled theirs. From this it was concluded that when consumers believe that they have come a long way (in relation to achieving a goal) it increases their commitment.

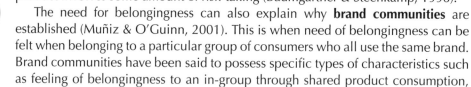

Key Terms

Brand communities
When groups of people feel they belong together due to using the same brands.

Framing effect
The way information is 'framed' or presented affects the way in which decisions are made.

Heuristics
Mental short cuts or rules of thumb that can be quickly and effortlessly applied in decision-making.

Inertia
Repeated purchase of products due to habit and because consumers lack motivation to consider potentially better alternatives.

Lay scientism
When consumers focus on objective attributes.

Summary

The consumer decision-making process is complex because it is affected by many different factors. Consumers often make use of heuristics when deciding what to buy. Some of the more common types of heuristics that are subconsciously used include prediction, persuasion and choice heuristics. Heuristics are partially the reason why consumers do not always make rational decisions. Emotions can at times also misguide consumers. This is because they may associate products with how they feel at a particular point in time, even though their mood is caused by an entirely different source. Consumers can be encouraged to make rational decisions by trying to make them more involved with the product or brand.

Decisions can also be affected by specific product attributes and the accessibility-diagnosticity model can be used to shed some light on why certain attributes are likely to be used in the decision-making process.

Consumers sometimes make the decision to repeatedly purchase a particular brand, which is known as brand loyalty. Individuals from collectivist cultures are more likely to become brand loyal when they know a particular brand has the approval of their peers.

Discussion questions

1 How might a marketer use heuristics to their advantage?

2 Is the use of heuristics the same as being irrational?

3 Is it possible for decisions not to be affected by emotions? Can consumers genuinely separate themselves from how they feel when making a decision?

4 Why do brand loyal consumers have a high level of involvement with their preferred brand?

5 Can brand loyalty really be achieved by using incentives?

CHAPTER

10

The Internet

Introduction

The use of the Internet is in itself a consumption activity. Participation in online activities is constantly on the increase, demonstrating a broadening of the appeal of the Internet. This chapter will look at factors that affect how Internet shoppers gather information and how they go about making their online decisions. However, since the Internet is not only used for shopping purposes, this chapter also examines how the Internet can be used as a social tool by making use of chat rooms and social networking sites such as Facebook. The chapter concludes by taking a brief look at how there is a downside to the Internet in that people can become addicted to it.

Internet use

Internet use has grown rapidly since the mid-1990s. It has been estimated that over 120 million people use the Internet worldwide (CommerceNet, 1999). For a summary of Internet usage statistics, see Table 10.1.

The commercial success of websites such as eBay and Amazon are testament to how Internet business can be highly profitable. The importance of e-commerce is becoming ever more evident and Gordon Brown stated in 2009 that the British government intends to boost the digital communications industry as it contributes approximately £50 billion to the economy on a yearly basis (BBC, 2009).

The Internet is good for consumers, marketers, manufacturers and retailers alike. From a consumer perceptive it enables the consumer to extensively research

TABLE 10.1 Internet use statistics

	Europe	USA	Australia
Usage	393,373,000	220,141,000	16,736,000
Usage growth 2000–2008	274%	130%	153%

Adapted from: http://www.internetworldstats.com/europa2.htm

products and services (e.g. Schwartz, 2004) and simplifies price comparison (e.g. Baker, Marn, & Zawada, 2001; Kambil, Wilson, & Agrawal, 2002). Marketers and manufacturers can also take advantage of simple price comparisons in that it enables them to track what competitors are doing and allows them to price their own products and services accordingly.

Retailers can benefit from putting their 'stores' online as it allows them to keep a close eye on their customers because they can follow the movements of visitors using their websites, and collect data about the type of purchases that they make. But perhaps one of the greatest advantages is that for manufacturers and marketers it provides an opportunity to reach a wide range of consumers that they may not otherwise be able to reach.

The Internet user

Because the Internet is so widely used, it is not possible to say that there is a certain type of Internet user. Men and women of all ages (Rogers & Fisk, 2000) use or are interested in using the Internet, which is why it is so attractive for marketers and manufacturers in that they do not necessarily have to limit their target audience. However, it is worth bearing in mind that not all age groups will be equally able to process the information presented to them online. For example, there is evidence to suggest that older adults will not be able to deal with as much online information as a young person due to diminished working memory capacity and difficulty in storing information (see Chapter 2). Consequently older consumers are likely to search for and generally 'read' less information than younger ones (e.g. Cole & Balasubramanian, 1993; Lin & Lee, 2004).

It is also difficult to pinpoint the type of consumers who are reluctant to engage in online shopping. But research has found that consumers who have a tendency to grumble about online shopping are those who don't actually shop online (Yang & Lester, 2004). So if they can be motivated to change their behaviours, they are also more likely to have a positive attitude towards it. However, let's not forget that the Internet is not only used for consumption purposes but also for a wide range of other reasons (see Table 10.2). One such reason is for social communication. Many online users these days are frequent Internet consumers because it gives them the opportunity to communicate with others.

Internet consumption

There are differences as well as similarities between Internet shopping and traditional in-store shopping. One key difference is that with Internet shopping there are no location and time constraints (Sheth & Sisodia, 1999), meaning that consumers can source products from other countries if needed and shop at a time of their convenience. Expediency has been identified as one of the main reasons why individuals choose to shop online as well as the possibility of purchasing products

TABLE 10.2 The many uses of the Internet

Objective	Examples
Research/information	By using search engines such as Google and Yahoo.
Entertainment	Browsing the web without no particular aim.
Games	Allows interactive gaming between players.
Socializing	May be achieved through chat rooms, social networking sites or email.
Communication	By using email set up by providers such as Yahoo, Google or Hotmail.
Shopping	Can be done through the endless number of shopping sites online such as eBay or perhaps through sites directly linked to shops (e.g. Ikea).
Watching movies	Downloading movies and television programmes from the net.
Educational	To learn about new subject areas. This may be done by using websites such as www.topmarks.co.uk or www.kidsknowit.com

at a discounted price (Ernst & Young, 1999). It is therefore hardly surprising that when consumers think that in-store shopping is inconvenient, their intention to shop online is greater (Chiang & Dholakia, 2003).

Another factor that also increases the likelihood of online shopping is the type of product that the consumer intends to buy. When consumers are shopping for goods that require personal inspection prior to purchase, such as perfume, they are less likely to shop online. However, when consumers intend to purchase products that can be thoroughly researched online without needing personal inspection (such as books), they are more likely to shop by using the Internet (Chiang & Dholakia, 2003).

In order to understand the Internet consumption process fully it is important to look at how consumers search for information and how they go about making purchase decisions.

Information search

Researching products online is a common everyday activity. A survey found that as many as 93 per cent of consumers have researched products online (Yankelovich Partners, & Harris Interactive, 2001). Consumers tend to think more extensively about the products they find on the Web and request more information than they would if they were exposed to the same products in printed advertisements (Schlosser, 2003). This was found when 143 participants had to evaluate two fictitious advertisements (one for a sports car and one for a fast food restaurant) either by seeing them on a computer or as a printed advertisement. Participants who had viewed the advertisements on the computer sought more information and mentioned more attributes than those in the print condition. Such findings suggest that the mere presence of a computer makes people think more about the product encountered, which might be because people have been conditioned into thinking that computers do provide detailed information (Schlosser, 2003). Just because people requested additional information in this study, it does not mean that consumers generally wish to gather vast amounts of information prior to every purchase they make. It is much more likely that consumers engage in limited information-gathering prior to making a cheaper type of purchase or one where the product will ultimately be the same regardless of which site they look at (i.e. books).

Limited information gathering

In certain circumstances, online shoppers appear to be engaging in a limited number of of pre-purchase information searches before deciding which product to buy. Even though research in this area is only in its infancy, there is evidence to suggest that many online consumers are loyal to a single site. For example, consumers shopping for CDs on the Internet on average only look at 1.3 sites prior to making a purchase, and both CD and book shoppers look at 1.2 book sites (Johnson et al., 2004). Consumers are also often inclined to make purchases from higher-priced vendors for products that are homogeneous (e.g. CDs and books) (Brynjolfsson & Smith, 2000) presumably because they are loyal to that site.

The underlying reason for using a limited amount of Internet resources when shopping for cheaper and homogenous products online may be explained by using the *human capital* model (Becker, 1993). The human capital model suggests that learning by doing is a key aspect of how humans acquire knowledge. Over time and through experience we obtain the skills we need to survive and thrive in the societies in which we live. When engaging in novel tasks we tend to have to make an effort. However, over time, and with practice, behaviours that were originally difficult and demanding become less so, and eventually become habitual. Consequently, the demands of the task decrease and cognitive resources can be used for other purposes (Murray & Häubl, 2003). Using a computer to shop for the first time can be demanding, but with practice the task becomes a lot easier and eventually will seem like second nature, because humans have the ability to learn from experience. Consequently, an Internet site that consumers have had previous experience of will be more useful in that it will decrease the mental effort put in. Although consumption activity increases, the time and effort to produce the activity decrease (Ratchford, 2001). The ease of using one particular website that consumers are familiar with means that consumers are ultimately learning to be loyal to one site, which explains why consumers fail to shop around online, even though it would be really easy to do (Murray & Häubl, 2003).

Reliance on multiple sources

Another reason why consumers choose not to gather a lot of information online about the products might be because they rely on multiple sources (e.g. Bettman & Park, 1980), meaning that they are unlikely to search for information only on the Internet. Additionally, the amount of effort that goes into researching products is also affected by how much previous knowledge the consumer has about the product. In fact, it has been proposed that there is an inverted-U relationship between product knowledge and the amount of search conducted (Bettman & Park, 1980). This means that those who are moderately knowledgeable about a product are those who are the most likely to conduct extensive product searches, while those with little or a lot of knowledge are the least likely to conduct searches.

Searching online/buying offline

Rather than purchasing their products online, some people prefer to purchase them in a traditional retail environment, even though they use the World Wide Web (WWW) to gather product information. This shopping strategy has certain advantages for in-store consumers, in that it can help them make a more informed choice while in store (Morton, Zettelmeyer, & Silva Russo, 2001), even though it is a disadvantage for online retailers. There are likely to be several underlying reasons why consumers engage in searching online and buying offline tactics. One explanation might be that when individuals have a '*need to touch*' products, they will not buy the product until they have had an opportunity to touch it (Citrin, Stem, Spangenberg, & Clark, 2003).

Another explanation can be because consumers are frequently presented with new ways to shop (Geyskens, Gielsen, & Dekimpe, 2002). With multiple options (e.g. the Internet, catalogue and in-store) consumers often rely on more than one product source, presenting certain difficulties to the seller (e.g. Stone, Hobbs, & Khaleeli, 2002). One problem in particular is that the trader may lose the customer at some point during the shopping process (Nunes & Cespedes, 2003). In light of this, it has been proposed that there are three different aspects that can explain why a potential customer may not conduct their purchase online (Verhoef, Neslin, & Vroomen, 2007).

1 It may be a 'tradition' that the Internet tends to have a strong *search attribute advantage* (ease of gathering information), while shops have a strong *purchase attribute advantage* (speed of obtaining a product).
2 Internet's lack of *channel lock-in* (the ability to retain customers across different stages such as search and purchase).
3 That *cross-channel synergy* (when searching for information from a particular source can enhance the purchase experience from another source) might occur between the Internet and traditional stores.

There are ways in which retailers can try to encourage consumers to purchase products online such as making them trust the website (Schlosser, Barnett-White, & Lloyd, 2006). Other examples include trying to increase channel lock-in, by using procedures such as remembering the customer's credit card and by offering immediate discounts (Verhoef, Neslin, & Vroomen, 2007).

Language

The language used on the Internet is also a factor that can affect how consumers gather information. Most websites are offered only in English (Fox, 2000), which raises the question how easy it is for non-native English speakers to gather information. It has been estimated that just under a third of all Web consumers will speak English as a first language (Crockett, 2000), meaning that the majority may not always fully understand the information they come across on the Internet. Language has been found to play an important role in consumers' perception of websites as it has the capacity to influence their attitudes towards them (Luna, Peracchio, & de Juan, 2003). This raises the possibility that language might also be a factor in whether or not consumers will search for information on sites that are not in their first language.

Internet decision-making

The consumer decision-making process (as discussed in the previous chapter) is complex. Naturally the same strategies that are used to make other types of decisions are also used to make shopping decisions online. However, there are some aspects of online decision-making that warrant further exploration. These include how Web information is presented and how the vast amount of choice available on the www can impact upon the purchase likelihood and outcome, as well as who consumers blame when making a bad purchase decision.

Web design

Purchasing decisions online are often constructed while navigating through Internet stores, meaning that the actual page layout can be a determining factor in predicting purchases (Mandel & Johnson, 2002). Design features have been found to operate implicitly upon the choices Internet users make. This is evident from a study conducted by Mandel and Johnson (2002) where they manipulated the background pattern of Internet car shopping sites. They altered the backgrounds so that they were designed to relate either to frugality or quality. Their findings showed that when participants had been exposed to backgrounds in line with thrift goals, they were more likely to choose an inexpensive but less safe car. However, those who had been exposed to backgrounds representative of safety goals (quality) showed a clear preference for more expensive but safer cars.

Knez and Niedenthal (2007) also produced findings that support the notion that altering the design of computer-related information can impact upon the user. In their study they tested if different types of lighting in games had the capacity to change the way the players felt and performed. They found that players performed best when exposed to warm coloured lighting (i.e. red) compared to cool coloured lighting (i.e. blue). The warm coloured lighting was also found to induce pleasantness in the players.

Amount of choice

Making purchase decisions online can be daunting as there are almost endless amounts of information that can be accessed (Schwartz, 2004). With a vast number of options to choose from consumers can feel uneasy (Schwartz, Ward, Monterosso, Lyubomirsky, White, & Lehman, 2002) which will in turn affect whether or not a decision is made (Iyengar & Lepper, 2000).

Too much choice can decrease the likelihood of purchase (Iyengar & Lepper,

2000) and if they do make a purchase, the item bought will be viewed as less satisfactory when it has been chosen from a larger selection (Diehl & Poynor, in press). The applicability of this to online purchases was shown in a study by Griffin and Broniarczyk (2008) when they asked participants to take part in an Internet search task. Participants were more likely to conduct extensive searches when options were **non-alignable** than when they were **alignable**. Non-alignable differences between products are unique, e.g. a house that has a pool versus one that has a garden, while alignable differences relate to a single dimension, such as a 40 ft garden versus a 60 ft garden. The authors concluded that the extensive search that participants engaged in when faced with non-alignable choices led to decreased satisfaction because of the difficult trade-offs they had to make. However, it needs to be remembered that online customers only tend to engage in extensive information searches for certain types of products, which means that the likelihood of feeling less satisfied is probably limited to certain product categories.

Who to blame for poor decision-making

When consumers use computers to assist in their purchase decisions they sometimes blame them when the decision does not turn out to be satisfactory (Moon, 2003). This is in line with the theory of **self-serving bias** that proposes that people have a tendency to take credit for positive outcomes and blame others or something else for negative outcomes (e.g. Nisbett & Ross, 1980; Snyder, Stephan, & Rosenfield, 1978). People engage in self-serving bias in order to protect their own self-esteem or self-concept. The retrospective positive or negative evaluation of the computer's performance is important in that it will most likely determine the likelihood of future purchases being made using the computer.

However, the pattern of blame changes when consumers have a history of intimate *self-disclosure* (the sharing of intimate information and feelings) with a computer. Relationships researchers have established that being sensitive and responsive to partners both develops and maintains relationships (Cross, Bacon, & Morris, 2000; Laurenceau, Barrett, & Pietromonaco, 1998). When closeness has been established to another person, an individual's self-concept expands so that it also incorporates the other (Aron & Aron, 1997). Bearing in mind that consumers can feel that non-animate objects are very important to them and a part of who they are (e.g. Belk, 1988; Dittmar, 2008b; Solomon, 1983), it is not surprising if they can also engage in self-disclosure with material possessions (Moon, 2003). Indeed, it has been found that when consumers come across computers they do treat them as social encounters (Moon, 2000; Nass & Moon, 2000) and consequently they can make social attributions toward the computer (e.g. Reeves & Nass, 1996). This is why the pattern of blame changes when consumers have a history of intimate self-disclosure with the computer. They are then more likely to accept responsibility and instead credit the computer for the positive decisions made (Moon, 2003).

The social Internet consumer

The Internet is naturally not just used by people for shopping purposes but also for reasons of a more social nature. The last decade in particular has demonstrated that it is easy to stay in touch with people by using email, chat rooms and social networking sites, meaning that it is a very useful tool when communicating with others. This is good news as it can allow Internet consumers to ensure that they never feel far away from their family and friends as well as providing them with the opportunity to make new friends and acquaintances.

The Internet as a means of communication

To date, not much has been written about how consumers use the Internet as a communicative tool (Zinkhan, Kwak, Morrison, & Peters, 2003). Researchers have identified that chatting on the Internet has increased a lot in recent years (Zinkhan, Kwak, & Pitt, 2001), and is consequently becoming an important aspect of Internet consumption. Chat rooms are such an integral part of 'Internet life' these days that many major companies have one so that their customers can air their views about the products and services that they provide. It has even been suggested that installing a chat room on a website can increase consumers' visits by approximately 50 per cent and online purchases by around 40 per cent (*Business Wire*, 1998).

Why chat online?

Not all consumers who use chat rooms are likely to engage with them simply because they can be perceived as unreal, and because there is no personal connection (Kwak, 2001). However, for those who do choose to chat online, there are many underlying reasons why they do it. Some do it in order to seek out information, to solve problems, or for social interaction (Kwak, 2001). Specific differences in regard to why men and women choose to chat online have been found. Women are more likely to do it for entertainment purposes, companionship, relaxation, and to kill time. Such information can benefit software companies in that it enables them to create programmes with specific purposes that are directly aimed at women (Zinkhan, Kwak, Morrison, & Peters, 2003).

MySpace and Facebook

It is common today for people to have a virtual image online that they have carefully created in order to show the world their most desirable self. Many of these virtual images are displayed on the increasingly popular social networking sites MySpace and Facebook (Thayer & Ray, 2006). These kinds of websites typically allow the user to post information about themselves, send messages to 'friends', post pictures and link their sites to friends' sites.

Estimates suggest that in 2006 there were approximately 20 million MySpace users and around 9.5 million Facebook users (CNN, 2006; Foxnews, 2006) and ever since somewhere in the region of 200,000 users have signed up every day. This has undoubtedly changed the way in which people interact and communicate since they can 'choose' the way in which they portray themselves to others.

Websites such as MySpace and Facebook are equally appealing to men and women as well as to most ethnic groups (Raacke & Bonds-Raacke, 2008). Most users of friend-networking sites employ them as a way of making new friends and to try and locate old ones (Raacke & Bonds-Raacke, 2008).

The way that an individual's personal page is perceived is very important, especially for young people. Valkenburg, Peter & Schouten (2006) found that there is a relationship between the use of social networking sites, self-esteem and well-being. They conducted a survey with over eight thousand people aged 10 to 19 who had an online profile and found that when they received positive feedback on their profiles, it enhanced their self-esteem and well-being. However, if they received negative feedback, their self-esteem decreased as did their well-being.

The relationships formed through networking sites are often of a shallow nature. It has been suggested that for many people, Facebook is only used to try and 'collect' online friends without wishing to establish any real contact with them. Such behaviour is consistent with narcissism (Buffardi & Campbell, 2008) and it may therefore be that particularly self-centred individuals use the sites to make themselves feel better in that they will appear popular to the online world.

The older Internet user

It would seem that the Internet would be the ideal tool for older individuals to stay in touch with others, especially since it is common that they have less and less contact with family and friends due to illness or long geographical distances (Victor, Scambler, Bond, & Bowling, 2000). The usefulness of using the Internet as a social communication tool for older people was investigated by Sum, Mathews, Hughes and Campbell (2008). In online questionnaires they asked 222 Australians aged 55 and over, about their Internet use and loneliness. Of the participants, 62 per cent were female and approximately 64 per cent lived with a partner or spouse, 90 per cent used the Internet for at least 4 hours every week, and around 96 per cent had used the Internet for more than a year. The findings showed that the Internet was mainly used for communication, information search and commerce. Most participants had low levels of loneliness (presumably because the majority were co-habiting) and men were found to experience more loneliness than the female participants. Though, when people reported that they did feel lonely, it correlated to the amount of time spent on the Internet, the more time spent on the net, the lonelier they were. It would therefore appear that the Internet is not a sufficient tool in reducing feelings of loneliness. However, the correlation found between loneliness and Internet use might be due to the type of sites that were used. Therefore the authors concluded that it would be useful to teach those over 55 years of age to use certain Internet functions in hope of reducing their feelings of loneliness.

Psychological well-being

One drawback of the Internet is that it can become addictive. Some Internet consumers are drawn to the www and chat rooms in particular because of their addictive nature (Kwak, 2001). Addiction to the Internet is not recognized by the current edition of the *Diagnostic Statistical Manual* but nevertheless there is plenty of data to suggest that Internet addiction is not uncommon, especially among teenagers. For example, it has been proposed that 7.5 per cent of the Taiwanese adolescent population (Ko, Yen, Yen, Lin, & Yang, 2007), 1.98 per cent of Norwegian adolescents (Johansson & Götestam, 2004), 8.2 per cent of Greek adolescents (Siomos, Dafouli, Braimiotis, Mouzas, & Angelopoulos, 2008) and approximately 2.4 per cent of Chinese teenagers (Gao & Su, 2007) suffer from Internet addiction.

Becoming addicted is not simply restricted to chat rooms but is applicable to the entire Internet. This was investigated by Young (1996) who approached the subject area as if it were similar to gambling. She modified a questionnaire normally used to identify compulsive gamblers to establish how many out of 600 participants were potentially addicted to the Internet (for an example of the questions asked, see Table 10.3). Young found that approximately 66 per cent of the participants were 'dependent' on the Internet and that they spent around 38 hours a week online. The 38 hours spent on the Internet did not include academic or employment-related activities. Interestingly enough, most of those who were classified as 'dependent' were relatively new to online activities, about 83 per cent had only used the Internet for a year or less, while those who were not dependent were mainly individuals who had used the Internet for a long time. Such findings may indicate that it may be the 'novelty' of using the Internet that is making some hooked but as users are becoming used to it they find it less entertaining and subsequently spend less time online. Nevertheless, it is worth questioning how healthy it is for any user to spend the equivalent amount of time to a full working week on the Internet.

TABLE 10.3 Examples of questions used by Young (1996)

Have you lied to family members, therapists, or others to conceal the extent of involvement with the Internet?

Do you stay online longer than originally intended?

Do you feel the need to use the Internet with increasing amounts of time in order to achieve satisfaction?

Do you feel preoccupied with the Internet (think about previous online activity or anticipate the next online session)?

Key Terms

Alignable options
When options are similar in nature, e.g. a vase that is identical but differs slightly in size.

Non-alignable options
When options are distinctive.

Self-serving bias
People tend to take credit for positive outcomes and blame others (or something else) for negative ones.

Summary

Online shopping provides consumers with a greater freedom to source products from further afield and at a time of their convenience. The amount of information gathered about products through using the Internet appears to vary depending on what kind of product the consumer intends to purchase. Consumers are often loyal to a particular shopping site and this can be explained by the human capital model. It is also common that consumers do not rely just on the Internet to provide them with product information but instead they seek out additional information from a wide range of sources. There are also times when consumers only use the Internet to search for product information and then purchase the products in a shop instead. Searching online and purchasing offline is more likely to happen because shops have a strong purchase attribute advantage, the Internet lacks channel lock-in and cross-channel synergy can take place between the two. Online decisions are affected by the website designs, the amount of choice available and because at times people blame the computer when making a decision that they are not happy with. The Internet is also used to communicate with friends and to make new social contacts, which is often done by using sites such as Facebook. Spending too much time on the Internet can lead to addiction but it is not clear if it is an 'Internet novice' condition that will wear off once the user becomes used to it.

Discussion questions

1 How does online shopping differ to shopping in a store?
2 What kind of lock-in strategies can be used to increase the likelihood of online purchases? Try to think of alternatives to those mentioned in the text.
3 Is the way in which consumers gather information online rational?
4 Should the amount of time children spend on the Internet be controlled?
5 Is it a good idea for individuals who feel lonely to engage in social networking sites?

Children as consumers

Introduction

This chapter looks at a wide variety of aspects of children and consumption. It will introduce how children's media literacy is cultivated in parallel with their cognitive development. In particular, you will be introduced to aspects such as Piaget's traditional theory of cognitive development, and research that demonstrates how complete comprehension of what is viewed on television is a gradual process. Additionally, the chapter also includes sections on how violent television programmes can affect children, the pros and cons of the Internet and whether it is ethically right to market products to children.

Children and consumption

Children are, like adults, avid consumers. Sales figures from both the USA and the UK clearly demonstrate that children are from an early age socialized to be a part of the consumer society in which we live. In 1997, sales figures in America showed that children under the age of 12 spent over $24 billion of their own money on numerous products and services. The same year, children were also found to influence the spending of an additional $188 billion (McNeal, 1998). In the UK, the toy industry was estimated to be worth approximately £2 billion (British Toy and Hobby Association, 2007).

It is not just the monetary value of consumption that demonstrates how dedicated children are to consuming but also the amount of time they invest in certain consumer activities. On average children watch 2–5 hours of television daily, spend around 2–3 hours using a computer, and approximately 5 hours listening to music or the radio (e.g. Larson & Verma, 1999; Ofcom, 2007; Roberts, Foehr, Rideout, & Brodie, 1999). This means that many children today will spend considerably more time engaging in consumer activities than they will going to school. Consequently it is inevitable that their social and cognitive skills will be affected by the consumer activities in which they engage.

How children differ cognitively from adults

Children's cognitive abilities develop throughout their childhood which means that they differ from adults in the way that they deal with the information they encounter. This means that children often do not perceive marketing messages and mainstream media in the same way as adults. They also tend to focus on different types of stimuli and at times (depending on age), children misunderstand what they have seen or heard. It is therefore essential for marketers and consumer psychologists to know at what age children develop different cognitive skills so that they can communicate effectively with young consumers.

Cognitive development

Piaget's (e.g. 1936, 1951) theory of cognitive development clearly demonstrates that children have limited cognitive capabilities compared to those of an adult (Ginsburg & Opper, 1988). He proposed that children go through four main stages of development: (1) *sensorimotor stage* (birth to 2 years); (2) *pre-operational stage* (2 to 7 years); (3) *concrete operational* (7 to 11 years); and (4) *formal operational* (11 through to adulthood) (see Table 11.1). Each stage demonstrates that children's cognitive abilities differ greatly depending on age. During the sensorimotor stage the child mainly focuses on immediate sensory and motor experiences and only has a rudimentary capacity for thinking. The second stage, the pre-operational, is divided into two periods, pre-conceptual (2–4 years) and intuitive period (4–7 years). The pre-conceptual period shows children's abilities to deal with relatively basic internal and symbolic thought. In the latter part of the pre-conceptual period, children have developed the mental operations of classifying and quantifying stimuli and experiences in a more systematic way, even though they are unable to explain why they have done it. During the pre-operational stage children tend to focus on a single dimension which is known as *centration*. For example, they may focus their attention on the colour of an object rather than the shape. Hence,

TABLE 11.1 Piaget's stages of intellectual development

Stage	Age	Characteristics
Sensori-motor	0–2	Child knows about the world through sensory information and actions. Learns to differentiate themselves from the environment and develop capacity to form internal mental representations.
Pre-operational	2–7	Child learns to understand basic internal and symbolic thought. Towards the end of this stage they begin to understand about classification of objects.
Concrete operational	7–12	Children can classify and organize objects. Within limitation, they can perform logical mental operations.
Formal operational	12+	Abstract reasoning starts. Have the capacity to formulate and test hypotheses.

marketing to children needs to be simple and clear so that children can extract the key information from the message encountered. Piaget called the third stage concrete operational because a child's thinking processes can only be applied to tangible present objects. Their reliance on the immediate environment means that they have difficulty dealing with abstract concepts. However, at this stage, children manage to consider several dimensions of a stimulus and consequently marketing messages can make use of a few more elements than they can during the preoperational stage. Only by the time children reach 11 years of age do they have the capacity to process information in a more adult-like pattern in that they can deal with complex thoughts and hypothetical scenarios. This is what is outlined in the final formal operational stage.

It is worth noting that in more recent years researchers have found that Piaget's stages are not entirely correct in that some aspects of cognitive development happen slightly earlier or later than he originally proposed (e.g. Baillargeon & DeVos, 1991; Bower, 1982; Wimmer & Perner, 1983). However, the general idea of Piaget's cognitive development remains intact and is worth paying attention to when marketing to children.

Impact of mainstream media

Research into children's consumer behaviour started during the 1950s and 1960s, when aspects such as brand loyalty (Guest, 1955) and comprehension of marketing messages (McNeal, 1964) were investigated. These days, children are continuously exposed to different types of media. Most commonly they are exposed to television, radio and the Internet on a daily basis. Through such sources they learn about the world in general and are frequently exposed to marketing messages. In parallel with the increase of media exposure, research looking at links between consumption, cognitive development, behaviour affects, and social influences has become more common. Some areas have been more popular than others, e.g. the impact of television viewing upon behaviour.

Television

Television viewing on a regular basis normally begins between the ages of 2½ and 3 (Huston, Donnerstein, Fairchild, Feshbach, Katz, Murray, et al., 1992). At the same time children also develop clear preferences for different types of television programmes. In a study conducted by Lyle and Hoffman (1972) it was found that approximately four-fifths of children as young as 3 years of age could name a favourite programme and this increased to almost a hundred per cent by the age of 5.

The amount of viewing increases gradually as children become older and peaks approximately at the age of 12. After that the amount watched tends to decline as teenagers tend to spend more time outside of the household (Comstock & Scharrer, 2001).

Becoming television literate

Young children do not deal with what they see on television in the same way as adults do. This is hardly surprising bearing in mind that research clearly shows that children gradually develop the cognitive skills (e.g. Baillargeon & DeVos, 1991; Bower, 1982; Piaget, 1951) that are required to fully understand and process the information they see on the small screen. It takes them a good ten years to get to the point where they can fully process and comprehend what they have watched (see Table 11.2).

Children younger than 6 lack the ability to understand the theoretical aspects of television programmes (Van den Broek, Lorch, & Thurlow, 1996). Hence they tend to focus on the actual behaviour that they observe on the screen, meaning that they often misunderstand the intended meaning of a programme. This is partially the reason why at that age they fail to comprehend that television is not real life, something that most children realize once they are approximately 7 years old (Wright, Huston, Alvarez, Truglio, Fitch, & Piemyat, 1995). Even with such a realization, they often fail to understand that what is seen on television is not an accurate portrayal of real life (Wright et al., 1995), meaning that their view of real life can become skewed.

Before the age of 8 or 9, children process the content of programmes in a piecemeal fashion. Rather than looking at a programme continuously they are temporarily captivated by fast-paced action, loud music, highly salient cues and rapid cuts between scenes (Alwitt, Anderson, Lorch, & Levin 1980; Schmitt, Anderson, & Collins, 1999). This is particularly applicable to younger children (aged 2 or 3) whose attention can be captured by elements such as vivid colours that may not

TABLE 11.2 Stages of television literacy

Age	Characteristics
6	Prior to the age of 6, children are still to develop the cognitive skills required to shift from perceptional to conceptual processing. Children above the age of 6 have the capacity to consider conceptual and abstract information in a plot, while the younger ones focus mainly on concrete behaviour.
7	Children below the age of 7 do not fully understand that television is not real life.
8	May know that television programmes are fiction but still view programmes as accurate portrayals of real life.
8–9	Children process programme content in a piecemeal fashion. They are captivated by fast-paced action, loud music and fast-paced cuts. During slower scenes they direct their attention elsewhere.
10	Able to draw inferences about scenes that are separated in time.

At a very young age they fail to watch programmes from the beginning to the end. Instead they tend to concentrate on fast moving scenes and those with bright colours, meaning that they often miss out on scenes containing people 'just talking' which can contain vital information when it comes to understanding the plot of the programme or advert.

necessarily be extraneous to the plot. For example, a bright red outfit may be the focal point, while the actions of the person wearing it might be totally ignored.

Similarly to highly salient cues, fast moving scenes can also capture people's attention, but unlike stimuli such as bright colours, this works from infancy through to adulthood. It has been found that if people are not looking when the fast-paced action occurs, they are likely to start watching. This is most likely due to the fact that humans have an acute sensitivity of peripheral vision to movement (Alwitt et al., 1980).

Not until they are around 10 years old are children able to draw conclusions about scenes that are separated in time (Van den Broek, 1997). For example, if a character 'acts' as if they are nice just so they can con another character later on, a child may fail to realize that the character is bad as they fail to make the connection between the two events.

Violent television programmes

The most commonly researched aspect of how watching television affects children is the influence of violence upon behaviour. Even though the influence of violence upon children is the only negative aspect of television viewing that will be discussed here, it is important to acknowledge that there are also other unconstructive consequences. For example, avid television viewers tend to be less creative (Kubey, 1986) and have been found to be poorer at reading comprehension (Koolstra, van der Voort, & van der Kamp, 1997; Wright et al., 2001).

In the late 1990s it was estimated that approximately 40 per cent of all children's television programmes contained acts of violence (Gunter & Harrison, 1997). Bearing in mind that children are also exposed to a high amount of violent content through the adult television programmes that they watch, it is hardly surprising that children are likely to see over 8,000 murders and over 100,000 violent acts before they reach late adolescence (Bushman & Anderson, 2001). The continuous exposure to violent acts are said to cause **desensitization** to violence in children, meaning that they are less likely to respond to real-life aggression and violence (Drabman & Thomas, 1974).

Because young children's ability to process information differs from adults, they often incorrectly believe that what they have seen on television is comparable to real life (Bushman & Huesmann, 2001). This can leave some children thinking that they live in a society where violence is highly prevalent. Similarly this has also been found for children's ability to deal with moral aspects of television programmes. Since they do not develop a clear moral understanding until they are aged at least 10 (Kohlberg, 1969, 1976; Piaget, 1932), a steady stream of television violence may also encourage them to replicate the behaviour they have seen, especially if the bad behaviour is rewarded in some way (Bandura, 1986, 2002). This was found in a classic series of studies conducted by Albert Bandura known as the 'Bobo doll experiments'. In one of the studies a group of pre-school children saw a film of an adult model hitting and kicking an inflated Bobo doll, while another group saw an aggression-free film (Bandura, Ross, & Ross, 1963). Once they had watched the film they were left alone in a room with the same doll that they had seen on the film. The children who had observed the aggressive model showed significantly more aggressive behaviour towards the Bobo doll than did the children from the control group. Additionally the children exposed to the aggressive model also exhibited aggressive actions that had not been modelled, meaning that observing aggressive and violent models also led to **disinhibition** in children. Bandura concluded from his studies that children learn socially to become aggressive (*social learning theory*) and that the chances of aggressive acts being replicated increase when people are seen to be rewarded for aggressive acts.

How to combat unwanted influences

One way to deter children from replicating violent and aggressive behaviour is by showing the true consequences of violence. They are then much less likely to replicate the behaviour they have seen on the small screen (Bandura, 1986; Schechter, 2000).

Another way to deal with potentially negative effects of television viewing is to teach children to view television critically. This can be facilitated by thoughtful questions being posed by parents, such as discussing the purpose of a particular message or encourage children to discuss details of programs (e.g. American Academy of Pediatrics, 1999; Singer & Zuckerman 1990). By doing so children can feel less concerned and upset after discussions about what they have seen, are able to differentiate between what is real and what is fantasy and can better understand commercial messages and identify less with aggressive characters (e.g. Brown, 2001; Hobbs & Frost, 2003; Rosenkoetter, Rosenkoetter, Ozretich, & Acock, 2004).

Positive impacts of television programmes

Violent television programmes are not the only programmes that affect children. There is also a string of other types of programmes that can have a positive impact upon a young child. When children are allowed to watch programmes containing pro-social behaviours, such as altruistic and friendly interactions between people, it has been found that they are more likely to imitate the behaviour they have seen (e.g. Hearold, 1986; Mares & Woodard, 2001).

Children can also be taught to have a positive interracial viewpoint of other nationalities if they are shown programmes such as *Sesame Street* where different races are frequently figured (Greenfield, 1984). Educational programmes (including *Sesame Street*) can also have a positive impact upon learning abilities. Provided there are genuine learning elements included, such as reading and counting, it can help children learn to read and count quicker and more effectively (Rice, Huston, Truglio, & Wright, 1990; Zill, Davies, & Daly, 1994).

Computers

Today computers are part of most people's lives, including children of all ages. The use of computers in a school environment has been found to aid learning and make it more fun for children (e.g. Clements & Nastasi, 1992; Collis, 1996). Additionally computers can also increase social interaction between young students, in that students are more likely to ask others for help when they are faced with an exigent task (Nastasi & Clements, 1993; Weinstein, 1991). Such research findings clearly show that the use of computers can be beneficial from an educational and social point of view.

Even though computers can have a positive impact on children there are also areas of computing such as the Internet and game playing that can be of some concern.

The Internet

For most children in western societies, using the Internet is as common as watching television and using mobile phones. Most children spend more time online than adults (Lenhart, Madden, & Hitlin, 2005) and teenagers aged 12–17 tend to be the most avid users of the Internet. The usage pattern has been found to be similar for children across the globe (e.g. Lenhart et al., 2005; Qrius, 2005).

Due to the fact that children spend a considerable amount of time on the Internet, they are likely to be affected by what they are exposed to. Many worry that they may be more vulnerable to online materials as they often access it unsupervised. However, it needs to be remembered that just as with most media, there are pros and cons to letting children use the Internet.

An educational source

Letting children use the Internet can provide them with a plethora of information that they may not otherwise have access to. This gives them the opportunity to learn about things in an easier manner than children used to. The vast amount of information that can be accessed has been found to be especially beneficial for children from low-income families. This was found in a study by Jackson et al. (2006) whereby African American children in their early teens, who lived in households with an income of approximately $15,000, were provided with a computer and access to the Internet. They found that those who used the Internet more performed better on reading tests after as little as 6 months than did those who used the Internet less. The findings may be explained by the fact that a high amount of Internet material is heavily text-based.

Even though there is evidence that children can benefit from accessing information on the Internet, it is worth remembering that not all the information on the Web is accurate. Consequently children may learn things that are inaccurate. Researchers have found that Web readers are persistently weak at judging whether information is trustworthy (Leu, Coiro, Castek, Hartman, Henry, & Reinking, 2008). In one study, Leu and colleagues asked 50 seventh-graders from different parts of the USA to assess the reliability of a website that looked at 'endangered Pacific Northwest Tree Octopus'. Even though the site was a hoax, the majority of the children claimed it was scientifically valid. Afterwards the researchers informed the children that the site was a joke; even so, approximately half were obdurate that it was truthful.

Social networking

The Internet has also been found to provide children with the opportunity to generate closer bonds with already existing friends (Valkenburg & Peter, 2007). Communicating via instant messaging provides young individuals with the opportunity to stay in constant touch with their friends and to have 'confidential conversations' that could be overheard if they were held on the phone. Because instant messaging and chat rooms make face-to-face interaction redundant, using the Internet also appeals to those who may be socially anxious. In some cases it helps individuals to open up and divulge personal information which they may not otherwise dare to do (Valkenburg & Peter, 2007).

But just as the Internet can be a useful social tool, it can also be detrimental to young individuals in that they may be lured into unfitting social interactions with older and/or deviant people through chat rooms. Some adolescents use the Internet specifically to form relationships with people they have never previously had any contact with (Wolak, Mitchell, & Finkelhor, 2003). Those with existing troubled relationships to others are more likely to make potentially dangerous connections to individuals on the Internet (Cynkar, 2007). Luckily the majority of children stick to communicating with people and organizations they are already familiar with, such as school friends (Gross, 2004) and subsequently are less likely to make inappropriate social connections.

Another potential downside to socializing is that some young children spend so much time on the Internet that they fail to interact frequently with family and friends (Mitchell, Becker-Blease, & Finkelhor, 2005), which in turn leads to social isolation.

Computer games

Throughout the 30-year history of computer games there has been a continuous increase in computer game playing among children. In particular, it has been identified as a high frequency activity among adolescents (Funk, 1993). For a long time computer games were of more interest to boys (e.g. Griffiths, 1991; Kaplan, 1983), as the contents of games were mainly aimed at a male audience (Morlock, Yando, & Nigolean, 1985). However, this is gradually changing with game consoles such as Wii which comes with a number of games that clearly target a female audience. It is often debated whether or not playing computer games is good or bad, especially those of a violent nature. The reality is that research to date has not proved conclusively one way or another and it appears that playing games can be both detrimental and advantageous to children's behaviour and development (see Figure 11.1).

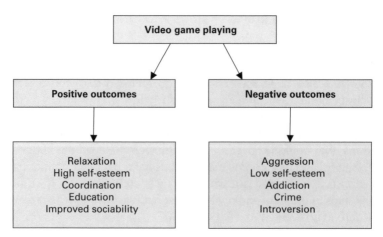

FIGURE 11.1 The positive and negative effects of computer games on children.

Positive influences

Research has found that computer games can help development of spatial awareness and general cognitive skills in young boys (Greenfield, Brannon, & Lohr, 1994). This has even been found to be applicable to simple games such as Tetris (a game that requires the player to rapidly rotate and place different shaped blocks into a wall of inconsistently placed blocks; see Figure 11.2). When children play Tetris, an increase in their mental rotation and spatial visualization time has been found on computer-based performance tests (Okagaki & Frensch, 1994).

Other positive research findings for computer games include an increase in non-verbal performance on IQ tests (Greenfield, 1998) and making children relax (Harris, 2001). Additionally it has also been suggested that playing violent and

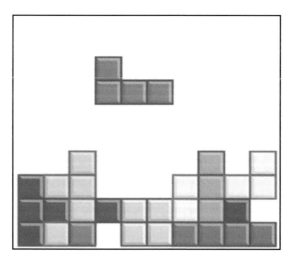

FIGURE 11.2 Example of the game Tetris.

aggressive games allows the player to release stress and aggression which prevents them from taking it out on real-life objects and individuals (e.g. Bowman & Rotter, 1983; Kestenbaum & Weinstein, 1985).

Negative influences

Negative aspects of frequently playing computer games include feelings of discontent by gamers (Roberts et al., 1999) and that they become isolated from their parents (Bonnafont, 1992, as cited in Goldstein, 1994). The underlying reason as to why there is a breakdown in communication between parents and children is presumably because parents often do not understand the games that the child is playing and consequently the child ends up playing on their own. The fact that they play on their own is also likely to be the cause for feeling less satisfied as social researchers have frequently established that social interaction is essential for people's well-being.

Other potential problems include that children who spend an excessive amount of time playing computer games run the risk of becoming addicted to them (e.g. Anderson & Ford, 1986). Computer game addiction is just like any other addiction in that individuals engage in compulsive playing, lose interest in other activities, and suffer physical and mental withdrawal symptoms if they try to stop the behaviour (Soper & Miller, 1983). To date, it is not certain why some children become addicted to playing games, however, it is possible that certain personality types are more likely to be hooked on gaming (Griffiths & Dancaster, 1995).

A final concern about playing a lot of computer games is that a high proportion of them contain some form of violence (Provenzo, 1991) and consequently many people are concerned about the effects it may have upon the person playing the game. Violent computer games have, just like violent television programmes, been used to explain why some children engage in seriously violent behaviours. Irwin and Gross (1995) conducted a study where they observed children playing either a game containing physical aggression or one that depicted no interpersonal aggression. They found that those who had played the 'aggressive' game were much more likely to exhibit object aggression during free play and inter-personal aggression during a frustrating situation than those who had played a non-aggressive game. The aggressive behaviour displayed after playing violent or aggressive games can be explained by social learning theory (Schutte et al., 1988).

It is possible that the interactive nature of computer games (especially online gaming) encourages violent behaviour more than a television programme as children actively have to perform the violent acts (Larson, 2001). For example, the game Doom was said to be the inspiration for two teenagers shooting students at Columbine High School in America in 1999 (Glick et al., 1999). However, not all researchers agree that aggressive computer games produce violent and aggressive behaviour in children. Just as with computer game addiction, some people believe it is more likely to be due to particular personality traits (Winkel et al., 1987). Consequently, it is possible that it is the type of personality that people have that predicts whether or not they will play aggressive games and in turn replicate the behaviour they see in the game.

Stereotyping

Children learn through the media about other individuals' behaviour (Clifford, Gunter & McAleer, 1995), meaning that any stereotypical images they come across will often be accepted as a fact in terms of what certain groups of people are like. Television is particularly influential when it comes to presenting children with stereotypes (Berry, 2000). From television programmes they learn about the way in which men and women are meant to behave (Durkin, 1985a) as well as specific characteristics applicable to groups of people (Holloway & Valentine, 2000).

Women are normally under-represented on children's programmes. In cartoons, men tend to outnumber women by four or five to one (Signorielli, 1984, 1991) and they are normally presented in very stereotypical roles (Levinson, 1975).

Minority groups such as Asians or Africans are often depicted in a non-realistic way. Since children are often unlikely to meet the minority groups portrayed on TV in real life, there is nothing to counterbalance what they have seen. Consequently, they form early stereotypical images of those groups which they later make use of when they encounter them in real life (Holloway & Valentine, 2000).

Advertising

Understanding advertising

Children watch around 20,000 ads a year (Kunkel & Roberts, 1991). Unlike adults, children of a young age do not understand that the information they come across through the media is not always factual and representative of real life. Advertising messages are often believed by children aged younger than 7 or 8 to be simply informative (e.g. Isler, Popper, & Ward, 1987; Lawlor & Prothero, 2003). Once they have turned 8, they no longer tend to believe that commercials are providing them with truthful and accurate information (Ward, 1972). Robertson and Rossiter (1974) found that approximately 52 per cent of children aged 6–7 years of age knew that advertisements were trying to persuade them to purchase something. The percentage increased to 87 per cent when children were aged 8–9 and to 99 per cent for those aged 10–11.

The older children become, the more sceptical their beliefs are with regards to how 'truthful' advertisements are and by the time they reach their teenage years the majority think that advertising hardly ever tells the truth (e.g. Bever, Smith, Bengen, & Johnson, 1975; Ward, Wackman, & Wartella 1977). However, understanding that deceit may be part of the advertising techniques used does not necessarily mean that children are less susceptible to the persuasive influences of the messages they are exposed to (Christenson, 1982; Ross et al., 1984).

Brand names and symbolism

Children learn about products and brands from an early age. Their awareness of brand names and how easily remembered they are gradually increases with age, from early to middle childhood (e.g. Rossiter, 1976; Ward et al., 1977). By the age of 2 or 3 they are able to recognize familiar packages in a store (Derscheid, Kwon, & Fang, 1996). It is also around the age of 3 that they start to realize that different brands have a symbolic value (McAlister & Cornwell, 2008). This means that they have an understanding for the meaning attributed to brands that are somehow relevant to their own lives. Within another couple of years they are also able to recollect brand names that they have seen advertised, especially if the adverts contained salient stimuli that are easily associated with the product (Macklin, 1996).

In parallel with learning to remember and recognize brands, they also start to develop preferences for brands. During the pre-school years they often prefer branded goods over general products (Hite & Hite, 1995) and such preference escalates as children become older (Ward et al., 1977).

Product categorization

Categorizing how products and services belong together or differ from one another requires insightfulness in regard to how underlying product attributes influence dissimilarity or similarity. Although children learn to group certain products together at an early age, they tend to rely on visible perceptual attributes to do so (John & Lakshmi-Ratan, 1992; Klees, Olson, & Wilson, 1988). This means that the way in which products are categorized may not necessarily be categorized the same as they would be by an adult or even older children. The age difference in product categorization was demonstrated in a study by John and Sujan (1990). They found that children aged 4–5 grouped different types of drinks together based on the similarity of the packaging, while older children aged 9–10 categorized them based on attributes such as taste and carbonation.

Is it ethically correct to target children as consumers?

Academics, politicians, marketers and others have in the past debated whether or not it is ethically correct to market products and services directly to young consumers. This is also a dilemma for psychologists who (just like others) have questioned whether they ought to help advertisers manipulate children into purchasing more products they have seen advertised (Kanner & Kasser, 2000).

Advertisers have admitted to taking advantage of the fact that it is easy to make children feel that they are losers if they do not own the 'right' products. Clever advertising informs children that they will be viewed by their peers in an unfavourable way if they do not have the products that are advertised and by doing so playing on their emotional vulnerabilities (Ruskin, 1999). The constant feelings of inadequateness created by advertising have been suggested to contribute to children becoming fixated with instant gratification and beliefs that material possessions are important (Kanner & Gomes, 1995).

The continuous desire children have to acquire more goods can also make parents feel pressured and for those who are economically disadvantaged, it can be very difficult. When children do not have their own money to spend, they tend to try and persuade their parents to purchase the goods for them (e.g. Tinsley, 2002).

Food advertising

A high proportion of advertising aimed at children worldwide advertises food-related products (Kunkel & Gantz, 1992), and many of those are for sweets and foods containing a lot of sugar and fats. This can be considered a serious ethical issue since the number of children experiencing weight problems has increased considerably since the 1990s (The Information Centre, 2006; Kids Health, 2005). Some suggest that there is a strong relationship between television viewing and childhood obesity (e.g. Crespo et al., 2001), and it may be partially caused by the invitation to consume the junk food they have seen advertised. Most advertising containing unhealthy foods tends to incorporate brief messages that state that such foods should only be consumed in moderation. However, such messages are not processed by young children as they simply fail to understand the meaning of them (e.g. Stern & Resnik, 1978).

Creating unrealistic expectations

Perhaps the most commonly debated aspect of the media creating unrealistic expectations in children is the impact of 'skinny role models' on young girls. From a very early age, girls are bombarded with beauty messages informing them (implicitly or explicitly) that they should be thin. It often starts with dolls such as Barbie that has a body that is impossible for a real life woman to achieve (Thompson, Heinberg, Altabe, & Tantleff-Dunn, 1999). Early exposure to ideal beauty images such as Barbie dolls has been found to damage girls' body image and in turn may contribute to eating disorders (e.g. Dittmar, Halliwell, & Ive, 2006).

Key Terms

Desensitization
When people have been repeatedly exposed to a specific type of stimuli so that they no longer respond to it.

Disinhibition
Reduction in the 'learned controls' that prevent people from behaving inappropriately.

Summary

It is evident from Piaget's theory of cognitive development that children will deal differently with consumer matters depending on what age they are. Not until they reach approximately the age of 11 will they be able to fully understand and process the information they encounter. Two good examples of this are how well children understand what they have seen on the television and how well they comprehend advertising messages. Children below the age of 11 go through phases whereby they lack the capacity to understand the theoretical aspect of the content and fail to realize it is often not representative of real life.

A lot of consumer activities such as watching television, using the Internet and playing computer games are double-edged swords. Provided they are used in moderation and used appropriately (e.g. watching an educational programme rather than a soap opera), they can have a positive influence on children.

Because some types of consumption are not always good for children, it has been debated whether or not it is ethically correct to market products and services directly to children.

Class exercise

Watch an episode of a television programme that is popular with children. Think about the story line, the order in which the events are presented, and how the characters come across. Discuss this with reference to how children's cognitive abilities develop and how they become television literate. You may wish to try and answer the following questions:

1 What would a young child focus on? Would it be different from that of a 10 year old?

2 Who is the intended audience for the programme and should it be watched by children of all ages?

Consumption and happiness

Introduction

Can happiness be found in material goods and services? Advertisers would most certainly like us to think so. However, this is debatable as psychological research often appears to indicate otherwise. It has been increasingly suggested that consumers are purchasing products and services in the hope that they will function as a substitute for factors that make people truly happy. This chapter explores whether or not consumption is detrimental to people's happiness and if the link between happiness and consumption extends to all types of shopping experiences.

Shopping for happiness

Why people consume will vary depending on what type of products and services are being purchased. One thing that most purchases have in common is that people no longer consume purely for practical purposes (Campbell, 2004). Instead it appears that consumers are purchasing products and services in the hope of expressing who they are (Dittmar & Beatty, 1998), to gain social status (McCracken, 1990), and in hope of becoming happy (Csikszentmihalyi, 2000; Wood & Bettman, 2007). When 'shopping for happiness' it is, however, debatable whether it extends to practical goods such as vacuum cleaners and a high number of fast-selling consumer goods.

Some have suggested that people try to achieve happiness through consumption because the consumer cultures in which we live encourage people to be materialistic as well as underpinning that material comfort will bring happiness (e.g. Luthar, 2003). This may to a certain extent explain why those who consume a lot tend to be individuals who seek pleasure or self-satisfaction (e.g. Campbell, 1987; Wachtel, 1983).

Consuming for happiness is one angle that is often used by marketers in the hope of selling certain products and services. They know that everybody wants to be happy and consequently they remind consumers that certain purchases are more likely to make them achieve happiness. This is done in an indirect or a direct way. When indirectly trying to persuade consumers, it could be in the form of an advert informing the audience that purchasing a particular product will give them benefits that they believe the consumer thinks will lead to a happier life. For example, a perfume ad may suggest that by using it they will become attractive to the opposite sex. On the other hand, the direct approach will simply tell the consumer that purchasing a particular product or brand will make them happy. An example of the use of happiness in marketing could be seen in the form of a small ad for Fox's biscuits that was attached to shopping trolleys at Sainsbury's supermarket stores. The ad clearly states that buying a packet of biscuits will make you happier. So how accurate are claims that consumption can make people happy?

What makes people happy is a huge question in itself and to widen it further in the hope of also more specifically explaining how consumption affects it, makes it even more complex. Nonetheless, a number of psychologists have attempted to explore the link between the two. So far, many have chosen to focus on the downside of consumption rather than looking at testing whether or not consumer activities might positively contribute to people's well-being.

Example of an advert that is trying to persuade consumers that purchasing biscuits will make them happy. The advert was placed on shopping trolleys in supermarkets.

FIGURE 12.1 Persuading consumers that products can make them happy.

Source: Courtesy of Northern Foods.

What is happiness?

There are several definitions of what happiness is and it may come as no surprise that the use of the term happiness varies somewhat between psychologists and marketers. Psychologists mainly work on the assumption that happiness is meant to emulate overall life satisfaction while marketers often link happiness to how satisfied customers are with the product and services they have purchased. However, happiness is not necessarily the same as consumer satisfaction (Desmeules, 2002). Instead consumer happiness may be better viewed as a summation of consumer activities that is affected by both positive and negative emotional experiences that in turn make people feel good or bad about themselves.

What makes people happy and what they think makes them happy are often not the same thing. For example, it has been found that individuals have a tendency to overestimate the usefulness of how much they will earn in the future (Easterlin, 2001), even though no positive correlations have been found between happiness and high income levels (e.g. Kasser & Ryan, 1993). Unfortunately, people also often underestimate the importance of personal interactions (Frey & Stutzer, 2004), something that has been found repeatedly to make people happier (Csikszentmihalyi, 1999).

Happiness measurements

Happiness is commonly measured in the form of subjective well-being. Many think that this is a suitable way to estimate how satisfied individuals are with their lives in general (e.g. Frey & Stutzer, 2002). A number of varied measures are used to tap into people's subjective sense of well-being, some make use of images while others mainly use questions, but it all amounts to the same thing in that it generates a response that indicates how people feel about their lives (Myers & Diener, 1996). What makes people feel happy with their lives overall is complex and many variables come into play (Myers, 2004). However, is it possible that there is another kind of happiness that may be worth exploring, one that is not necessary long-lasting and life changing?

It would be naïve to debate if there is such a thing as overall life happiness but it is worth thinking about whether or not overall life satisfaction can determine fleeting moments of happiness that consumers may experience from certain products and services. Most people have experienced immense temporary pleasure from consumer activities at some point, perhaps a fabulously tasty meal, a massage, or even just a great tasting cup of coffee. The question is whether or not they can be defined as transitory moments of happiness. If such experiences are a form of happiness, then perhaps most types of happiness measurements are not adequate to measure and establish if consumption can make people happy.

Disadvantageous consumption

Since the early 1990s there has been an increase in research that investigates different aspects of consumer societies that do not impact well on individuals. It would be nice to be able to say that somebody in particular is to blame for why some consumers clearly are affected negatively by their consumer behaviours, but the reality is somewhat different. The fact is that industrialized societies are generally encouraging people to consume regardless of whether or not they already have more possessions than they really need. Fierce marketing campaigns contribute extensively to people believing that if they buy more products they will somehow improve their lives which in turn will make them happier. So also do the people around us, in that we observe their consumer behaviour and assume that having endless amounts of possessions is the norm (Du Nann Winter, 2003). Consequently, many people feel that they have to compete in order to make them appear to be desirable individuals (Zahavi, 1975).

Television watching is also likely to fuel consumers' feelings that it is important to own certain material possessions. Unfortunately that is not the only problem with consuming too much television. It is well known that watching TV is a common consumer activity that many overindulge in (Kubey & Czikszentmihalyi, 2002). In the light of this, some have speculated that it may be because it becomes a habit (Christakis & Zimmerman, 2006) or even an addiction (e.g. Kubey & Czikszentmihalyi, 2002; McIlwraith, 1998). Watching too much television has been found to decrease overall life satisfaction (Frey et al., 2007), demonstrating that it is one type of consumption that is likely to lead to some level of unhappiness, whether it is due to the fact that it is because people become addicted or because it is a solitary activity that does not encourage social interactions. So clearly there are specific consumer activities that are more likely to cause unhappiness. This is an area that still requires more research before it is possible to map out which specific consumption activities may lower life satisfaction.

Other factors that clearly demonstrate that consumption can be disadvantageous are when people become overly materialistic and when they become 'addicted' to consumption. As you will find out, there are similarities between very materialistic individuals and shopaholics.

Materialistically oriented consumers

There are several products that can be consumed that clearly have the ability to cause misery in some form or another to consumers. Nevertheless, due to the fact that consumers often act in non-rational ways, people still choose to engage in such consumption activities. This is particularly evident from alcohol, drug and tobacco consumption, which often creates habits that consumers fail to control. However, it is not just particular products that might cause misery in some form; consumers can also be detrimentally affected when they become overly engaged with a number of different products, which is what materialism is all about.

Materialism can be defined as 'the importance a consumer attaches to worldly possessions' (Belk, 1984, p. 291). Many things have been written about how detrimental it can be for individuals to have high materialistic value orientations (MVO). One of the biggest drawbacks is that they are likely to own more credit cards and get into debt which can have psychological as well as practical life repercussions (Watson, 2003).

It seems that those who become materialistic try to make use of products and services in the hope of compensating for something in their lives that is missing. For example, individuals who were socio-economically disadvantaged during their childhood (Cohen & Cohen, 1996) or whose parents divorced (Rindfleisch, Burroughs & Denton, 1997) have been found to be more likely to become materialistic later in life.

The onset of materialism varies: some become materialistic during their childhood years while for others it happens during adulthood. Teenagers have been found to display a higher level of materialistic values than younger children (Chaplin & John, 2007), which may indicate that peer pressures, a desire to be independent as well as lack of parental support and how many possessions are owned during the early years are factors that may contribute to whether or not people become materialistic.

In adults, materialism has been linked to those who are generally unhappy, have serious doubts about their own competence and who suffer from life fears in general (Chang & Arkin, 2002; Diener & Biswas-Diener, 2002). It is possible that such factors may stem from childhood and consequently it is a reflection of already existing values and beliefs. However, another possibility is that when people stumble upon difficult life situations they look for a quick fix to console themselves and consequently try to find some comfort by purchasing something they think will make them feel better, which may have nothing to do with earlier life experiences. Instead it may be that other day-to-day activities such as television watching indirectly encourage them to consume in order to console themselves. Those who spend a lot of time watching television have been found to be more likely to think that material possessions are important (Frey, Benesch, & Stutzer, 2007), demonstrating that it may be a contributory factor in why consumers use material possessions to make themselves feel better.

The fact that research has found materialists to be debt-ridden, using consumption to compensate for childhood losses and as 'pick me ups' in adulthood clearly demonstrates that materialism is not something positive. Consequently, one may be inclined to assume that consumption can be negative for people's overall happiness.

Compulsive buying

Engaging in excessive buying patterns is not exactly common but neither is it so unusual that one hardly ever reads about individuals who do it. Estimates in a number of countries suggest that the number of compulsive shoppers varies. For example, it has been suggested that there are somewhere in the region of half a million people in the UK who suffer from compulsive buying behaviour (Black, 1996), while in the USA the prevalence is somewhere between 5.9 to 10 per cent (e.g. Faber & O'Guinn, 1992; Trachtenberg, 1988, as cited in Hanley & Wilhelm, 1992). Researchers who made use of longitudinal data found that there has been a substantial increase in compulsive consumption in Germany since 1991 (Neuner, Raab, & Reisch, 2005). Such data seem to indicate that compulsive buying behaviour is on the increase.

However, it is possible that greater awareness of compulsive buying in general may be the underlying reason why a higher number of individuals are being diagnosed with the condition (Faber, 2003). In recent years the media in particular have written quite a lot about what it means to be a 'shopaholic' and have consequently contributed, perhaps inadvertently, to greater awareness occurring among psychologists as well as those with the condition who will therefore in turn be more likely to seek professional help.

Currently there is not a single definition of what **compulsive buying** is but generally it is agreed that it involves an involuntary behaviour that is in some way destructive (Faber & O'Guinn, 1992). Most spend a lot of time and money buying products that they often don't need and they keep this behaviour up, regardless of how it affects their lives. On average most compulsive buyers make two or three shopping trips a week (e.g. Christenson, Faber, de Zwaan, Raymond, Specker, Ekern, et al., 1994), but this may vary.

A common problem for compulsive buyers is that they get into debt (Scherhorn, Reisch, & Raab, 1990), something that is likely to be inflamed further by the easy access to credit (Drentea & Lavrakas, 2000). Other difficulties include getting involved in embezzlement and losing social relationships (e.g. Dittmar, 2004b; Faber, O'Guinn, & Krych, 1987).

Who becomes addicted to shopping?

There is some evidence suggesting that those with high MVOs are more likely to be prone to becoming addicted to shopping (e.g. Yurchisin & Johnson, 2004). Consequently, it would appear that how much people value material possessions may be one of the bases of becoming addicted. However, to date, there is not enough research evidence to fully support such a conclusion. What is more certain is that there is definitely a link between low self-esteem and compulsive consumption (Richins & Dawson, 1992). This may in turn also partially explain the relationship found between high MVOs and addiction, in that individuals may believe that they will feel more confident if they own certain possessions.

Researchers have also found that those who are narcissistic are more likely to fall into the addictive consumption trap (Rose, 2007) due to their desire to be admired by others (Campbell & Foster, 2007). The idea is that owning certain possessions will make others become envious of those who are narcissistic because others yearn to own the very same belongings.

Advantageous consumption

So far it seems that the link between consumption and happiness is a negative one. However, consumption does not have to be all doom and gloom as can be seen from the following section. First, it is worth pointing out that the constant negative relationship found between consumption levels and happiness could possibly be related to the fact that people often fail to accurately report on their own happiness or unhappiness and that they are often unaware of what caused it (Weiss & Brown, 1977). The easiest way to measure people's levels of happiness is to directly ask them about it, but if people genuinely do not know what causes it, there is nothing to say that the correlations found are the same as cause and effect. This is a common problem with correlational research as just because there is a significant relationship, it does not mean that one factor is directly causing the other.

A second point that is also worth making is that the links investigated between happiness and consumption are not necessarily representative of all types of consumption. Often research fails to take smaller aspects of consumption into account that may not necessarily cause people to feel miserable. For example, measuring if there is a correlation between MVOs and well-being is not necessarily the same as asking people if going on holiday somewhere makes them feel more relaxed, invigorated and temporarily happier. Perhaps consumption and happiness research should focus a little bit less on the accumulation of material goods (which is the focus of MVO) and instead look at whether alternative non-lasting consumption can make them feel better about themselves. To date, not much research has been conducted in this area. Nevertheless there are some indicators that consuming does not have to be detrimental to consumers' well-being.

Reasons that can shed some light on why consumption should not always be seen from a negative perspective and that it can increase happiness include evolutionary perspectives of consumption, distinguishing between different types of consumer activities, the influence of previous experiences and how marketing techniques contribute to consumer happiness.

Consumption as a part of evolution

What if consumption is simply part of the evolutionary process? And what if it is actually something useful in that it allows humans to use products to somehow set them apart? Surely then consumption should be considered to be something positive?

Based upon Darwin's work, evolutionary psychologists propose that behaviour can be explained in terms of how humans adapt to a constantly changing environment. For example, a commonly made distinction is sex differences between men and women. These can be explained by how men and women have faced different challenges over hundreds of years and how they have adapted in order to be able to deal with the challenges so that they can survive to pass on their genes through reproduction. According to evolutionary psychologists, reproduction is one of the main ambitions in life. In such a context it may be that consumers have an innate desire to have products and make use of services that can signal to others that they are desirable mates (Zahavi, 1975), meaning that consumption fills a practical function in the evolutionary process. For example, a man who drives an expensive car and wears an expensive watch will clearly signal to women that he can afford to look after their offspring and consequently he will be seen as a more desirable mate than a man who may not display the same kind of wealth.

The evolutionary process can also explain why some people are badly affected by living in a consumer society. Bearing in mind that evolution is suggesting that only the fittest people survive and reproduce, it is possible that those who fall into the 'trap of detrimental consumption' are simply not meant to pass on their genes. It is difficult to prove whether or not material possessions are just another pawn in the evolutionary process but it is not impossible.

Different types of consumption

Research has shown that it is worth distinguishing between different types of consumption when trying to determine the effect it has upon people's general well-being. One particular type of consumption that has been linked to happiness is the kind where consumers purchase experiences rather than possessions. Van Boven and Gilovich (2003) investigated this in a series of separate studies. In one of the studies they wanted to explore if purchasing life experiences over material possessions would make people happier. This was done by asking 97 individuals, through the use of a survey, to describe and evaluate the most recent experiential and material purchases they had made for more than $100. The results showed that experiential purchases made people happier and were viewed as a better investment than money spent on material possessions. These findings were also supported by a follow-up study that made use of a more diverse range of subjects, consisting of 1,263 men and women from a different cultures and socio-economically diverse groups. Hence research clearly demonstrates that certain types of consumption can contribute to overall consumer happiness. However, it is worth noting that it is not the same as saying that material possessions cannot make people happy.

Why experiential purchases make people happy

There are three possible explanations why purchasing experiences make people happy (Van Boven, 2005).

1 *Experiences are more likely to be interpreted in a positive manner.* Retrospectively, experiences can give people pleasure as they remember the 'good times'. This is often the case even when the actual experience was not as good as we may have originally wanted it to be. For example, on a visit to Nevada in the USA, I had organized a trip to the Grand Canyon which included a plane, helicopter and boat ride. I had eagerly anticipated that this would be a marvellous experience. However, the travel agent had somehow

managed to mess things up and I only got a brief plane ride over the Grand Canyon. At the time this was utterly disappointing in comparison to what I originally had planned to do. Even though the experience itself was below par, I now often think rather fondly of my trip to Nevada, because when I think back on the trip I tend to focus on the magnificent sight of the Grand Canyon rather than on the disappointment I felt at the time. The above experience is not uncommon and consumers often alter their memories of events afterwards so that they are remembered in a more favourable manner (Mitchell, Thompson, Peterson, & Cronk, 1997). Consequently consumers tend to remember consumption experiences differently to how they remember disappointing product purchases.

2 *Experiences can foster good social relationships.* The mentioned Grand Canyon trip has on several occasions come up as a topic of conversation at social gatherings. Telling people about your 'life' experiences can help to foster social relationships in that it can open up and prolong conversations. However, if you had bought a new jumper recently you are less likely to talk about it when out for a drink with friends and if you do, they are less likely to reciprocate in a positive fashion. This is because people generally hold positive stereotypes of those who like experiences (Van Boven, Campbell, & Gilovich, 2008), while those who are perceived to be materialistic are associated with negative stereotypes (Richins, 1994).

Another reason why experiential purchases can foster social relationships is because most such activities are undertaken with other people. For example, when we travel or go to the theatre, we are much more likely to do it together with others than we would be if we go shopping for a jumper or shampoo.

3 *Experiences are less likely to be disadvantageously compared to other experiences.* Social comparison studies have shown that when individuals compare themselves in some way to others, the outcome can be negative (e.g. Easterlin, 1995; Frank, 1999). For example, getting a pay increase at work may seem less satisfying if you find out that your best friend, work colleague or neighbour got a much bigger one. Hence, something that should have made you feel good subsequently makes you feel bad. Similarly, this is often the case with product purchases. Most consumer have unrealistic expectations of the products they buy and when these don't live up to them, they feel dissatisfied and unhappy (Schwartz, 2004). However, it is very difficult to compare experiences in the same way as you would a pay increase or a product that you bought. Consequently experiential purchases are less likely to cause people to feel unhappy.

Impact of marketing strategies on happiness

Researchers have found that certain marketing actions can influence happiness by using strategies to ensure that the overall consumption experience is satisfactory.

Three useful marketing methods will be discussed: (1) the use of autobiographical advertising to ensure that prior negative experiences of some sort do not overshadow future positive consumption experiences; (2) the impact of price on product efficacy; and (3) how too much choice can affect consumer happiness.

Autobiographical advertising

Previous experiences can play a significant role in how particular types of consumption are perceived (Elster & Loewenstein, 1992). For example, if eating peas is associated with negative memories, then it will naturally reflect negatively upon the way in which you think and feel about eating peas in the future. This is often the case even though the memories themselves may not have any direct link to the peas themselves. It may be that as a child you were told off by your parents while eating them and consequently a negative association was formed.

Negative memories in particular can be unfortunate if a consumer lets one bad incident dictate whether or not they will engage in a particular consumer activity again that could potentially be a great experience. The memories then become obstacles to consumer happiness in that they may prevent consumers from purchasing experiences that could increase their overall happiness, especially if the memories keep them from engaging in experiential purchases.

It may appear impossible to alter people's perception of product experiences if they have previous negative memories that affect what they think of products and brands. However, advertising research suggests that it is possible to alter people's memory by using autobiographical advertising (use of scenes that appear to show past personal experiences). This was proven when participants in a study were tested to see if nostalgia created by the use of autobiographical advertising can make people believe they had experienced what they saw in the ads (Braun, Ellis, & Loftus, 2002). Participants were shown an ad for Disney that suggested that they had shaken hands with Bugs Bunny during their childhood. Even though Bugs Bunny is a Warner Bros. character, it was found that people thought they had indeed shaken Bugs Bunny's hand at a Disney resort, demonstrating that the use of autobiographical advertising can alter people's memories of certain events. Such memory changes most likely occur as the result of the advertisement being used as a cue to remember past experiences and events. Bearing in mind that memories are constructive, marketers can make use of autobiographical images when they want to ensure that consumers will perceive certain experiences and products favourably as well as establishing a personal relationship with them.

Price

Price can also play a part in how effective products are in their applications which in turn also may affect how positively evaluated they are and how happy consumers feel about their purchase. For example, the price of a product can act as a placebo effect that activates certain expectations in regard to the efficacy of the product. In a study consisting of three separate experiments it was established that when consumers paid less for an energy drink, they were less able than those who paid the full price to solve fewer puzzles (see Figure 12.2), and hence demonstrating the placebo effect of price. The underlying idea being that energy drinks will make people more mentally alert (Shiv, Carmon, & Ariely, 2005).

The fact that marketing actions can impact subconsciously on how effective a product becomes is also likely to affect how satisfied a consumer will be with their purchase. If they come to believe that the product is inferior to other competitive brands, the satisfaction level and likelihood of repeat purchase will decrease. Such beliefs may in turn generate feelings of unpleasantness that may be interpreted as temporary unhappiness. So if consumers are pleased with their purchases, then the likelihood of experiencing unpleasant feelings that may be interpreted as unhappiness may be avoided.

Choice

Economic approaches to choice work on the assumption that people have a much better chance to satisfy their individual needs when there are plenty of products to choose from. From an economic perspective, the fact that people have the freedom to choose virtually anything they want should lead to greater life satisfaction. From a psychological perspective, it may not seem so obvious that small factors such as the amount of choice available would impact upon consumers' overall happiness and well-being. However, research in the area does demonstrate also that smaller consumer-related factors such as the amount of choice can contribute to how a person feels.

It has been found that too much choice can be demotivating (Iyengar & Lepper, 2000). If consumers have a high number of options to choose from, they are much more likely to feel dissatisfied than they would if they only had to choose from just a

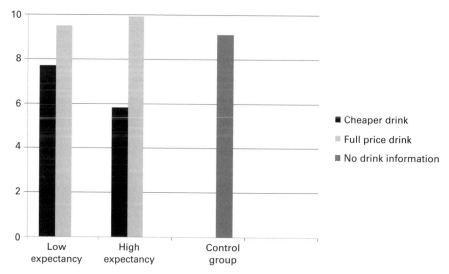

FIGURE 12.2 Impact of pricing upon puzzle performance.

Source: Adapted from Shiv, Carmon, and Ariely (2005).

few options. This is most likely due to the fact that the choice process becomes much more complex when a high number of products are involved. In some instances having any more than one option can even cause the consumer to feel less happy (Hsee & Leclerc, 1998). This seems to be particularly applicable in situations where the consumer is faced with the choice of two particularly good options. They will then have to deal with the fact that both options have limitations that only the other option can accommodate and consequently regardless which option they go for, they will feel as if they have missed out on what the other option had to offer. In such situations, consumers will feel dissatisfied regardless of which option they choose. The way to avoid feeling unhappy about the choice made would be not to scrutinize both options as consumers will then not be fully aware of what they may miss out on (Carmon, Wertenbroch, & Zeelenberg, 2003). However, that may be difficult for individuals with a desire to get the most out of their purchases. They are also the ones who are particularly prone to feeling unhappy with their choices when they have too many products to choose from (Schwartz et al., 2002).

Another way of combating people's unease with multiple choices can be to let others make the decisions for them. This is particularly applicable in situations where all the choices appear to be undesirable (Botti & Iyengar, 2004). Choosing between undesirable options induces negative feelings, and similar to having to choose between two good choices, it will make consumers feel uneasy after the decision has been made.

To sum up, it seems as if too much variety may be too much of a good thing (Lehmann, 1998). However, the relationship between amount of choice and happiness is not a linear one. Instead it has been proposed that the relationship is almost like an inverted-U shape (Desmeules, 2002) (see Figure 12.3).

Does consumption make us happy?

It is not easy to say whether or not consumption makes us happy or unhappy. Research seems to suggest that it can increase as well as decrease overall well-being depending on what type of consumer activities are being studied. There are different levels of happiness: the kind that makes your life better overall, and short-term temporary happiness which is more to do with instant gratification and satisfaction. Overall life happiness is not likely to be achieved through accumulation of possessions but temporary moments of happiness most likely can be achieved through consumption. Continuous life satisfaction is more likely to depend on factors such as good social relationships. However, it needs to be remembered that some consumer activities can contribute to maintaining existing relationships as well as fostering new ones.

Too much of a good thing can also make people miserable which is noted from those engaging in excessive consumption behaviour. It is unlikely that a 'consumer paradise' would occur if everybody could buy what they wanted at all times. Being able to get your hands on exactly what you want and when you want it without any

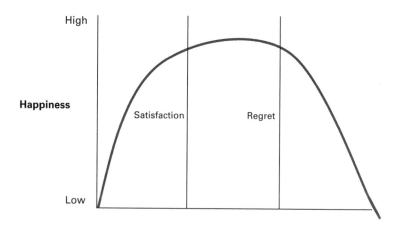

Amount of choice

The inverted U-shape can be viewed as consisting of three parts: (1) an upward sloping section which leads to a high level of satisfaction; (2) a middle part with a relatively flat plateau; and (3) a downward sloping section. The most satisfaction is experienced after a number of options. However, the feeling of happiness continues to increase as the consumer adds a few options to their consumer experience. This is because they believe they are more likely to find what they ideally want.

FIGURE 12.3 Relationship between amount of choice and happiness.

Source: Adapted from Desmeules (2002).

financial repercussions, would most likely make you feel euphoric, but only for a short while (Campbell, 1975). Before long, you would adjust to being able to consume all you want and consequently it would no longer be anything out of the ordinary, meaning that it would become the norm and would not make you feel any happier.

Key Terms

Compulsive buying
A destructive kind of behaviour where individuals engage in frequent unnecessary shopping bouts.

Summary

People are increasingly consuming in the hope that it will make them happy. Whether or not it is possible to achieve happiness through consumption partially depends on how happiness is defined and measured. It is clear from research that those who are highly materialistic or engaged in compulsive buying patterns are not generally happy. Materialistic individuals use products and service in the hope of compensating for something that is missing in their lives, while compulsive buyers often get into serious debt. Looking at those who are negatively affected by consumption might make it seem as if consumption is the devil in disguise. However, it is possible that consumption is simply part of evolution and hence something that those who are stronger are more equipped to deal with in order to pass on their genes.

Purchasing experiences such as holidays can make people happy. This is because they are interpreted in a positive way, can foster social relationships and are less prone to negative comparisons. Making use of autobiographical marketing techniques, charging a competitive price and reducing the amount of choice available can also generate a happier consumption experience.

Discussion questions

1 Is it a good idea to present consumers with a high number of product and brand choices? Is it possible to control the amount of choice consumers are faced with in a competitive market?

2 What can marketers do in the hope of ensuring consumer happiness?

3 Why is it that people with high materialistic value orientations are generally unhappier?

4 Should compulsive shoppers be used as an example that consumption can make you unhappy?

5 Is it consumption itself or the underlying reasons why products and services are purchased that make people unhappy?

CHAPTER 13

Consumers and the environment

Introduction

The environmental consequences of consumption are not commonly discussed by consumer psychologists. However, it is important to recognize that pro-ecologically driven campaigns either by the media, individual activist groups, and governments are affecting the way consumers view certain products and services and to what extent they engage in environmentally friendly behaviour. It is also important to be aware that they influence the way in which products are marketed and manufactured. This chapter seek to address different aspects of environmentally linked consumption that can shed some light on how intertwined consumer behaviours are with environmental issues.

Environmental issues

People around the world are showing an increasing interest in and becoming more concerned with environmental issues (e.g. Hodgkinson & Innes, 2000; Roodman, 1999). This is particularly evident from the number of articles published in news papers, and by the work of individuals such as Al Gore who made a film entitled 'The inconvenient truth' about it (which also helped him get a Nobel prize). It is therefore hardly surprising that such awareness also affects consumer industries. Many companies these days are aware that consumers are concerned about environmental issues and consequently they wish to be seen to do what they can to ensure that their products represent those values and beliefs. When companies are involved in schemes to improve the environment, they readily advertise such facts. For example, GAP has printed a statement at the bottom of their bags that they contain '15% post consumer recycled material' while Primark's bags state that they are 'made from 100% recycled material and [are] biodegradable'. Other companies such as Starbucks print on their bags that they 'care about the environment'.

Even though consumers are environmentally concerned, some studies say women are more so than men (Grankvist, 2008; Iyer & Kashyap, 2007), but it is rare that products high on ethical attributes are among the top selling brands in their product categories. This shows that what consumers actually buy is often incongruent with their value systems. Naturally this raises questions such as why people do not buy products that are pro-environmentally friendly and how it is possible to get them to do so.

The impact of consumption upon the environment

In the past decade a lot has been written about how consumer practices affect our environment badly. The fact is that in most Western societies people are now so accustomed to having a mobile phone, their own washing machine, microwave, television and computer that a world without them would seem incomprehensible. Unfortunately all the aforementioned products are in one way or another (together with most other types of products and a high number of services) depleting our environment. In the UK alone there has been a steady increase in consumption of numerous products since the late 1990s (Figure 13.1) and it does not appear to be slowing down. This, in combination with the increase in consumption that has taken place in several other countries, makes it easy to see how it may be a significant contributor to environmental issues. What makes matters worse is that currently only a small amount of the world's population (around 20 per cent) use the majority of Earth's non-renewable resources (approximately 80 per cent) (Dürr, 1994). And with a high number of less industrialized countries striving to reach the same consumption levels as Europe and the USA, the strain on natural resources is bound to be devastating.

It would be impossible to cover all angles of the proposed detrimental relationship between consumption and the environment here. So what follows are brief

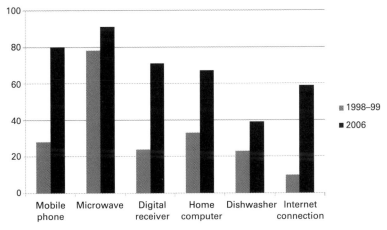

FIGURE 13.1 Increase in consumer durables between 1998–99 and 2006 (%).

Source: Information adapted from National Statistics (2008a).

outlines of some of the areas that can demonstrate that consumer consumption can play a role in environmental deterioration.

Depletion of natural resources

Rather scarily it has been estimated that if the entire world's population were to use the same amount of natural resources as Western societies are currently using, three planet Earths would be required (Wackernagel & Rees, 1996). This is rather alarming bearing in mind that nations such as China and India are rapidly expanding their consumption rate and hence contributing to the speed with which natural resources are diminishing. There are many natural resources that are getting close to disappearing or are diminishing rapidly, and two of the more commonly discussed ones are oil and forests.

Oil is one natural resource that many are particularly concerned about. Transportation would be particularly badly affected if the world were to run out of oil. Without it there would be a drastic decrease in transportation. Flying is the most fuel-inefficient way to travel of all the alternatives and it is therefore unfortunate that so many people are increasingly flying. Never before have people (and Europeans in particular) flown as much as they do today, hence helping to ensure that the oil supply is rapidly disappearing. Of course, other areas would also be badly affected by a serious decrease in the oil supply as it is used for many different purposes, i.e. heating and manufacturing of various products.

There is great variation in how much oil different countries consume; for example, in America approximately 18 barrels of oil per person are used annually while Australians use around 6 per person (Sheehan, 2001). Some believe that once the world starts running out of oil and water, it is likely that conflict between countries will erupt and war will be inevitable (Homer-Dixon, 1991; Lang & Heasman, 2004). Others have claimed that this has already happened with the invasion of Iraq (Gray, 2003).

Deforestation is another problem that is linked to consumption. Paper consumption is a serious contributor to the world's diminishing forests. Every year mail-order catalogues, junk mail, newspapers, magazines, Christmas cards, shopping bags, writing paper, etc. are thrown away in their billions. Most paper-based products are not the kind that will be used for long periods of time, instead a high percentage is used for things such as packaging (Mattoon, 2000), which is rapidly discarded by most people. Many seemed to think that paper use would be greatly reduced with the introduction of computers in most parts of societies. Unfortunately paper use did not decrease but has instead increased since the early 1990s (see Figure 13.2).

The reason why people should be worried about deforestation is because forests produce oxygen while helping to absorb carbon emissions, shelter animal wildlife and help prevent landslides and flooding (Abramovitz & Mattoon, 1999) and consequently the world cannot afford to get rid of them without serious ecological consequences.

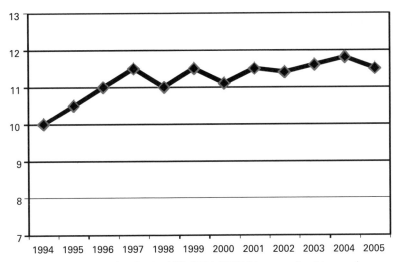

FIGURE 13.2 Paper consumption in the UK, 1994–2005 (thousands of tonnes).

Global warming

Our planetary home is getting gradually warmer due to the fact that a high level of carbon dioxide (CO_2) is released into the air. Every time an organic substance such as oil, gas or wood is burned, more CO_2 emissions are released, preventing less warm air from escaping, while letting warm sunlight in, and hence causing the Earth to become hotter. Increasing temperatures have been linked to flooding, extreme droughts, and severe storms around the world (Flavin & Dunn, 1999). Some are even suggesting that global warming can cause the West Antarctic ice sheet to melt which in turn would mean that large parts of the USA such as New Orleans and New York would be flooded (Schneider, 1997). Bearing in mind that the Antarctic ice has already started melting and that Earth's temperature increased 0.51°C from the 1950s until 1999 compared to only 0.57°C between 1866 and 1950 (Dunn, 2000), it is not hard to imagine the entire West Antarctic ice sheet melting.

Manufacturing products and keeping our homes heated with gas are examples of consumption-related practices that contribute to global warming. Transportation is another; not only is it bad news for resource depletion but it is also the fastest growing contributor to the increase of carbon emissions (Sheehan, 2001). In 1971, 52 per cent of all the households in the UK had access to a car compared to 75 per cent in 2004, an increase of 23 per cent. Over the same period the increase in households having two or more cars went up from 8 to 31 per cent (National Statistics, 2008b). The British and European populations only drive approximately half the distance compared to Americans, meaning that US carbon emissions are even higher.

Sustainability

One of the recent 'buzz' phrases in research concerning environmentally friendly consumption is 'sustainable consumption'. Sustainability can be defined as 'using the world's resources in ways that will allow human beings to continue to exist on Earth with an adequate quality of life' (Oskamp, 2000, p. 496). It is worth noting that sustainable consumption is not about consuming less but that it is about consuming in an efficient manner. The recent interest in sustainable consumption by governments and academics alike has generated an increase in more pro-environmentally friendly ways to produce goods (Michaelis, 2003).

Sustainable consumption is not easily achieved and it has been suggested that the promotion of such practices by governments can only be successful when it does not conflict with the economic growth of a country (Christensen, Godskesen, Gram-Hanssen, Quitzau, & Røpke, 2007). This may be unfortunate as government policies are often demanding when it comes to ensuring that the majority of a population is aware of certain issues and since governments are always more likely to put economic growth first, the extent to which they will promote sustainable consumption is bound to be limited. However, this is only important if sustainable consumption is the genuine solution to the ecological problems the world is facing. This may be questionable if one considers that resources such as oil cannot be regenerated and its continued use (in whatever form) will simply continue to decrease the supply, and once it has been used up, it will be gone forever. Consequently, sustainable consumption may simply not be enough to solve all the environmental problems but it is likely to be useful in resolving some consumer issues and to create more awareness.

Recycling

An important part of sustainable consumption is recycling. How products are recycled varies depending on what kind of product it is. Some are handed in to be reused (wholly or partially) in the production of other goods, while some are given to charity shops or perhaps sold in flea markets (known as **lateral recycling**). Environmentalists are generally most concerned with the type of products that can be productively reused but for one reason or another end up in the bin rather than being recycled.

The biggest obstacle to people choosing to recycle appears to be linked to how easy or difficult it is to do. Research has found that when people perceive it to be difficult, they are much less likely to recycle, regardless of whether or not they believe it is important to do so (Bagozzi & Dabholkar, 1994). Hence, it is imperative that recycling points are readily available on most street corners, as is the case in places such as downtown Toronto, in order to ensure that people will not find it difficult to recycle. Even though making it easy to recycle will undoubtedly encourage consumers to do so, it is also important that they genuinely believe that it will make a difference to the environment (Pieters, 1991). If they believe that it will not make a difference, then even if it is easy to do, it is unlikely that they will recycle. However, to induce such beliefs may be difficult.

Although recycling is on the increase in most Western societies, most countries could be doing much better than they are. There is little consistency between how much and what different countries recycle (Thøgersen, 1993) and this may be due to cultural differences in consumption style. Greece is the worst EU country when it comes to recycling and is closely followed by Ireland. Austria, Germany, and the Netherlands are among the countries that recycle the most (Defra, 2004). In the UK, the majority of the possessions discarded are still included in the general household waste (as can be noted from Figure 13.3), even though it is likely that a high proportion could be recycled.

Even though awareness of recycling practices is high, it appears that there is a long way to go before most nations are thoroughly engaged in recycling.

Pro-environment products – a complicated issue

What is deemed to be environmentally friendly consumption is rather complex. Some say that organically produced products are good for our environment, while others may focus on whether or not something can be recycled or what amount of CO_2 emissions were released into the air during its production. However, even if consumers know exactly what the products or services they purchase should represent, they may not always end up choosing the most environmentally friendly

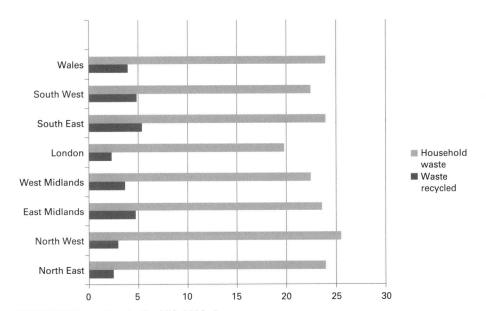

FIGURE 13.3 Recycling in the UK, 2003–4.

Note: Household waste and proportion recycled are shown in kilograms per household per week.

alternative. For example, they may have a preference for organic food, but upon purchase they may not check where the food was produced and hence may end up buying something that has been imported from a country far away. Consequently the particular food product bought may be contributing unnecessarily to pollution. It is often difficult to make a totally informed consumption decision as it can be confusing and complicated. Perhaps this may be one of the reasons why environmentally friendly products are not always perceived in a positive manner as consumers are aware that they may not be helping the environment in the way that they would like to.

How do consumers perceive environmentally friendly products?

It appears that there are cultural differences to how people perceive products that are better for the environment. Perhaps this is a reflection of the fact that different countries deal with the environment in different ways. For example, it has been suggested that German consumers view humans as an integral part of the ecological system while Northern Americans have a desire to master their environment (Homma, 1991). It may therefore come as no great surprise that consumers in the USA perceive ethically superior products (includes products made from recycled materials, that are biodegradable, represent fair labour, and so forth) as being less effective than those that are not (Luchs, Walker Naylor, Irwin, & Raghunathan, 2008). Northern Europeans appear to have a more positive view of pro-environmentally friendly products than the Americans. For example, Swedish consumers have been found to have positive attitudes towards organically produced products (Magnusson, Arvola, Koivisto Hursti, Åberg, & Sjödén, 2001). Unfortunately, a positive perception of pro-environmental products and services does not necessarily translate into consumption behaviour. Apart from the fact that attitudes do not always predict behaviour, there may also be other explanations why this is the case, such as environmentally friendly products are not always easily identified and hence it is more difficult for consumers to choose which product to buy. This has been found to be the case for food products, which is unfortunate bearing in mind that the food industry has been suggested to be one area where consumers can make a difference to several environmentally linked problems (Stern, Dietz, Ruttan, Socolow, & Sweeney, 1997). In many countries (e.g. the UK, Germany and Austria) food products have labels that show if they have been organically produced and farmed. However, many other aspects that consumers may wish to know about such as transport distance and conservation practices (Jungbluth, Tietje, & Scholz, 2000) are not clearly labelled on food packaging, making it a lot more difficult for consumers to choose. It has been suggested that one way of simplifying the product choice process for pro-environment goods and services may be to make use of only one label rather than presenting consumers with an array of several product dimensions (Tanner & Jungbluth, 2003).

Can non-environmentally friendly consumption be reduced?

To date, not much research has been conducted by psychologists looking at how non-environmentally friendly consumption can be reduced, even though there appears increasing interest in the subject area. That is not to say that the foundation has not been laid for the kind of techniques that can be useful when it comes to tackling consumer awareness and behaviour in favour of the ecological system. Looking at previously used methodologies deriving from social, cognitive and behavioural approaches, these can shed some light on what can be done to encourage more environmentally responsible consumption (Du Nann Winter, 2000, 2003).

The social approach

It has been suggested that in order to understand and explain environmental behaviour it is essential to understand the social environment in which it is developed (e.g. Vorkinn & Riese, 2001). There is little doubt that people are affected by their social environments in that they wish to be perceived by others in a certain way and they will replicate the behaviour of those they admire and respect, consequently also shaping environmentally friendly consumption. For example, factors that are often the product of socialization procedures such as having close, warm relationships with others have been found to correlate with whether or not people have a preference for ethically produced goods (Grankvist, 2008).

One way to make people interested in pro-environmental consumption may be through **modelling**, which is a form of vicarious learning whereby people observe a real-life or symbolic model and replicate their actions, attitudes, behaviour and emotional responses (e.g. Bandura, 1973). The people who are most likely to inspire others to replicate behaviours are those who appear to be rewarded for it. For example, when a person who is popular and famous campaigns for an end to whale hunting, people will link the two together and think that it is a good thing to campaign to save the whales. Since people are subconsciously continuously comparing themselves to others, and in particular to those whom they like and admire (e.g. Festinger, 1954; Wheeler, 1991), it can be very effective to make use of 'role models' in pro-environmental consumption campaigns, as people are then more likely to follow suit. Therefore making use of popular celebrities (perhaps through advertising) to persuade consumers to change their shopping patterns may have the desired effect.

It would also be good to encourage individuals not to compare themselves to those who clearly over-consume. People's self-esteem tends to increase or decrease depending upon who they are comparing themselves to (e.g. Marsh, Kong, & Hau, 2000). Because people tend to value material possessions in industrialized societies, it can make certain individuals feel inadequate when they compare themselves to those who own things to which they aspire but cannot afford. People in the public eye who are particularly associated with an affluent lifestyle ruled by which designer clothes they wear, the exotic holidays they have or the kind of expensive cars they drive, often become role models that make over-consumption the norm. Such role models can not only lower people's self-esteem but they also function as an obstacle to reducing the amount people are consuming as they tend to consume in line with others (Leonard-Barton, 1981) and this in turn decreases the likelihood of pro-environmental consumption.

Making consumers feel as if their consumer behaviours are *deviating from the norm* might also work. Schachter (1951) found that those who express a different opinion to groups tend to be under a lot of social pressure to conform to what the group believes. If the person with the different opinion fails to conform, they can find themselves rejected by the group. Hence, making it appear to be the norm to engage in environmentally friendly consumption may pressurize others into doing the same or they may feel left out and unwanted. That is not to say that this would be easy to do, especially since the current norm held by most groups appears to be that it is acceptable to accumulate material possessions and to ignore ethically produced goods.

The cognitive approach

The cognitive approach emphasizes how information that is framed and presented in a particular way affects how it is processed and perceived. In order to encourage environmentally friendly consumption, it is essential to alter people's perception and how they think about pro-environmental products and services and one way of doing so is through education. Educating people environmentally can be done in many different ways, such as through traditional schooling, advertising, discussion groups, or the media. Education has often been considered the key to changing people's thoughts and attitudes towards particular subject areas, but unfortunately it has not always been proved to be very successful (Dwyer, Leeming, Cobern, Porter, & Jackson, 1993; Howard, 2000; McKenzie-Mohr, 2000). This seems to be regardless of the kind of educational methods used. Geller (1981) found that educational workshops had little impact on reducing energy use and Heberlein (1975) noted that giving people booklets about how to save energy was also ineffective. However, on occasion educational messages have been found to impact upon individuals but unfortunately such campaigns may for other reasons have been deemed unsuccessful. For example, this was found to be the case when pro-environmental messages shown on television were investigated by Syme, Seligman, Kantola, and Macpherson (1987). They studied the effects of an intense four-week television campaign aimed at reducing petrol consumption in three Australian cities. One campaign emphasized the money-saving aspect while another pointed out that it would make people 'good citizens'. Even though a small statistically significant relationship was found between the campaigns and pro-petrol conservation attitudes, the authors concluded that campaigns had not been cost effective.

The lack of a clear relationship between pro-environmental attitudes and actual behaviour may not necessarily be due to inefficient educational campaigns. It may very well be that those exposed to such messages intend to change their consumption behaviours but that societal structures are preventing them from doing so (Stern, 2000). For example, the lack of public transport to outer city shopping centres means that people have to drive even if they don't want to.

Other reasons why education has not proved to be effective can be how the actual information is presented as well as how and when people are being targeted with pro-environmental messages. If advertising campaigns are used to teach consumers about pro-environmental consumption, it may be that the messages are not attracting enough attention by making use of vivid stimuli, which have specifically been found to be able to increase pro-environment behaviour (Gonzales, Aronson, & Costanzo, 1988) or that they fail to encourage elaborative processing, which in turn decreases the likelihood of attitudes being generated in favour of the message presented (Petty & Cacioppo, 1986a). (For more information about advertising and elaboration, see Chapter 8).

Another issue related to commercial messages is that they can on occasion undermine other factors that are also important, such as those caused by everyday behaviour. In particular this can be the case when vivid images are used to represent environmental problems (Du Nann Winter, 2000). For example, seeing colourful, strong images of how the ice melting in the Arctic circle is causing severe environmental problems can make the use of free plastic bags seem insignificant in comparison. Consequently, people will fail to reduce the kind of non-environmentally friendly consumption that they can actually do something about.

A final thought on the matter is that the weak relationship between education and pro-environmental consumption is due to the fact that education is simply geared towards altering consumers' attitudes. Generally, people in both the USA and Europe are concerned about the state of the environment (Cohen & Horm-Wingerd, 1993; Dunlap & Mertig, 1995; Wall, 1995) but nevertheless the correlation between such attitudes and behaviour is weak or at times non-existent (e.g. Geller, Winnett, & Everett, 1982; Newhouse, 1990). Hence, simply informing people about environmental disasters is not enough to change behaviour (Stern, 2000); instead it may be better to try and implement behavioural change strategies.

The behavioural approach

Nobody is claiming that changing human behaviour is easy but behaviourists have come up with two particular approaches that may be useful when it comes to trying to get consumers to engage in environmentally friendly consumption. The first is stimulus control management and the second is contingency management (Geller, 1987). **Stimulus control management** is about exposing individuals to stimuli such as models, specific cues and instructions prior to engaging in a particular behaviour in the hope that it will prevent them from doing something.

This has been found to be successful for reducing both water consumption (Aronson & O'Leary, 1982–1983) and littering (Geller, 1980). **Contingency management** is when people make use of methods such as rewards or fines after individuals have engaged in a particular behaviour, something that has been found to be useful for things such as the reduction of energy use (Walker, 1979).

There are some obstacles to the effectiveness of behavioural methods such as stimulus control and contingency management. First, it is worth noting that it is very difficult to reduce people's consumption patterns when they are living in societies that are actively encouraging people to over-consume. Advertising is luring consumers to buy, buy, buy, people see their friends and family continuously buying products and even governments publicize how good it is for the economy when we spend, spend, spend. But what makes it the most difficult to resist may be the short-term benefits consumption can provide which consumers clearly notice while they fail to recognize the long-term environmental costs, a phenomenon

known as '**Tragedy of the Commons**' (Hardin, 1968, 1998). Put simply, this is when the short-term benefits of consumption seem more obvious than the long-term costs. Examples may include receiving airmiles every time they fly, two-for-one offers, and severely discounted goods and services for limited time periods. This is a serious problem, especially since many consumers do not fully understand or are unaware of what the environmental costs of consumption are.

Hardin suggested that the way to control people's behaviour so that they do not go for simple short-term solutions, is by using some kind of coercion that is enforced by an external source. The coercion may occur in terms of additional charges for a particular service. Take the Internet as an example. Users are generally not specifically charged for the volume they use and hence individuals who over-consume can cause blocking to occur, inconveniencing many other users (Huberman & Lukose, 1997). However, if people were charged for the exact amount used and perhaps even for accessing specific sites, congestion at critical junctions could be avoided as it would act as a deterrent. This may work, especially if one considers that it has been suggested that the commons tragedy can be viewed as a 'social trap' that can be analysed in terms of rewards and punishments (Platt, 1973). There are two types of social traps that are particularly applicable to environmentally friendly consumption: (1) *individual good – collective bad trap*; and (2) *missing hero trap*. The first refers to when a group is competing for a precious resource. If only one or two people engage in a destructive behaviour, it will have little impact upon the resource, but if the entire group engages in the same behaviour, the consequences may be disastrous. For example, individuals who live in countries where there is a water shortage may continue to consume large amounts of water because they do not wish to feel dirty and thirsty. Hence they think that the short-term reward of feeling clean and hydrated is more important than the long-term consequence of everyone else consuming lots of water. The second type of trap focuses on actions that consumers fail to engage in due to being concerned about the short-term punishment that they will be subjected to. For example, people don't want to use their car less, as it would be harder work to have to walk even though the long-term benefits will include less pollution and lower oil consumption.

However, not everybody is convinced that rewards and punishments are the answer to making people engage in environmentally friendly behaviours as there are many other factors that can come into play (e.g. Axelrod & Lehman, 1993; Edney, 1980). Nevertheless, environmentally based consumption research still shows that rewards in particular can be successful in combating certain types of behaviours as long as the immediate benefits are clear to the consumer. For example, different types of awards, such as cash, have been found to be good incentives to encourage people to drive less (Foxx & Hake, 1977). Similarly, this has also been found when participants in studies were given lottery tickets (Reichel & Geller, 1980). Another reward strategy that appears to encourage people to recycle is to give people a small financial incentive for returning bottles and cans that can be recycled (Wolf & Feldman, 1991), a method that has been implemented in many places such as New York, Australia and Sweden.

Is one psychological approach better than another?

At this point in time it is difficult to say for certain if a specific psychological approach should be taken to encourage consumers to engage in pro-environmental consumption. The best solution may be to draw on the successes from different types of psychology research in the hope of reaching the best possible result. This would naturally also include evolutionary (belief that consumption is a way to adapt and that it is fuelled by sexual competition) and psychodynamic perspectives (over-consumption is part of the instinctive urges people have that drive them unconsciously towards destruction), even though these approaches are not discussed in this chapter. In particular, the use of rewards seems encouraging as it is very well tried and tested in many areas of psychology, but naturally it can be an expensive affair to reward each consumer for resisting certain ecologically destructive behaviours or consuming only those products and services deemed to be environmentally friendly.

Key Terms

Contingency management
When rewards or punishments are introduced after people have engaged in a particular behaviour.

Lateral recycling
Products that are reused either partially or fully.

Modelling
Learning by observation of others.

Stimulus control management
Altering behaviour by exposing people to stimuli prior to engaging in a behaviour.

Tragedy of the Commons
When immediate benefits appear to outweigh the long-term costs.

Summary

Consumption of various products and services contributes to a great extent to harming the natural resources of our planetary home. Since the 1990s researchers have started to look at how sustainable consumption can help to resolve some of the environmentally linked issues. Recycling can be a good way of ensuring that valuable materials do not go to waste but it needs to be made easy for people or they are likely to put their 'rubbish' into the bin instead. There also seem to be great cultural differences in how and why people recycle. The influence of culture can also be noted in the way in which environmentally friendly products are perceived. Some countries have been found to have a more positive outlook on eco-friendly products while others do not necessarily see them in a positive light. Even though there is little research on how to increase pro-environmentally friendly consumption, it should be possible to make use of already established techniques from different psychological approaches that have been found to be useful in changing people's thoughts and behaviours. Such techniques include modelling, norm deviation, stimulus control management and contingency management.

Discussion questions

1 Why should consumer psychologists be interested in environmental issues?
2 Give at least two examples of consumption practices that were not mentioned in this chapter, that have a bad impact upon the environment.
3 How do you think pro-ecological products may be perceived in very different cultures such as India and Italy?
4 What kind of techniques could be effective when it comes to encouraging consumers to buy environmentally friendly products?
5 Why might it be that Americans think that ethically produced products are inferior to those that are not?

References

Aaker, D.A., & Keller, K.L. (1990). Consumer evaluations of brand extensions. *Journal of Marketing, 54,* 27–41.

Aaker, J.L. (1997). Dimensions of brand personality. *Journal of Marketing Research, 34,* 342–352.

Aaker, J.L. (1999). The malleable self: The role of self-expression in persuasion. *Journal of Marketing Research, 36,* 45–57.

Aaker, J.L., & Williams, P. (1998). Empathy versus pride: The influence of emotional appeals across cultures. *Journal of Consumer Research, 25,* 241–261.

Abraham, M.M., & Lodish, L.M. (1990). Getting the most out of advertising and promotion. *Harvard Business Review, 68,* 50–60.

Abramovitz, J.N., & Mattoon, A.T. (1999). Reorienting the forest products economy. In L.R. Brown, C. Flavin, H.F. French & L. Starke (Eds.), *State of the world 1999: A Worldwatch Institute report on progress toward a sustainable society* (pp. 60–77). New York: Worldwatch Institute.

Adams, H.F. (1916). *Advertising and its mental laws.* New York: Macmillan.

Adaval, R. (2001). Sometimes it just feels right: The differential weighting of affect-consistent and affect-inconsistent product information. *Journal of Consumer Research, 28,* 1–17.

Ajzen, I. (1985). From intentions to actions: A theory of planned behaviour. In J. Kuhl & J. Beckmann (Eds.), *Action control: From cognition to behaviour* (pp. 11–39). New York: Springer.

Ajzen, I. (2008). Consumer attitudes and behaviour. In C.P. Haugtvedt, P.M. Herr & F.R. Kardes (Eds.), *Handbook of consumer psychology* (pp. 525–548). New York: Lawrence Erlbaum Associates.

Alba, J.W., & Hutchinson, J.W. (1987). Dimensions of consumer expertise. *Journal of Consumer Research, 13,* 411–454.

Alba, J.W., Hutchinson, J.W., & Lynch, J.G. (1991). Memory and decision making. In T.S. Robertson & H.H. Kassarjian (Eds.), *Handbook of consumer behaviour* (pp. 1–49). Englewood Cliffs, NJ: Prentice-Hall.

Allen, C.T. & Madden, T.J. (1985). A closer look at classical conditioning. *Journal of Consumer Research, 12,* 301–315.

Allison, R.I., & Uhl, K.P. (1964). Influence of beer brand identification on taste perception. *Journal of Marketing Research, 1,* 36–39.

Alpers, G.W., & Gerdes, A.B.M. (2006). Another look at 'Look-Alikes': Can judges match belongings with their owners? *Journal of Individual Differences, 27,* 38–41.

Alwitt, L.F., Anderson, D.R., Lorch, E.P., & Levin, S.R. (1980). Preschool children's visual attention to attributes of television. *Human Communication Research, 7,* 52–67.

American Academy of Pediatrics (1999). *Understanding the impact of media on children and teens.* Elk Grove Village: Media Matters.

Anderson, C.A., & Ford, C.M. (1986). Affect of the game player: Short term effects of highly and mildly aggressive video games. *Personality and Social Psychology Bulletin, 12,* 390–402.

Anderson, C.A., & Godfrey, S.S. (1987). Thoughts about actions: The effects of specificity and availability of imagined behavioral scripts on expectations about oneself and others. *Social Cognition, 5,* 238–258.

Anderson, J.R. (1983). *The architecture of cognition.* Cambridge, MA: Harvard University Press.

Anderson, J.R. (1993). *Rules of the mind.* Hillsdale, NJ: Lawrence Erlbaum Associates.

Andrade, E.B. (2005). Behavioral consequences of affect: Combining evaluative and regulatory mechanisms. *Journal of Consumer Research, 32,* 355–362.

Andrews, J. (1988). Motivation, ability, and opportunity to process information: Conceptual and experimental manipulation issues. In M.J. Houston (Ed.), *Advances in consumer research* (vol. 15, pp. 219–225). Provo, UT: Association for Consumer Research.

Archer, D., Iritani, B., Kimes, D.D., & Barrios, M. (1983). Face-ism: Five studies of sex differences in facial prominence. *Journal of Personality and Social Psychology, 45*, 725–735.

Arkes, H.R., Herren, L.T., & Isen, A.M. (1988). The role of potential loss in the influence of affect on risk-taking behaviour. *Organizational Behavior and Human Decision Processes, 42*, 181–193.

Arnold, J., Robertson, I.T., & Cooper, C.L. (1995). *Work psychology: Understanding human behaviour in the workplace* (2nd ed.). London: Pitman.

Aron, A., & Aron, E.N. (1997). Self-expansion motivation and including other in the self. In S. Duck (Ed.), *Handbook of personal relationships: Theory, research, and intervention* (2nd ed., pp. 251–270). Chichester: Wiley.

Aronson, E. (1992). The return of the repressed: Dissonance theory makes a comeback. *Psychological Inquiry, 3*, 303–311.

Aronson, E. (1998). Dissonance, hypocrisy, and the self-concept. In E. Harmon-Jones & J.S. Mills (Eds.), *Cognitive dissonance theory: Revival with revisions and controversies* (pp. 21–36). Washington, DC: American Psychological Association.

Aronson, E., & O'Leary, M. (1982–1983). The relative effectiveness of models and prompts on energy conservation: A field experiment in a shower room. *Journal of Environmental Systems, 12*, 219–224.

Arthur, W., Jr., & Benjamin, L.T. (1999). Psychology applied to business. In A.M. Stec & D.A. Bernstein (Eds.), *Psychology: Fields of application*. Boston: Houghton Mifflin Company.

Atkin, C.K. (1977). Effects of campaign advertising and newscasts on children. *Journalism Quarterly, 54*, 503–558.

Atkinson, R.C., & Shiffrin, R.M. (1968). Human memory: A proposed system and its control processes. In K.W. Spence & J.T. Spence (Eds.), *The psychology of learning and motivation* (vol 2). London: Academic Press.

Axelrod, L.J., & Lehman, D.R. (1993). Responding to environmental concerns: What factors guide individual action? *Journal of Environmental Psychology, 13*, 149–159.

Baddeley, A. (1990). *Human memory*. Needham Heights, MA: Allyn and Bacon.

Baddeley, A.D., & Hitch, G.J. (1974). Working memory. In G.H. Bower (Ed.), *The psychology of learning and motivation* (vol. 8). London: Academic Press.

Bagozzi, R.P., & Dabholkar, P.A. (1994). Consumer recycling goals and their effect on decisions to recycle: a means–end chain analysis. *Psychology & Marketing, 11*, 313–340.

Baillargeon, R., & DeVos, J. (1991). Object permanence in young infants: further evidence. *Child Development, 62*, 1227–1246.

Baker, J., Levy, M., & Grewal, D. (1992). An experiential approach to making retail store environmental decisions. *Journal of Retailing, 68*, 445–460.

Baker, J., Parasuraman, A., Grewal, D., & Voss, G.B. (2002). The influence of multiple store environment cues on perceived merchandise value and patronage intentions. *Journal of Marketing, 66*, 120–141.

Baker, M.J., & Churchill, G.A. Jr. (1977). The impact of physically attractive models on advertising evaluations. *Journal of Marketing Research, 14*, 538–555.

Baker, W., Marn, M., & Zawada, C. (2001). Price smarter on the net. *Harvard Business Review*, February, 122–127.

Balcetis, E., & Dunning, D. (2006). See what you want to see: Motivational influences on visual perception. *Journal of Personality and Social Psychology, 91*, 612–625.

Balderjahn, I. (1988). Personality variables and environmental attitudes as predictors of ecologically responsible consumption patterns. *Journal of Business Research, 17*, 51–56.

Bamossy, G., Scammon, D.L., & Johnston, M. (1983). A preliminary investigation of the reliability and validity of an aesthetic judgement test. In R. Bagozzi and A Tybout (Eds.), *Advances in consumer research*. (vol. 10, pp. 685–690). Ann Arbor, MI: Association for Consumer Research.

Bandura, A. (1965). Influence of models' reinforcement contingencies on the acquisition of imitative responses. *Journal of Personality and Social Psychology, 1*, 589–595.

Bandura, A. (1969). *Principles of behavior modification*. New York: Holt, Rinehart & Winston.

Bandura, A. (1973). *Aggression: A social learning analysis*. Englewood Cliffs, NJ: Prentice Hall.

Bandura, A. (1977). *Social learning theory*. Englewood Cliffs, NJ: Prentice Hall.

Bandura, A. (1986). *Social foundations of thought and action: A social cognitive theory.* Englewood Cliffs, NJ: Prentice-Hall.

Bandura, A. (1997). *Self-efficacy: The exercise of control.* New York: Freeman.

Bandura, A. (2002). Social cognitive theory of mass communication. In J. Bryant and D. Zillman (Eds.), *Media effects: Advances in theory and research* (2nd ed., pp. 121–153). Mahwah, NJ: Lawrence Erlbaum Associates, Inc.

Bandura, A., Ross, D., & Ross, S.A. (1963). Imitation of film-mediated aggressive models. *Journal of Abnormal and Social Psychology, 66,* 3–11.

Bargh, J.A. (1997). The automaticity of everyday life. In R.S. Wyer, Jr. (Ed.), *Advances in social cognition: The automaticity of everyday life* (vol. 10, pp. 1–61). Mahwah, NJ: Lawrence Erlbaum Associates, Inc.

Bargh, J.A., Chaiken, S., Govender, R., & Pratto, F. (1992). The generality of the automatic attitude activation effect. *Journal of Personality and Social Psychology, 62,* 893–912.

Bargh, J.A., McKenna, K.Y.A., & Fitzsimons, G.M. (2002). Can you see the real me? Activation and expression of the 'true self' on the Internet. *Journal of Social Issues, 58,* 33–48.

Barnow, E. (1975). *Tube of plenty: The evolution of American television.* London: Oxford University Press.

Barone, M.J., Miniard, P.W., & Romeo, J.B. (2000). The influence of positive mood on brand extension evaluations. *Journal of Consumer Research, 26,* 386–400.

Bartlett, F.C. (1932). *Remembering: A study in experimental and social psychology.* Cambridge: Cambridge University Press.

Bassili, J.N. (1996). Meta-judgemental versus operative indexes of psychological attributes: The case of measures of attitude strength. *Journal of Personality and Social Psychology, 71,* 637–653.

Batra, R., & Ray, M.L. (1986a). Situational effects of advertising repetition: The moderating influence of motivation, ability, and opportunity to respond. *Journal of Consumer Research, 12,* 432–445.

Batra, R., & Ray, M.L. (1986b). Affective responses mediating acceptance of advertising. *Journal of Consumer Research, 13,* 234–249.

Baumgartner, H., & Steenkamp, J-B.E.M. (1996). Exploratory consumer buying behaviour: Conceptualization and measurement. *International Journal of Research in Marketing, 13,* 121–137.

Bayen, U.J., & Murnane, K. (1996). Aging and the use of perceptual and temporal information in source memory tasks. *Psychology and Aging, 11,* 293–303.

BBC (2009). Plans target digital Britain push. Retrieved February 8, 2009, from http://news.bbc.co.uk/1/hi/technology/7857402.stm

Becker, G. (1993). *Human capital.* Chicago: University of Chicago Press.

Belch, G.E., & Belch, M.A. (1984). An investigation of the effects of repetition on cognitive and affective reactions to humorous and serious television commercials. In T. Kinnear (Ed.), *Advances in consumer research* (vol. II). Ann Arbor, MI: Association for Consumer Research.

Belen del Rio, A., Vacquez, R., & Iglesias, V. (2001). The effects of brand association on consumer response. *Journal of Consumer Marketing, 18,* 410–425.

Belk, R.W. (1984). Three scales to measure constructs related to materialism: reliability, validity and relationships to measures of happiness. In T. Kinnear (Ed.), *Advances in consumer research* (vol. 11, pp. 291–297). Provo, UT: Association for Consumer Research.

Belk, R.W. (1988). Possessions and the extended self. *Journal of Consumer Research, 15,* 139–168.

Belk, R.W. (1993). Materialism and the making of the modern American Christmas. In D. Miller (Ed.), *Unwrapping Christmas* (pp. 75–104). Oxford: Clarendon Press.

Belk, R.W. (2008). Consumption and identity. In A. Lewis (Ed.), *Handbook of psychology and economic behaviour* (pp. 199–226). Cambridge: Cambridge University Press.

Belk, R.W., Mayer, R.N., & Bahn, K.D. (1982). The eye of the beholder: Individual differences in perceptions of consumption symbolism. *Advances in Consumer Research, 9,* 523–530.

Belk, R.W., Sherry, J.F. Jr, & Wallendorf, M. (1988). A naturalistic inquiry into buyer and seller behaviour at a Swap Meet. *Journal of Consumer Research, 14,* 449–470.

Bellizzi, J.A., & Martin, W.S. (1982). The influence of national versus generic branding on taste perceptions. *Journal of Business Research, 10,* 385–396.

Bello, D.C., Pitts, P.E., & Etzel, M.J. (1983). The communication effects of controversial sexual content in television programs and commercials. *Journal of Advertising, 12*, 32–42.

Bem, D.J. (1972). Self-perception theory. In L. Berkowitz (Ed.), *Advances in experimental social psychology* (vol. 6, pp. 1–62). New York: Academic Press.

Benjamin, L.T., & Baker, D.B. (2004). *From séance to science: A history of the profession of psychology in America*. Belmont, CA: Wadsworth/Thompson.

Benjamin, L.T. Jr., Rogers, A.M., & Rosenbaum, A. (1991). Coca-Cola, caffeine, and mental deficiency: Harry Hollingworth and the Chattanooga trial of 1911. *Journal of the History of the Behavioral Sciences, 27*, 42–45.

Bennett, R. (1996). Effects of horrific fear appeals on public attitudes towards AIDS. *International Journal of Advertising, 15*, 183–202.

Berlyne, D.E. (1971). *Aesthetics and psychobiology*. New York: Appleton-Century-Crofts.

Berlyne, D.E., & Parham, L.C.C. (1968). Determinants of subjective novelty. *Perception and Psychophysics, 3*, 415–423.

Berman, B., & Evans, J.R. (1995). *Retail management: A strategic approach* (6th ed). Englewood Cliffs, NJ: Prentice-Hall.

Berns, G.S., Cohen, J.D., & Mintun, M.A. (1997). Brain regions responsive to novelty in the absence of awareness. *Science, 276*, 1272–1275.

Berry, G.L. (2000). Multicultural media portrayals and the changing demographic landscape: The psychosocial impact of television representations on the adolescent of color. *Journal of Adolescent Health, 27*, 57–60.

Bettman, J.R. (1979). *An information processing theory of consumer choice*. Reading, MA: Addison-Wesley.

Bettman, J.R., & Park, C.W. (1980). Effects of prior knowledge and experience and phase of the choice process on consumer decision processes: A protocol analysis. *Journal of Consumer Research, 7*, 234–248.

Bever, T.G., Smith, M.L., Bengen, B., & Johnson, T.G. (1975). Young viewers' troubling response to TV ads. *Harvard Business Review, 53*, 109–120.

Biehal, G.J., & Chakravarti, D. (1986). Consumers' use of memory and external information in choice: Macro and micro processing perspectives. *Journal of Consumer Research, 12*, 382–405.

Bitner, M.J. (1990). Evaluating service encounters: The effects of physical surroundings and employee responses. *Journal of Marketing, 54*, 69–82.

Black, D.W. (1996). Compulsive buying. *Journal of Clinical Psychiatry, 57*, 50–54.

Blaney, P.H. (1986). Affect and memory – A review. *Psychological Bulletin, 99*, 229–246.

Bloch, P. (1995). Seeking the ideal form: Product design and consumer response. *Journal of Marketing, 59*, 16–29.

Bloch, P.H. (1981). An exploration into the scaling of consumers' involvement with a product class. In K.B. Monroe (Ed.), *Advances in consumer research* (vol. 8., pp. 61–65). Provo, UT: Association for Consumer Research.

Bolls, P.D., & Muehling, D.D. (2003). The effects of television commercial pacing on viewers' attention and memory. *Journal of Marketing Communications, 9*, 17–28.

Bone, P.F., & Ellen, P.S. (1999). Scents in the marketplace: Explaining a fraction of olfaction. *Journal of Retailing, 75*, 243–262.

Boorstin, D.J. (1973). *The Americans: The democratic experience*. New York: Vintage Books.

Bornstein, R.F., & D'Agostino, P.R. (1992). Stimulus recognition and the mere exposure effect. *Journal of Personality and Social Psychology, 63*, 545–552.

Botti, S., & Iyengar, S.S. (2004). The psychological please and pain of choosing: When people prefer choosing at the cost of subsequent outcome satisfaction. *Journal of Personality and Social Psychology, 87*, 312–326.

Boush, D.M., & Loken, B. (1991). A process-tracing study of brand extension evaluation. *Journal of Marketing Research, 28*, 16–28.

Bower, G.H. (1991). Mood congruity of social judgement. In J. Forgas (Ed.), *Emotion and social judgement* (pp. 31–54). Oxford: Pergamon.

Bower, G.H., Clark, M.C., Lesgold, A.M., & Winzenz, D. (1969). Hierarchical retrieval schemes in recall of categorical word lists. *Journal of Verbal Learning and Verbal Behavior, 8,* 323–343.

Bower, G.H., & Cohen, P.R. (1982). Emotional influences in memory and thinking: Data and theory. In M.S. Clark & S.T. Fiske (Eds.), *Affect and cognition.* Hillsdale, NJ: Lawrence Erlbaum.

Bower, G.H., & Forgas, J.P. (2000). Affect, memory, and social cognition. In E. Eich, J.F. Killstrom, G.H. Bower, J.P. Forgas & P.M. Niedenthal (Eds.), *Cognition and emotion* (pp. 87–168). New York: Oxford University Press.

Bower, G.H., Gilligan, S.G., & Montiero, K.P. (1981). Selectivity of learning caused by affective states. *Journal of Experimental Psychology: General, 110,* 451–473.

Bower, T.G.R. (1982). *Development in infancy* (2nd ed). San Francisco: W.H. Freeman.

Bowman, R.P., & Rotter, J.C. (1983). Computer games: Friend or foe? *Elementary School Guidance and Counselling, 18,* 25–34.

Boynton, R.M., & Smallman, H.S (1990). Visual search for basic vs. nonbasic chromatic targets. *Proceedings of the SPIE Conference on Human Vision, Visual Processing and Digital Display, 1250,* 9–18.

Bradley, M.M., Greenwald, M.K., Petry, M.C., & Lang, P.L. (1992). Remembering pictures: Pleasure and arousal in memory. *Journal of Experimental Psychology: Learning Memory and Cognition, 18,* 379–390.

Brannon, L.A., & Brock, T.C. (1994). The subliminal persuasion controversy. In S. Shavitt & T.C. Brock (Eds.), *Persuasion: Psychological insights and perspectives* (pp. 279–293). Needham Heights, MA: Allyn & Bacon.

Bransford, J.D., & Johnson, M.K. (1972). Contextual prerequisites for understanding: Some investigations of comprehension and recall. *Journal of Verbal Learning and Verbal Behavior, 11,* 717–726.

Braun, K.A., Ellis, R., & Loftus, E.F. (2002). Make my memory: How advertising can change our memories of the past. *Psychology & Marketing, 19,* 1–23.

Breckler, S.J., & Wiggins, E.C. (1989). On defining attitude and attitude theory: Once more with feeling. In A.R. Pratkanis, S.J. Breckler, & A.G. Greenwald (Eds.), *Attitude structure and function* (pp. 407–427). Hillsdale, NJ: Lawrence Erlbaum Associates.

Brewer, M.B. (2001). The many faces of social identity: Implications for political psychology. *Political Psychology, 22,* 115–125.

Brewer, M.B., & Gardner, W. (1996). Who is this 'We'? Levels of collective identity and self representation. *Journal of Personality and Social Psychology, 71,* 83–93.

Bridges, J.S. (1993). Pink or blue: Gender stereotypic perceptions of infants as conveyed by birth congratulations cards. *Psychology of Women Quarterly, 17,* 193–205.

British Toy and Hobby Association (2007). UK toy industry worth £2.2 billion after strong performance in 2006. Retrieved 5 October 2008 from http://www.btha.co.uk/press/industry_worth.php?PHPSESSID=edfb519a1697e943767e86abdbd0e181

Brown, J.A. (2001). Media literacy and critical television viewing in education. In D.G. Singer & J.L. Singer (Eds.), *Handbook of children and the media* (pp. 681–697). Thousand Oaks, CA: Sage Publications.

Brunel, F.F., Tietje, B.C., & Greenwald, A.G. (2004). Is the Implicit Association Test a valid and valuable measure of implicit consumer social cognition? *Journal of Consumer Psychology, 14,* 385–404.

Brutt, H., & Crockett, T. (1928). A technique for psychological study of poster board advertising and some preliminary results. *Journal of Applied Psychology, 12,* 43–55.

Brynjolfsson, E., & Smith, M. D. (2000). Frictionless commerce? A comparison of internet and conventional retailers. *Management Science, 46,* 4.

Buckley, K.W. (1989). *Mechanical man: John Broadus Watson and the beginnings of behaviorism.* New York: Guilford Press.

Buffardi, L.E., & Campbell, W.K. (2008). Narcissism and social networking web sites. *Personality and Social Psychology Bulletin, 34,* 1303–1314.

Bundesen, C., & Pedersen, L.F. (1983). Color segregation and visual search, *Perception and Psychophysics, 33*, 487–493.

Burke, R.R., & Srull, T.K. (1988). Competitive interference and consumer memory for advertising. *Journal of Consumer Research, 15*, 55–68.

Busch, P.S., & Houston, M.J. (1985). *Marketing strategic foundations*. Homewood, IL: Richard D. Irwin.

Bushman, B.J., & Anderson, C.A. (2001). Media violence and the American public: Scientific facts versus media misinformation. *American Psychologist, 56*, 477–489.

Bushman, B.J. & Bonacci, A.M. (2002). Violence and sex impair memory for television ads. *Journal of Applied Psychology, 87*, 557–564.

Bushman, B.J., & Huesmann, L.R. (2001). Effects of televised violence on aggression. In D.G. Singer & J.L. Singer (Eds.), *Handbook of children and the media* (pp. 223–254). Thousand Oaks, CA: Sage.

Bushnell, E.W., & Boudreau, J.P. (1991). The development of haptic perception during infancy. In M.A. Heller & W. Schiff (Eds.), *The psychology of touch* (pp. 139–161). Hillsdale, NJ: Lawrence Erlbaum Associates.

Business Wire. (1998). Unveils Internet's first real-time 3D chat technology. Retrieved December 3, 1998, from www.businesswire.com

Caballero, M.J., & Pride, W.M. (1984). Selected effects of salesperson sex and attractiveness in direct mail advertisements. *Journal of Marketing, 48*, 94–100.

Cacioppo, J.T., Petty, R.E., Kao, C.F., & Rodriguez, R. (1986). Central and peripheral routes to persuasion: An individual difference perspective. *Journal of Personality and Social Psychology, 51*, 1032–1043.

Campbell, C. (1987). *The romantic ethic and the spirit of modern consumerism*. New York: Basil Blackwell.

Campbell, C. (2004). I shop therefore I know that I am. The metaphysical basis of modern consumption. In K. Ekström & H. Brembeck (Eds.), *Elusive consumption* (pp. 27–44). Oxford: Berg.

Campbell, D.T. (1975). On the conflicts between biological and social evolution and between psychology and moral tradition. *American Psychologist, 30*, 1103–1126.

Campbell, W.K., & Foster, J.D. (2007). The narcissistic self: Background, an extended agency model, and ongoing controversies. In C. Sedikides, & S. Spencer (Eds.), *Frontier in social psychology: The self* (pp. 115–138). Philadelphia, PA: Psychology Press.

Cantril, H., & Allport, G.W. (1935). *The psychology of radio*. New York: Harpers and Brothers.

Carlson, J.G., & Hatfield, E. (1992). *Psychology of emotion*. New York: Harcourt Brace Jovanovich.

Carlson, N.R. (1987). *Discovering psychology*. London: Allyn & Bacon.

Carmon, Z., Wertenbroch, K., & Zeelenberg, M. (2003). Option attachment: When deliberating makes choosing feel like losing. *Journal of Consumer Research, 30*, 15–29.

Cartwright, D., & Harary, F. (1956). Structural balance: A generalisation of Heider's theory. *Psychological Review, 63*, 277–293.

Celsi, R.L., & Olson, J.C. (1988). The role of involvement in attention and comprehension processes. *Journal of Consumer Research, 15*, 210–224.

Cerella, J. (1985). Information processing rates in the elderly. *Psychological Bulletin, 98*, 67–83.

Chaffee, S.H., Jackson-Beeck, M., Durall, J., & Wilson, D. (1977). Mass communication in political communication. In S.A. Renshon (Ed.), *Handbook of political socialization: Theory and research* (pp. 223–258). New York: Free Press.

Chaiken, S. (1980). Heuristic versus systematic information processing and the use of source versus message cues in persuasion. *Journal of Personality and Social Psychology, 39*, 752–766.

Chaiken, S. (1987). The heuristic model of persuasion. In M.P. Zanna, J.M. Olsen & C.P. Herman (Eds.), *Social influence: The Ontario symposium* (vol. 5, pp. 3–39). Hillsdale, NJ: Lawrence Erlbaum Associates.

Chaiken, S., Liberman, A., & Eagly, A.H. (1989). Heuristic and systematic processing within and beyond the persuasion context. In J.S. Uleman & J.A. Barg (Eds.), *Unintended thought* (pp. 215–252). New York: Guilford Press.

Chaiken, S., & Maheswaran, D. (1994). Heuristic processing can bias systematic processing: Effects of source credibility, argument ambiguity, and task importance on attitude judgement. *Journal of Personality and Social Psychology, 66,* 460–473.

Chang, L.C., & Arkin, R.M. (2002). Materialism as an attempt to cope with uncertainty. *Psychology & Marketing, 19,* 389–406.

Chaplin, L.N., & John, D.R. (2007). Growing up in a material world: Age differences in materialism in children and adolescents. *Journal of Consumer Research, 34,* 480–493.

Chattopadhyay, A., Dahl, D.W., Ritchie, R.J.B., & Shahin, K.N. (2003). Hearing voices: The impact of announcer speech characteristics on consumer response to broadcast advertising. *Journal of Consumer Psychology, 13,* 198–204.

Chebat, J-C., Chebat, C.G., & Vaillant, D. (2001). Environmental background music and in-store selling. *Journal of Business Research, 54,* 115–123.

Chebat, J-C. & Michon, R. (2003). Impact of ambient odors on mall shoppers' emotions, cognition, and spending: A test of competitive causal theories, *Journal of Business Research, 56,* 529–539.

Chernev, A. (2001). The impact of common features on consumer preferences: A case of confirmatory reasoning. *Journal of Consumer Research, 27,* 475–488.

Chiang, K-P., & Dholakia, R.R. (2003). Factors driving consumer intention to shop online: An empirical investigation. *Journal of Consumer Psychology, 13,* 177–183.

Childers, T.L., & Houston, M.J. (1984). Conditions for a picture-superiority effect on consumer memory. *Journal of Consumer Research, 11,* 643–654.

Christakis, D.A., & Zimmerman, F.J. (2006). Early television viewing is associated with protesting turning off the television at age 6. *Medscape General Medicine, 8,* 63.

Christensen, T., Godskesen, M., Gram-Hanssen, K., Quitzau, M-B, & Røpke, I. (2007). Greening the Danes? Experience with consumption and environment policies. *Journal of Consumer Policies, 30,* 91–116.

Christenson, G.A., Faber, R.J., de Zwaan, M., Raymond, N.C., Specker, S.M., Ekern, M.D. et al. (1994). Compulsive buying: descriptive characteristics and psychiatric comorbidity. *Journal of Clinical Psychiatry, 55,* 5–11.

Christenson, P.G. (1982). Children's perceptions of TV commercials and products: The effects of PSAs. *Communication Research, 9,* 491–524.

Cialdini, R.B. (1993). *Influence: Science and practice.* New York: HarperCollins.

Cialdini, R.B., Cacioppo, J.T., Bassett, R., & Miller, J.A. (1978). Low-ball procedure for producing compliance: Commitment then cost. *Journal of Personality and Social Psychology, 36,* 463–476.

Citrin, A.V., Stem, D.E., Spangenberg, E.R., & Clark, M.J. (2003). Consumer need for tactile input: An internet retailing challenge. *Journal of Business Research, 56,* 915–922.

Clark, M.D., & Teasdale, J.D. (1982). Diurnal variation in clinical depression and accessibility of memories of positive and negative experiences. *Journal of Abnormal Psychology, 91,* 87–95.

Clements, D.H., & Nastasi, B.K. (1992). Computers and early childhood education. In M. Gettinger, S.N. Elliott, & T.R. Kratochwill (Eds.), *Advances in school psychology: Preschool and early childhood treatment directions* (pp. 187–246). Hillsdale, NJ: Lawrence Erlbaum Associates.

Clifford, B.R., Gunter, B. & McAleer, J. (1995). *Program evaluation, comprehension and impact.* Hillsdale, NJ: Lawrence Erlbaum Associates.

Cline, T.W., & Kellaris, J.J. (2007). The influence of humor strength and humor-message relatedness on ad memorability. *Journal of Advertising, 36,* 55–67.

CNN (2006). *MySpace cowboys.* Retrieved August 15, 2006, from http://money.cnn.com/magazines/fortune/fortune_archive/2006/09/04/8384727/index.htm

Cohen, J.B., & Andrade, E.B. (2004). Affective intuition and task-contingent affect regulation. *Journal of Consumer Research, 31,* 358–367.

Cohen, J.B., Tuan Pham, M., & Andrade, E.B. (2008). The nature and role of affect in consumer behaviour. In C.P. Haugtvedt, P.M. Herr & F.R. Kardes (Eds.), *Handbook of consumer psychology* (pp. 297–348). New York: Lawrence Erlbaum Associates.

Cohen, P. & Cohen, J. (1996). *Life values and adolescent mental health.* Mahwah, NJ: Lawrence Erlbaum Associates.

Cohen, S., & Horm-Wingerd, D. (1993). Children and the environment: Ecological awareness among preschool children. *Environment and Behavior, 25,* 103–120.

Cole, C.A., & Balasubramanian, S.K. (1993). Age differences in consumers' search for information: Public policy implications. *Journal of Consumer Research, 20,* 157–169.

Collins, A.M., & Loftus, E.F. (1975). A spreading-activation theory of semantic processing. *Psychological Review, 82,* 407–428.

Collis, B.A. (1996). *Children and computers at school.* Mahwah, NJ: Lawrence Erlbaum Associates.

CommerceNet (1999). *World wide statistics.* Retrieved August 16, 1999 from www.commerce.net/research/stats/wwstats.html

Comstock, G., & Scharrer, E. (2001). The use of television and other film-related media. In D.G. Singer & J.L. Singer (Eds.), *Handbook of children and the media.* Thousand Oaks, CA: Sage Publications.

Costley, C., Das, S., & Brucks, M. (1997). Presentation medium and spontaneous imaging effects on consumer memory. *Journal of Consumer Psychology, 6,* 211–232.

Cowan, R.S. (1983). *More work for mother: The ironies of household technology from the open hearth to the microwave.* New York: Basic Books.

Cowley, E., & Janus, E. (2004). Not necessarily better but certainly different: A limit to the advertising misinformation effect on memory. *Journal of Consumer Research, 31,* 229–235.

Cowley, E., & Mitchell, A.A. (2003). The moderating effect of product knowledge on the learning and organization of product information. *Journal of Consumer Research, 30,* 443–454.

Craik, F.I.M. (1986). A functional account of age differences in memory. In F. Klix & H. Hagendorf (Eds.), *Human memory and cognitive capabilities, mechanisms and performances* (pp. 409–422). New York: Elsevier.

Crespo, C.J., Smit, E., Troiano, R., Bartlett, S.J., Macera, C.A., & Andersen, R.E. (2001). Television watching, energy intake, and obesity in U.S. children: Results from the third national health and nutrition examination survey, 1988–1994. *Archives of Pediatric and Adolescent Medicine, 155,* 360–365.

Crockett, R.O. (2000). Surfing in tongues. *Business Week,* Dec. 11, 18.

Cronley, M.L., Posavac, S.S., Meyer, T., Kardes, F.R., & Kellaris, J.J. (2005). A selective hypothesis testing perspective on price-quality inference inference-based choice. *Journal of Consumer Psychology, 15,* 159–169.

Cross, S.E., Bacon, P.L., & Morris, M.L. (2000). The relational-interdependent self-construal and relationships. *Journal of Personality and Social Psychology, 78,* 791–808.

Csikszentmihalyi, M. (1999). If we are so rich, why aren't we happy? *American Psychologist, 54,* 821–827.

Csikszentmihalyi, M. (2000). The cost and benefits of consuming. *Journal of Consumer Research, 27,* 267–272.

Csikszentmihalyi, M., & Rochberg-Halton, E. (1981). *The meaning of things: Domestic symbols and the self.* Cambridge: Cambridge University Press.

Cynkar, A. (2007). Socially wired. *Monitor on Psychology, 38,* 47–49.

Dahl, D.W., Frankenberger, K.D., & Manchanda, R.V. (2003). Does it pay to shock? Reactions to shocking and nonshocking advertising content among university students. *Journal of Advertising Research, 43,* 268–280.

Damasio, A.R. (1994). *Descartes' error: Emotion, reason and the human brain.* New York: Grosset/Putnam.

Darwin, C.J., Turvey, M.T., & Crowder, R.G. (1972). An auditory analogue of the Sperling partial report procedure: Evidence for brief auditory storage. *Cognitive Psychology, 3,* 255–267.

Davies, G.M., & Patel, D. (2005). The influence of car and driver stereotypes on attributions of vehicle speed, position on the road, and capability in road accident scenario. *Legal and Criminological Psychology, 10,* 45–62.

Davies, P.G., Spencer, S.J., Quinn, D.M., & Gerhardstein, R. (2002). Consuming images: How television commercials that elicit stereotype threat can restrain women academically and professionally. *Personality and Social Psychology Bulletin, 28,* 1615–1628.

Decci, E.L., & Ryan, R.M. (1985). *Intrinsic motivation and self-determination in human behaviour.* New York: Plenum.

Deci, E.L. (1971). Effects of externally mediated rewards on intrinsic motivation. *Journal of Personality and Social Psychology, 18,* 105–115.

Deci, E.L. (1972). The effects of contingent and noncontingent rewards and controls on intrinsic motivation. *Organizational Behavior and Human Performance, 8,* 217–229.

Defra (2004). Waste management in the EU. Retrieved May 12, 2004 from http://www.defra.gov.uk

Denburg, N.L., Tranel, D., & Bechara, A. (2005). The ability to decide advantageously declines prematurely in some older persons. *Neuropsychologica, 43,* 1099–1106.

Derry, S.J. (1990). Learning strategies for acquiring useful knowledge. In B. Jones & L. Idol (Eds.), *Dimensions of thinking and cognitive instruction.* Hillsdale, NJ: Lawrence Erlbaum Associates.

Derscheid, L.E., Kwon, Y., & Fang, S. (1996). Preschoolers' socialization as consumers of clothing and recognition of symbolism. *Perceptual and Motor Skills, 82,* 1171–1181.

Desmeules, R. (2002). The impact of variety on consumer happiness: Marketing and the tyranny of freedom. *Academy of Marketing Science Review,* 1–20.

de Veer, M., Gallup, G.G., Theall, L.A., van den Bos, R., & Povinelli, D.J. (2003). An 8-year longitudinal study of mirror self-recognition in chimpanzees. *Neuropsychologica, 41,* 229–234.

De Vries, J. (1975). Peasant demand patterns and economic development: Friesland, 1550–1750. In W.N. Parker & E.L. Jones (Eds.), *European peasants and their markets: Essays in agrarian economic history.* Princeton, NJ: Princeton University Press.

De Wick, H. (1935). The relative effectiveness of visual and auditory presentations of advertising material. *Journal of Applied Psychology, 19,* 245–264.

Dick, A., Chakravarti, D., & Biehal, G. (1990). Memory-based inferences during choice. *Journal of Consumer Research, 117,* 82–93.

Dickinson, A. (1980). *Contemporary animal learning theory.* Cambridge: Cambridge University Press.

Dickinson, S., & Holmes, M. (2008). Understanding the emotional and coping responses of adolescent individuals exposed to threat appeals. *International Journal of Advertising, 27,* 251–278.

Diehl, K., & Poynor, C. (in press) Great expectations ?! Assortment size, expectations and satisfaction. *Journal of Marketing Research.*

Diener, E., & Biswas-Diener, R. (2002). Will money increase subjective well-being? *Social Indicators Research, 57,* 119–169.

Dion, K., Berscheid, E., & Walster, E. (1972). What is beautiful is good. *Journal of Personality and Social Psychology, 24,* 285–290.

Dittmar, H. (1992). *The social psychology of material possessions: To have is to be.* Hemel Hempstead: Harvester Wheatsheaf.

Dittmar, H. (2004a). Are you what you have? Consumer society and our sense of identity. *Psychologist, 17,* 206–210.

Dittmar, H. (2004b). Understanding and diagnosing compulsive buying. In R. Coombs (Ed.), *Handbook of addictive disorders: A practical guide to diagnosis and treatment* (pp. 411–450). New York: Wiley.

Dittmar, H. (2008a). I shop therefore I am? Compulsive buying and identity seeking. In H. Dittmar (Ed.), *Consumer culture, identity and well-being* (pp. 95–120). Hove: Psychology Press.

Dittmar, H. (2008b). Understanding the impact of consumer culture. In H. Dittmar (Ed.), *Consumer culture, identity and well-being* (pp. 1–23). Hove: Psychology Press.

Dittmar, H., & Beatty, J. (1998). Impulsive and excessive buying behaviour. In P. Taylor-Gooby (Ed.), *Choice and public policy: The limits to welfare markets* (pp. 123–144). London Macmillan.

Dittmar, H., Halliwell, E., & Ive, S. (2006). Does Barbie make girls want to be thin? The effect of experimental exposure to images of dolls on the body image of 5- to 8-year old girls. *Developmental Psychology, 42,* 283–292.

Dittmar, H., & Howard, S. (2004). Thin-ideal internalization and social comparison tendency as moderators of media models' impact on women's body-focused anxiety. *Journal of Social and Clinical Psychology, 23,* 747–770.

Dodge, A.F. (1938). What are the personality traits of the successful sales-person? *Journal of Applied Psychology, 22,* 229–238.

Doll, J., & Ajzen, I. (1992). Accessibility and stability of predictors in the theory of planned behaviour. *Journal of Personality and Social Psychology, 63*, 754–765.

Donahue, E.M., Robins, R.W., Roberts, B.W., & John, O.P. (1993). The divided self: Concurrent and longitudinal effects of psychological adjustment and social roles on self-concept differentiation. *Journal of Personality and Social Psychology, 64*, 834–846.

Donnerstein, E., & Berkowitz, L. (1981). Victim reactions in aggressive erotic films as a factor in violence against women. *Journal of Personality and Social Psychology, 41*, 710–724.

Dougherty, M.R.P., Gronlund, S.D., & Gettys, C.F. (2003). Memory as a fundamental heuristic for decision-making. In S.L. Schneider & J. Shanteau (Eds.), *Emerging perspectives on judgment and decision research* (pp. 125–164). New York: Cambridge University Press.

Drabman, R.S., & Thomas, M.H. (1974). Does media violence increase children's toleration of real-life aggression? *Developmental Psychology, 10*, 418–421.

Drentea, P., & Lavrakas, P.J. (2000). Over the limit: The association among health, race and development. *Social Science and Medicine, 50*, 517–529.

Dube, L., Chebat, J-C., & Morin, S. (1995). The effect of background music on consumers' desire to affiliate in buyer seller interactions. *Psychology & Marketing, 12*, 305–319.

Dudley, S.C. (1999). Consumer attitudes toward nudity in advertising. *Journal of Marketing Theory and Practice, 79*, 89–96.

Du Nann Winter, D. (2000). Some big ideas for some big problems. *American Psychologist, 55*, 516–522.

Du Nann Winter, D. (2003). Shopping for sustainability: Psychological solutions to overconsumption. In T. Kasser & A.D. Kanner (Eds.), *Psychology and consumer culture: The struggle for a good life in a materialistic world* (pp. 69–87). Washington, DC: American Psychological Association.

Dunlap, R.E., & Mertig, A.G. (1995). Global concern for the environment: Is affluence a prerequisite? *Journal of Social Issues, 51*, 121–137.

Dunn, S. (2000). Global temperature drops. In L.R. Brown, M. Renner, & B. Halweil (Eds.), *Vital signs, 2000: The environmental trends that are shaping our future* (pp. 64–65). New York: Norton.

Durkin, K. (1985a). Television and sex-role acquisition: Effects. *British Journal of Social Psychology, 24*, 191–210.

Durkin, K. (1985b). Television and sex-role acquisition: Content. *British Journal of Social Psychology, 24*, 101–113.

Dürr, H.P. (1994). Sustainable, equitable economics, the personal energy budget. In P.B. Smith, S.E. Okoye, J. de Wilde & P. Deshnkar (Eds.), *The world at the crossroads, Towards a sustainable, equitable and liveable world*. London: Earthscan.

Dutton, D.G., & Aron, A.P. (1974). Some evidence for heightened sexual attraction under conditions of high anxiety. *Journal of Personality and Social Psychology, 30*, 510–517.

Dwyer, W.O., Leeming, F.C., Cobern, M.K., Porter, B.E., & Jackson, J.M. (1993). Critical review of behavioral interventions to preserve the environment: Research since 1980. *Environment and Behavior, 25*, 275–321.

Eagly, A.H., & Chaiken, S. (1975). An attributional analysis of the effect of communicator characteristics on opinion change: The case of communicator attractiveness. *Journal of Personality and Social Psychology, 32*, 136–144.

Eagly, A.H., & Chaiken, S. (1998). Attitude structure and function. In D.T. Gilbert, S.T. Fiske & G. Lindzey (Eds.), *The handbook of social psychology* (vol. 1, 4th ed. pp. 269–322). Boston: McGraw-Hill.

Earth Policy Institute (2002). Water scarcity spreading. Retrieved 12 June 2008 from http://www.earth-policy.org/Indicators/indicator7.htm

Easterlin, R. (1995). Will raising the incomes of all increase the happiness of all? *Journal of Economic Behavior and Organization, 27*, 35–47.

Easterlin, R.A. (2001). Income and happiness: Towards an unified theory. *Economic Journal, 111*, 465–484.

Eccles, J.S. (1987). Gender roles and women's achievement-related decisions. *Psychology of Women Quarterly, 11*, 135–172.

Edell, J.A., & Burke, M.C. (1987). The power of feelings in understanding advertising effects. *Journal of Consumer Research, 14,* 421–433.

Edney, J.J. (1980). The commons problem: Alternative perspectives. *American Psychologist, 35,* 131–150.

Edwards, S., & Shackley, M. (1992). Measuring the effectiveness of retail window display as an element of the marketing mix. *International Journal of Advertising, 11,* 193–202.

Effective Advertising 8 (2006). Sydney: Advertising Federation of Australia Advertising Effectiveness Awards.

Eibl-Eibesfeldt, I. (1988). The biological foundation of aesthetics. In I. Rentschler, B. Herzberger & D. Epstein (Eds.), *Beauty and the brain: Biological aspects of aesthetics* (pp. 29–55). Basel: Birkhäuser Verlag.

Eighmey, J., & Sar, S. (2007). Harlow Gale and the origins of the psychology of advertising. *Journal of Advertising, 36,* 147–158.

Elster, J., & Loewenstein, G. (1992). Utility from memory and anticipation. In G. Loewenstein & J. Elster (Eds.), *Choice over time* (pp. 213–234). New York: Russell Sage Foundation.

Emmons, R.A. (1996). Striving and feeling: Personal goals and subjective well-being. In P.M. Gollwitzer & J.A. Bargh (Eds.), *The psychology of action* (pp. 313–337). New York: Guilford.

Engel, J.F., Kollat, D.T., & Blackwell, R.D. (1968). *Consumer behaviour.* New York: Holt, Rinehart and Winston.

Englis, B.G., & Solomon, M.R. (1995). To be and not to be: Lifestyle imagery, reference groups, and the clustering of America. *Journal of Advertising, 24,* 13–28.

Erikson, E. (1968). *Identity: Youth and crisis.* London: Faber.

Ernst, M.O., & Banks, M.S. (2002). Using visual and haptic information for discriminating objects. *Perception, 31,* (supplement), 147b.

Ernst, M.O., Banks, M.S., & Bulthoff, H.H. (2000). Touch can change visual slant perception. *Nature Neuroscience, 3,* 69–73.

Ernst & Young (1999). *The second annual Internet shopping study.* Retrieved 18 October 2000, from http://ey.com/publicate/consumer/pdf/Internetshopp.pdf

Eysenck, M.W. (1993). *Principles of cognitive psychology.* Hove: Erlbaum.

Faber, R.J. (2003). Self-control and compulsive buying. In T. Kasser & A.D. Kanner (Eds.), *Psychology and consumer culture: The struggle for a good life in a materialistic world* (pp. 169–189). Washington, DC: American Psychological Association.

Faber, R.J., & O'Guinn, T.C. (1992). A clinical screener for compulsive buying. *Journal of Consumer Research, 19,* 459–469.

Faber, R.J., O'Guinn, T.C., & Krych, R. (1987). Compulsive consumption. In M. Wallendorf & P. Anderson (Eds.), *Advances in consumer research* (pp.132–135). Provo, UT: Association for Consumer Research.

Fairchilds, C. (1998). Consumption in early modern Europe: A review article. *Comparative Studies in Society and History, 35,* 850–858.

Fallon, A.E., & Rozin, P. (1985). Sex differences in perceptions of desirable body shape. *Journal of Abnormal Psychology, 94,* 102–105.

Fazio, R.H. (1986). How do attitudes guide behaviour? In R.M. Sorrentiono & E.T. Higgins (Eds.), *Handbook of social behaviour.* New York: Guilford.

Fazio, R.H. (1989). On the power and functionality of attitudes: The role of attitude accessibility. In A.R. Ptratkanis, S. Breckler, & A.G. Greenwald (Eds.), *Attitude, structure and function* (pp. 153–179). Hillsdale, NJ: Lawrence Erlbaum Associates.

Fazio, R.H. (1990). Multiple processes by which attitudes guide behaviour: The MODE model as an integrative framework. In M.P. Zanna (Ed.), *Advances in experimental social psychology* (vol. 23, pp 75–109). New York: Academic Press.

Fazio, R.H. (1995). Attitudes as object-evaluation associations: Determinants, consequences, and correlates of attitude accessibility. In R.E. Petty & J.A. Krosnick (Eds.), *Attitude strength: Antecedents and consequences* (pp. 247–282). Mahwah, NJ: Lawrence Erlbaum Associates.

Fazio, R.H., Blaschovich, J., & Driscoll, D.M. (1992). On the functional value of attitudes: The influence of accessible attitudes upon the ease and quality of decision making. *Personality and Social Psychology Bulletin, 18*, 388–401.

Fazio, R.H., Chen, J-M., McDonel, E.C., & Sherman, S.J. (1981). Attitude accessibility, attitude–behavior consistency, and the strength of the object–evaluation association. *Journal of Experimental Social Psychology, 18*, 339–357.

Fazio, R.H., & Olson, M.A. (2003). Implicit measures in social cognition research: Their meaning and uses. *Annual Review of Psychology, 54*, 297–327.

Fazio, R.H., Sanbonmatsu, D.M., Powell, M.C., & Kardes, F.R. (1986). On the automatic activation of attitudes. *Journal of Personality and Social Psychology, 50*, 229–238.

Fazio, R.H., & Zanna, M.P. (1978). Attitudinal qualities relating to the strength of the attitude–behaviour relation. *Journal of Experimental Social Psychology, 14*, 398–408.

Feather, N.T. (1959). Subjective probability and decision under uncertainty. *Psychological Review, 66*, 150–164.

Feinberg, R.A. (1986). Credit cards as spending facilitating stimuli: A Conditioning Interpretation. *Journal of Consumer Research, 12*, 384–356.

Feldman, J.M., & Lynch, J.G. (1988). Self generated validity and other effects of measurement on belief, attitude, intention, and behavior. *Journal of Applied Psychology, 73*, 421–435.

Feldwick, P. (1990). *Advertising works 5*. Henley-on-Thames: Institute of Practitioners in Advertising, NTC Publications.

Ferguson, L.W. (1934). Preferred positions of advertisements in the *Saturday Evening Post*. *Journal of Applied Psychology, 18*, 749–756.

Ferguson, L.W. (1935). The importance of the mechanical features of an advertisement. *Journal of Applied Psychology, 19*, 521–526.

Fessler, D.M.T., Pillsworth, E.G., & Flamson, T.J. (2004). Angry men and disgusted women: An evolutionary approach to the influence of emotions on risk taking. *Organizational Behavior and Human Decision Processes, 95*, 107–123.

Festinger, L. (1954). A theory of social comparison processes. *Human Relations, 7*, 117–140.

Festinger, L. (1957). *A theory of cognitive dissonance*. Evanston, IL: Row and Peterson.

Festinger, L., & Carlsmith, J.M., (1959). Cognitive consequences of forced compliance. *Journal of Abnormal and Social Psychology, 58*, 203–210.

Finlay, K., Marmurek, H.H.C., & Morton, R. (2005). Priming effects in explicit and implicit memory for textual advertisements. *Applied Psychology, 54*, 442–455.

Finucane, M.L., Peters, E., & Slovic, P. (2003). Judgment and decision-making: The dance of affect and reason. In S.L. Schneider & J. Shanteau (Eds.), *Emerging perspectives on judgement and decision research* (pp. 327–364). New York: Cambridge University Press.

Fischhoff, B., Lichtenstein, S., Slovic, P., Derby, S.L., & Keeney, R.L. (1981). *Acceptable risk*. New York: Cambridge University Press.

Fishbein, M. (1963). An investigation of the relationships between beliefs about an object and the attitude toward that object. *Human Relations, 16*, 233–240.

Fishbein, M. (1967). A consideration of beliefs and their role in attitude measurement. In M. Fishbein (Ed.), *Readings in attitude theory and measurement* (pp. 257–266). New York: Wiley.

Fishbein, M., & Ajzen, I. (1975). *Belief, attitude, intention and behaviour: An introduction to theory and research*. Reading, MA: Addison-Wesley.

Fishurn, P.C. (1974). Lexicographic orders, utilities and decision rules: A survey. *Management Science, 20*, 142–147.

Flavin, C., & Dunn, S. (1999). Reinventing the energy system. In L.R. Brown, C. Flavin, H. French, J. Abramovitz, S. Dunn, G. Gardner, et al., *State of the world 1999* (pp. 22–40). New York: Norton.

Forgas, J.P., & Bower, G.H. (1987). Mood effects on person-perception judgements. *Journal of Personality and Social Psychology, 53*, 53–60.

Fox, J. (2000). The triumph of English. *Fortune*, Sept. 18, 209–212.

Fox, S. (1984). *The mirror makers*. New York: Morrow.

Foxnews (2006). *Angry students lash out at Facebook.com privacy changes.* Retrieved 9 September 2006 from http://72.14.209.104/search?q_cache:G27bD-yC8BUJ:www.foxnews.com/story/0,293

Foxx, R.M., & Hake, D.F. (1977). Gasoline conservation: A procedure for measuring and reducing the driving of college students. *Journal of Applied Behavior Analysis, 10,* 61–74.

Francis, L. (1994). Laughter the best mediation: Humor as emotional management in interaction. *Symbolic Interaction, 17,* 147–163.

Frank, R.H. (1999). *Luxury fever: Why money fails to satisfy in an era of success.* New York: Oxford University Press.

Freitas, A., Kaiser, S., Chandler, J., Hall, C., Jung-Won, K., & Hammidi, T. (1997). Appearance management as border construction: Least favourite clothing, group distancing, and identity . . . not! *Sociological Inquiry, 67,* 323–335.

Frey, B.S., Benesch, C., & Stutzer, A. (2007). Does watching TV make us happy? *Journal of Economic Psychology, 28,* 283–313.

Frey, B.S., & Stutzer, A. (2002). What can economists learn form happiness research? *Journal of Economic Literature, 40,* 402–435.

Frey, B.S., & Stutzer, A. (2004). *Economic consequences of misprediciting utility.* IEW Working Paper No. 218.

Frey, D. (1986). Recent research on selective exposure to information. In L. Berkowitz (Ed.), *Advances in experimental psychology* (vol. 19, pp. 41–80). New York: Academic Press.

Frey, D., & Rosch, M. (1984). Information seeking after decisions: The roles of novelty of information and decision reversibility. *Personality and Social Psychology Bulletin, 10,* 91–98.

Frey, K.P., & Eagly, A.H. (1993). Vividness can undermine the persuasiveness of messages. *Journal of Personality and Social Psychology, 65,* 32–44.

Fried, C.B., & Johanson, J.C. (2008). Sexual and violent media's inhibition of advertisement memory: effect or artefact? *Journal of Applied Social Psychology, 38,* 1716–1735.

Friedman, H.H., Santeramo, M.J., & Traina, A. (1978). Correlates of trustworthiness for celebrities. *Journal of the Academy of Marketing Science, 6,* 291–299.

Friedman, M.A., & Brownell, K.D. (1995). Psychological correlates of obesity: Moving to the next research generation. *Psychological Bulletin, 117,* 3–20.

Frijda, N.H. (1986). *The emotions.* Cambridge: Cambridge University Press.

Frijda, N.H. (1993). Moods, emotions episodes, and emotions. In M.L. Haviland & J.M. Haviland (Eds.), *Handbook of emotions.* New York: Guilford.

Funk, J.B. (1993). Re-evaluating the impact of video games. *Clinical Paediatrics,* February, 86–90.

Gagnon, J.P., & Osterhaus, J.T. (1985). Research note: The effectiveness of floor displays on the sales of retail products. *Journal of Retailing, 61,* 104–116.

Gao, F., & Su, L. (2007). Internet addiction among Chinese adolescents: prevalence and psychological features. *Child Care Health & Development, 33,* 275–281.

Garber, L.L., & Hyatt, E.M. (2003). Color as a tool for visual persuasion. In L.M. Scott & R. Batra (Eds.), *Persuasive imagery: A consumer response perspective* (pp. 313–336). Mahwah, NJ: Lawrence Erlbaum Associates.

Gardner, B.B., & Levy, S.J. (1955). The product and the brand. *Harvard Business Review, 5,* 33–39.

Garner, R. (2005). What's in a name? Persuasion perhaps. *Journal of Consumer Psychology, 15,* 108–116.

Geer, J.H., Judice, S., & Jackson, S. (1994). Reading times for erotic material: The pause to reflect. *The Journal of General Psychology, 121,* 345–352.

Geer, J.H., & Melton, J.S. (1997). Sexual content-induced delay with double-entendre words. *Archives of Sexual Behavior, 26,* 295–316.

Gelb, B.D., & Zinkhan, G. M. (1986). Humor and advertising effectiveness after repeated exposure to a radio commercial. *Journal of Advertising, 15,* 15–34.

Geller, E. S. (1980). Applications of behavioral analysis for litter control. In D. Glenwick & L. Jason (Eds.), *Behavioral community psychology: Progress and prospects* (pp. 254–283). New York: Praeger.

Geller, E.S. (1981). Evaluating energy conservation programs: Is verbal report enough? *Journal of Consumer Research, 8,* 331–335.

Geller, E.S. (1987). Applied behavior analysis and environmental psychology: From strange bedfellows to a productive marriage. In D. Stokols & I. Airman (Eds.), *Handbook of environmental psychology* (vol. 1, pp. 361–388). New York: Wiley.

Geller, E.S., Winnett, R.A., & Everett, P.B. (1982). *Preserving the environment: New strategies for behavior change.* New York: Pergamon.

Gerbner, G., Gross, L., Morgan, M., & Signorielli, N. (1994). Growing up with television: The cultivation perspective. In J. Bryant & D. Zillman (Eds.), *Media effects: Advances in theory and research.* Hillsdale, NJ: Lawrence Erlbaum Associates.

Geyskens, I., Gielsen, K.J.P., & Dekimpe, M.G. (2002). The marketing valuation of internet channel additions. *Journal of Marketing, 66,* 102–119.

Giner-Sorolla, R., & Chaiken, S. (1997). Selective use of heuristic and systematic processing under defence motivation. *Personality and Social Psychology Bulletin, 23,* 84–97.

Ginsburg, H.P., & Opper, S. (1988). *Piaget's theory of intellectual development.* Englewood Cliffs, NJ: Prentice Hall.

Glanzer, M., and Cunitz, A.R. (1966). Two storage mechanisms in free recall. *Journal of Verbal Learning and Verbal Behavior, 5,* 351–360.

Glick, D., Keene-Osborn, S., Gegax, T.T., Bai, M., Clemetson, L., Gordon, D., et al. (1999). Anatomy of a massacre. *Newsweek,* May, *3,* p. 24.

Godden, D.R., & Baddeley, A.D. (1975). Context-dependent memory in two natural environments: On land and underwater. *British Journal of Psychology, 66,* 325–332.

Goethals, G.R., & Nelson, R.E. (1973). Similarity in the influence process: The belief-value distinction. *Journal of Personality and Social Psychology, 25,* 117–122.

Goffman, E. (1959). *The presentation of self in everyday life.* Garden City, NY: Doubleday.

Goldberg, M.E., & Gorn, G.J. (1974). Children's reactions to television advertising: An experimental approach. *Journal of Consumer Research, 1,* 69–75.

Goldsmith, R.E., & Flynn, L.R. (1995). The domain-specific innovativeness scale: Theoretical and practical dimensions. *Proceedings of the Association of Marketing Theory and Practice, 177*–182.

Goldstein, J.H. (1994). Sex differences in toy play and use of video games. In J.H. Goldstein (Ed.), *Toys, play and child development.* Cambridge: Cambridge University Press.

Gonzales, M.H., Aronson, E., & Costanzo, M.A. (1988). Using social cognition and persuasion to promote energy conservation: A quasi-experiment. *Journal of Applied Social Psychology, 18,* 1049–1066.

Goodwin, N., Nelson, J.A., Ackerman, F., & Weisskopf, T. (2005). *Microeconomics in context.* Boston: Houghton Mifflin.

Gordon, I.E. (1989). *Theories of visual perception.* Chichester: Wiley.

Gorn, G.J. (1982). The effects of music in advertising on choice behavior: A classical conditioning approach. *Journal of Marketing, 46,* 94–101.

Gorn, G.J., Goldberg, M.E., & Basu, K. (1993). Mood, awareness and product evaluation. *Journal of Consumer Psychology, 2,* 237–256.

Gorn, G.J., Pham, M.T., & Sin, L.Y. (2001). When arousal influences ad evaluation and valence does not (and vice versa). *Journal of Consumer Psychology, 11,* 43–55.

Gosling, S.D., Ko, S.J., Morris, M.E., & Thomas, M. (2002). A room with a cue: Personality judgements based on offices and bedrooms. *Journal of Personality and Social Psychology, 82,* 379–398.

Graf, P., & Schachter, D.L. (1985). Implicit and explicit memory for new associations in normal and amnesic subjects. *Journal of Experimental Psychology: Learning, Memory, and Cognition, 11,* 501–518.

Grankvist, G. (2008). *Values and preference for ethical alternatives.* Poster presented at the XXIX International Congress of Psychology, Berlin, July.

Gray, J. (2003). *Al Qaeda and what it means to be modern.* London: Faber.

Green, H. (1992). *The uncertainty of everyday life, 1915–1945.* New York: HarperCollins Publishers Inc.

Green, L. (2007). *Advertising works 15.* IPA Effectiveness Awards 2006, Henley-on-Thames: World Advertising Research Center.

Greenfield, P.M. (1984). *Mind and the media: The effects of television, video games and computers.* Aylesbury: Fontana.

Greenfield, P.M. (1998). The cultural evolution of IQ. In U. Neisser (Ed.), *The rising curve: Long-term gains in IQ and related measures* (pp. 81–123). Washington, DC: American Psychological Association.

Greenfield, P.M., Brannon, C., & Lohr, D. (1994). Two-dimensional representation of movement through three-dimensional space: The role of video game expertise. *Journal of Applied Developmental Psychology, 15,* 87–104.

Greenwald, A.G. (1980). The totalitarian ego: Fabrication and revision of personal history. *American Psychologist, 35,* 603–618.

Greenwald, A.G., & Farnham, S.D. (2000). Using the Implicit Association Test to measure self-esteem and self-concept. *Journal of Personality and Social Psychology, 79,* 1022–1038.

Greenwald, A.G., & Leavitt, C. (1984). Audience involvement in advertising: Four levels. *Journal of Consumer Research, 11,* 581–592.

Greenwald, A.G., & Ronis, D.L. (1978). Twenty years of cognitive dissonance: Case study of the evolution of a theory. *Psychological Review, 85,* 53–57.

Gregory, W.I., Cialdini, R.B., & Carpenter, K.M. (1982). Self-relevant scenarios as mediators of likelihood estimate and compliance: Does imagining make it so? *Journal of Personality and Social Psychology, 43,* 89–99.

Grewal, D., Baker, J., Levy, M., & Voss, G.B. (2003). The effects of wait expectations and store atmosphere on patronage intentions in service-intensive retail stores. *Journal of Retailing, 79,* 259–268.

Griffin, J.G., & Broniarczyk, S.M. (2008). The slippery slope: The impact of feature alignability on search and satisfaction. Retrieved October 10, 2008 from http://www.business.ualberta.ca/MBEL/marketing_seminar_series/2008–09=SlipperySlope-paper.pdf

Griffiths, M.D. (1991). The observational analysis of adolescent gambling in UK amusement arcades. *Journal of Community and Applied Social Psychology, 1,* 309–320.

Griffiths, M.D., & Dancaster, I. (1995). The effect of type A personality on physiological arousal while playing computer games, *Addictive Behaviours, 20,* 543–548.

Gross, E.F. (2004). Adolescent Internet use: What we expect, what teens report. *Journal of Applied Developmental Psychology, 25,* 633–649.

Guest, L.P. (1955). Brand loyalty – Twelve years later. *Journal of Applied Psychology, 39,* 405–408.

Guest, L.P., & Brown, R.H. (1939). A study of the recall of radio advertising material. *Journal of Psychology, 89,* 381–387.

Gulas, C.S., & Schewe, C.D. (1994). Atmospheric segmentation: Managing store image with background music. In R. Acrol & A. Mitchell (Eds.), *Enhancing knowledge development in marketing* (pp. 325–330). Chicago: American Marketing Association.

Gunter, B., & Harrison, J. (1997). Violence in children's programs on British television. *Children and Society, 11,* 143–156.

Gustafson, B. & Yssel, J. (1994). Are advertisers practicing safe sex? *Marketing News,* March 14.

Hale, J.L., Lemieux, R., & Mongeau, P.A. (1995). Cognitive processing of fear-arousing message content. *Communication Research, 22,* 459–474.

Halliwell, E., & Dittmar, H. (2006). The role of appearance-related self-discrepancies for young adults' affect, body image, and emotional eating: A comparison of fixed-item and respondent-generated self-discrepancy measures. *Personality and Social Psychology Bulletin, 32,* 447–458.

Han, S., Lerner, J.S., & Keltner, D. (2007). Feelings and consumer decision making: The Appraisal-Tendency Framework. *Journal of Consumer Psychology, 17,* 158–168.

Han, S., & Shavitt, S. (1994). Persuasion and culture: Advertising appeals in individualistic and collectivistic societies. *Journal of Experimental Social Psychology, 30,* 326–350.

Hanley, A., & Wilhelm, M.S. (1992). Compulsive buying: An exploration into self-esteem and money attitudes. *Journal of Economic Psychology, 13,* 5–8.

Hardin, G. (1968). The tragedy of the commons. *Science, 162,* 1243–1248.

Hardin, G. (1998). Extensions of 'the tragedy of the commons'. *Science, 280,* 682–683.

Harris, J. (2001). *The effects of computer games on young children – A review of the research.* RDS Occasional paper No. 72. London: Home Office.

Harris, R.J. (1999). *A cognitive psychology of mass communication* (3rd ed.). Mahwah, NJ: Lawrence Erlbaum.

Hart, D., & Damon, W. (1986). Developmental trends in self-understanding. *Social Cognition, 4,* 388–407.

Harter, S. (2003). The development of self-representations during childhood and adolescence. In M.R. Leary & J.P. Tangney (Eds.), *Handbook of self and identity* (pp. 610–642). New York: Guilford Press.

Hartmann, T., & Klimmt, C. (2006). The influence of personality factors on computer game choice. In P. Vordereer & J. Bryant (Eds.), *Playing video games: Motives, responses, and consequences* (pp. 115–131). Mahwah, NJ: Lawrence Erlbaum Associates.

Hastak, M., & Olson, J.C. (1989). Assessing the role of brand-related cognitive responses as mediators of communication effects on cognitive structure. *Journal of Consumer Research, 15,* 444–456.

Haugtvedt, C.P., & Kasmer, J.A. (2008). Attitude change and persuasion. In C.P. Haugtvedt, P.M. Herr & F.R. Kardes (Eds.), *Handbook of consumer psychology.* New York: Lawrence Erlbaum Associates.

Haugtvedt, C.P., & Wegener, D.T. (1994). Message order effects in persuasion: An attitude strength perspective. *Journal of Consumer Research, 21,* 205–218.

Hawkins, S.A., & Hoch, S.J. (1992). Low-involvement learning: Memory without evaluation. *Journal of Consumer Research, 19,* 212–225.

Hearold, S. (1986). A synthesis of 1043 effects of television on social behavior. In G. Comstock (Ed.), *Public communications and behaviour* (vol. 1, pp. 65–133). New York: Academic Press.

Heberlein, T.A. (1975). Conservation information: The energy crisis and electricity consumption in an apartment complex. *Energy Systems and Policy, 1,* 105–117.

Hebl, M., & King, E. (2004). You are what you wear: An interactive demonstration of the self-fulfilling prophecy. *Teaching of Psychology, 31,* 260–262.

Hecker, S. (1984). Music for advertising effect. *Psychology & Marketing, 1,* 3–8.

Heckhausen, H. (1977). Achievement motivation and its constructs: A cognitive model. *Motivation and Emotion, 1,* 283–329.

Heckhausen, H. (1991). *Motivation and action.* Berlin: Springer-Verlag.

Heider, F. (1946). Attitudes and cognitive organisation. *Journal of Psychology, 21,* 107–112.

Heider, F. (1958). *The psychology of interpersonal relations.* New York: Wiley.

Held, R. (1970). Two modes of processing spatially distributed visual stimulation. In F.O. Schmidt (Ed.), *The neurosciences; Second study program,* New York: Rockefeller University Press.

Heller, M.A., (1982). Visual and tactual texture perception: Intersensory cooperation. *Perception and Psychophysics, 31,* 339–344.

Herr, P. (1989). Priming price: Prior knowledge and context effects. *Journal of Consumer Research, 16,* 67–76.

Herr, P.M., Farquhar, P.H., & Fazio, R.H. (1996). Impact on dominance and relatedness on brand extensions. *Journal of Consumer Psychology, 5,* 135–160.

Herzog, T.R. (1984). A cognitive analysis of preference for field-and-forest environments. *Landscape Research, 9,* 10–16.

Herzog, T.R., Kaplan, S., & Kaplan, R. (1982). The prediction of preference for unfamiliar urban places. *Population and Environment, 5,* 43–59.

Hess, T.M., Rosenberg, D.C., & Waters, S.J. (2001). Motivation and representational processes in adulthood: The effects of social accountability and information relevance. *Psychology and Aging, 48,* 37–44.

Higgins, E.T. (1987). Self-discrepancy: A theory relating self and affect. *Psychological Review, 94,* 319–340.

Higgins, E.T. (1989). Knowledge accessibility and activation: Subjectivity and suffering from unconscious sources. In J.S. Uleman & J.A. Bargh (Eds.), *Unintended thought* (pp. 75–123). New York: Guilford Press.

Higgins, E.T. (1998). Promotion and prevention: Regulatory focus as a motivational principle. In M.P. Zanna (Ed.), *Advances in experimental social psychology* (vol. 30, pp. 1–46). San Diego: Academic Press.

Hill, R.P., & Ward, J.C. (1989). Mood manipulation in marketing research: An examination of potential confounding effects. *Journal of Marketing Research, 26*, 97–104.

Hilles, W.S., & Kahle, L.R. (1985). Social contract and social integration in adolescent development. *Journal of Personality and Social Psychology, 49*, 1114–1121.

Hilton, M. (2007). Consumers and the state since the Second World War. *The Annals of the American Academy of Political and Social Science, 16*, 66.

Hines, J., Hungerford, H., & Tomera, A. (1987). Analysis and synthesis or research on environmental behaviour: A meta-analysis. *Journal of Environmental Education, 18*, 1–18.

Hirt, E.R., & Sherman, S.J. (1985). The role of prior knowledge in explaining hypothetical events. *Journal of Experimental Social Psychology, 21*, 519–543.

Hite, C.F., & Hite, R.E. (1995). Reliance on brand by young children. *Journal of the Market Research Society, 37*, 185–193.

Hobbs, R., & Frost, R. (2003). Measuring the acquisition of media-literacy skills. *Reading Research Quarterly, 38*, 330–355.

Hochberg, J.E. (1971). Perception I: Colour and shape. In J.W. Kling, & L.A. Riggs (Eds.), *Woodworth and Schlosberg's experimental psychology* (3rd ed). New York: Holt, Rinehart & Winston.

Hodgkinson, S., & Innes, J. (2000). The prediction of ecological and environmental belief systems: The differential contributions of social conservatism and beliefs about money. *Journal of Environmental Psychology, 20*, 285–294.

Hoegg, J., & Alba, J.W. (2008). A role for aesthetics in consumer psychology. In C.P. Haugtvedt, P.M. Herr & F.R. Kardes (Eds.), *Handbook of consumer psychology* (pp. 733–754). New York: Lawrence Erlbaum Associates.

Hogg, M.A., & Abrams, D. (1988). *Social identifications: A social psychology of intergroup relations and group processes*. London: Routledge.

Hogg, M.K., Bruce, M. & Hough, K. (1999). Female images in advertising: The implications of social comparison for marketing, *International Journal of Advertising, 18*, 445–473.

Hogg, M.K., & Fragou, A. (2003). Social comparison goals and the consumption of advertising: Towards a more contingent view of young women's consumption of advertising. *Journal of Marketing Management, 19*, 749–780.

Holbrook, M.B., & Batra, R. (1987). Assessing the role of emotions as mediators of consumer responses to advertising. *Journal of Consumer Research, 14*, 404–420.

Holden, S.J.S., & Vanhuele, M. (1999). Know the name, forget the exposure: brand familiarity versus memory of exposure context. *Psychology & Marketing, 16*, 479–496.

Hollingsworth, H.L. (1913). *Advertising and selling: Principles of appeals and responses*. New York: D. Appleton.

Holloway, S.L., & Valentine, G. (2000). Corked hats and Coronation Street: British and New Zealand children's imaginative geographies of the other. *Childhood, 7*, 335–357.

Homer-Dixon, T.F. (1991). On the threshold: Environmental changes as causes of acute conflict. *International Security, 16*, 76–116.

Homma, N. (1991). The continued relevance of cultural diversity. *Marketing and Research Today*, November, 251–259.

Hornik, J. (1992). Tactile stimulation and consumer response. *Journal of Consumer Research, 19*, 449–458.

Hothersall, D. (1984). *History of psychology*. New York: McGraw-Hill.

Hovde, H.T. (1931). Consumer preferences for small glass containers. *Journal of Applied Psychology, 15*, 346–357.

Hovland, C.I., Janis, I.L, & Kelley, H.H. (1953). *Communication and persuasion*. New Haven, CT: Yale University Press.

Hovland, C.I., & Weiss, W. (1951). The influence of source credibility on communication effectiveness. *Public Opinion Quarterly, 15*, 635–650.

Howard, G.S. (2000). Adapting human lifestyles for the 21st century. *American Psychologist, 55,* 509–515.

Hsee, C.K. (1999). Value-seeking and prediction-decision inconsistency: Why don't people take what they predict they'll like the most? *Psychonomic Bulletin and Review, 6,* 555–561.

Hsee, C.K., & Leclerc, F. (1998). Will products look more attractive when evaluated jointly or when evaluated separately? *Journal of Consumer Research, 25,* 175–186.

Hsee, C.K., Zhang, J., Yu, F., & Xi, Y. (2003). Lay rationalism and inconsistency between predicted experience and decision. *Journal of Behavioral Decision Making, 16,* 257–272.

Huberman, B.A., & Lukose, R.M. (1997). Social dilemmas and Internet congestion. *Science, 277,* 535–537.

Huesmann, L.R. (1986). Psychological processes promoting the relation between exposure to media violence and aggressive behaviour by the viewer. *Journal of Social Issues, 42,* 125–139.

Huesmann, L.R. (1988). An information processing model for the development of aggression. *Aggressive Behavior, 14,* 13–24.

Huesmann, L.R., & Miller, L.S. (1994). Long-term effects of repeated exposure to media violence in childhood. In L.R. Huesmann (Ed.), *Aggressive behaviour: Current perspectives* (pp. 153–186). New York: Plenum.

Hui, M.K., Dubé, L., & Chebat, J. (1997). The impact of music on consumers' reactions to waiting for services. *Journal of Retailing, 73,* 87–104.

Hull, C.L. (1943). *Principles of behaviour: An introduction to behaviour theory.* New York: Appleton Century.

Hull, C.L. (1952). *A behaviour system.* New Haven, CT: Yale University Press.

Huston, A.C., Donnerstein, E., Fairchild, H., Feshbach, N.D., Katz, P.A., Murray, J.P., et al., (1992). *Big world, small screen: The role of television in American society.* Lincoln, NE: University of Nebraska Press.

Hutchinson, J.W., & Eisenstein, E.M. (2008). Consumer learning and expertise. In C.P. Haugtvedt, P.M. Herr & F.R. Kardes (Eds.), *Handbook of consumer psychology* (pp. 103–132). New York: Lawrence Erlbaum Associates.

Insko, C.A. (1981). Balance theory and phenomenology. In R.E. Petty, T.M. Ostrom & T.C. Brock (Eds.), *Cognitive responses in persuasion* (pp. 309–338). Hillsdale, NJ: Lawrence Erlbaum Associates.

Insko, C.A. (1984). Balance theory, the Jordan paradigm, and the Wiest tetrahedron. In L. Berkowitz (Ed.), *Advances in experimental social psychology* (vol. 18, pp. 89–140). New York: Academic Press.

Insko, C.A., Drenan, S., Solomon, M.R., Smith, R., & Wade, T.J. (1983). Conformity as a function of the consistency of positive self-evaluation with being liked and being right. *Journal of Experimental Social Psychology, 19,* 341–358.

Irwin, A.R., & Gross, A.M. (1995). Cognitive tempo, violent video games and aggressive behaviour in young boys. *Journal of Family Violence, 10,* 337–350.

Isen, A.M. (1984). Toward understanding the role of affect in cognition. In R.S. Wyer & T.K. Srull (Eds.), *Handbook of social cognition* (vol. 3, pp. 179–236). Hillsdale, NJ: Lawrence Erlbaum Associates.

Isen, A.M., Clark, M.S., & Schwartz, M.F. (1976). Duration of the effect of good mood on helping: Footprints on the sands of time. *Journal of Personality and Social Psychology, 34,* 385–393.

Isen, A.M., Shalker, T.E., Clark, M., & Karp, L. (1978). Affect, accessibility of material in memory, and behaviour: A cognitive loop? *Journal of Personality and Social Psychology, 36,* 1–12.

Isler, L., Popper, E., & Ward, S. (1987). Children's purchase requests and parental responses: Results from a diary study. *Journal of Advertising Research, 27,* 28–39.

Iyengar, S.S., & Lepper, M.R. (2000). When choice is demotivating: Can one desire too much of a good thing? *Journal of Personality and Social Psychology, 79,* 995–1006,

Iyer, E.S. (1989). Unplanned purchasing: Knowledge of shopping environment and time pressure. *Journal of Retailing, 65,* 40–57.

Iyer, E.S., & Kashyap, R.K. (2007). Consumer recycling: role of incentives, information and social class. *Journal of Consumer Behaviour, 6,* 32–47.

Jackson, L.A., von Eye, A., Biocca, F.A., Barbatsis, G., Zhao, Y., & Fitzgerald, H.E. (2006). Does home

Internet use influence the academic performance of low-income children? *Developmental Psychology, 42*, 429–435.

Jacoby, J., & Chestnut, R. (1978). *Brand loyalty: Measurement and management*. New York: Wiley.

Jacoby, L.L., Kelley, C., Brown, J., & Jasechko, J. (1989). Becoming famous overnight: Limits on the ability to avoid unconscious influences of the past. *Journal of Personality and Social Psychology, 56*, 326–338.

James, W. ([1890] 1950). *The principles of psychology*. New York: Dover Publications.

Janis, I.L., Hovland, C.I., Field, P.B., Linton, H., Graham, E., Cohen, A.R., et al. (1959). *Personality and persuasibility*. New Haven, CT: Yale University Press.

Janiszewski, C. (1988). Preconscious processing effects: The independence of attitude formation and conscious thought. *Journal of Consumer Research, 15*, 199–209.

Janiszewski, C. (1990). The influence of print advertisement organization on affect toward a brand name. *Journal of Consumer Research, 17*, 53–65.

Jansson, C., Bristow, M., & Marlow, N. (2004). The influence of colour on visual search times in cluttered environments. *Journal of Marketing Communications, 10*, 183–193.

Jansson-Boyd, C.V., & Marlow, N. (2007). Not only in the eye of the beholder: Tactile information can affect aesthetic evaluation. *Psychology of Aesthetics, Creativity and the Arts, 1*, 170–173.

Jenkins, R. (1996). *Social identity*. London: Routledge.

Johansson, A., & Götestam, K.G. (2004). Internet addiction: characteristics of a questionnaire and prevalence in Norwegian youth (12–18 years). *Scandinavian Journal of Psychology, 45*, 223–229.

John, D.R., & Lakshmi-Ratan, R. (1992). Age differences in children's choice behaviour: The impact of available alternatives. *Journal of Marketing Research, 29*, 216–226.

John, D.R., & Sujan, M. (1990). Age differences in product categorization. *Journal of Consumer Research, 16*, 452–460.

Johnson, E.J., Moe, W., Fader, P., Bellman, S., & Lohse, G. L. (2004). On the depth and dynamics of online search behavior, *Management Science, 50*, 299–308.

Johnson, M.K., & Weisz, C. (1994). Comments on unconscious processing: Finding emotion in the cognitive stream. In P. Niedenthal & S. Kitayama (Eds.), *The heart's eye: Emotional influences in perception and attention* (pp. 145–164). San Diego: Academic Press.

Jones, E.E., & Goethals, G.R. (1971). Order effects in impression formation: Attribution context and the nature of the entity. In E.E. Jones, D.E. Kanouse, H.H. Kelley, R.E. Nisbett, S.Valins & B. Weiner (Eds.), *Attribution: Perceiving the causes of behaviour* (pp. 95–120). Morristown: General Learning Press.

Jordan, N. (1953). Behavioral forces that are a function of attitudes and behavioral organization. *Human Relations, 6*, 273–287.

Journal of Marketing (2008). Retrieved 22 June 2008 from http://www.marketingjournals.org/jm/

Jowett, G.S., & O'Donnell, V. (1986). *Persuasion and propaganda*. Beverly Hills, CA: Sage.

Judd, B.B., & Alexander, M.W. (1983). On the reduced effectiveness of some sexually suggestive ads. *Journal of the Academy of Marketing Science, 11*, 156–168.

Jungbluth, N., Tietje, O., & Scholz, R. (2000). The modular LCA: Environmental impacts of food purchases from the consumers' point of view. *International Journal of LCA, 5*, 134–142.

Kahle, L.R. & Homer, P.M. (1985). Physical attractiveness of the celebrity endorser: a social adaptation perspective. *Journal of Consumer Research, 11*, 954–961.

Kahle, L.R., Homer, P.M., O'Brien, R.M., & Boush, D.M. (1997). Maslow's hierarchy and social adaptation as alternative accounts of value structures. In L.R. Kahle & L. Chiagouris (Eds.), *Values, lifestyles, and psychographics* (pp. 111–137). Mahwah, NJ: Lawrence Erlbaum Associates.

Kahneman, D. (1973). *Attention and effort*. Englewood Cliffs, NJ; Prentice Hall.

Kahneman, D. (2002). Maps of bounded rationality: A perspective on intuitive judgment and choice. Nobel Prize lecture, December 8.

Kahneman, D., Knetsch, J. L., & Thaler, R. (1986). Fairness and the assumptions of economics. *Journal of Business, 59*, 285–300.

Kahneman, D., Slovic, P., & Tversky, A. (Eds.). (1982). *Judgement under uncertainty: Heuristics and biases.* Cambridge: Cambridge University Press.

Kahneman, D., & Tversky, A. (1982). The simulation heuristic. In D. Kahneman, P. Slovic, & A. Tversky (Eds.), *Judgment under uncertainty: Heuristics and biases* (pp. 201–208). Cambridge: Cambridge University Press.

Kambil, A., Wilson III, H.J., & Agrawal, V. (2002). Are you leaving money on the table? *The Journal of Business Strategy, 23,* 40–43.

Kang, Y., & Herr, P. (2006). Beauty and the beholder: Toward an integrative model of communication source effects. *Journal of Consumer Research, 33,* 123–130.

Kanner, A.D., & Gomes, M.E. (1995). The all-consuming self. In T. Roszak, M.E. Gomes & A.D. Kanner (Eds.). *Ecopsychology: Restoring the Earth, healing the mind.* San Francisco: Sierra Club Books.

Kanner, A.D., & Kasser, T. (2000). Stuffing our kids: Should psychologists help advertisers manipulate children? *The Clinical Psychologist, 53,* 16–20.

Kaplan, K.J., & Fishbein, M. (1969). The source of beliefs, their saliency, and prediction of attitude. *Journal of Social Psychology, 78,* 63–74.

Kaplan, S. (1987). Aesthetics, affect, and cognition: Environmental preferences from an evolutionary perspective. *Environment and Behaviour, 19,* 3–32.

Kaplan, S.J. (1983). The image of amusement arcades and differences in male and female video game playing. *Journal of Popular Culture, 16,* 93–98.

Kaptein, N.A., Theeuwes, J., & Van der Heijden, A.H.C. (1994). Search for conjunctively defined target can be selectively limited to a color-defined subset of elements. *Journal of Experimental Psychology: Human Perception and Performance, 21,* 1053–1069.

Kardes, F.R. (1994). Consumer judgement and decision processes. In R.S. Wyer & T.K. Srull (Eds.), *Handbook of social cognition* (vol. 2). Hillsdale, NJ: Lawrence Erlbaum Associates.

Karpinski, A., & Hilton, J.L. (2001). Attitudes and the implicit associations test. *Journal of Personality and Social Psychology, 81,* 774–788.

Kasser, T., & Kanner, A.D. (2003). Where is the psychology of consumer culture? In T. Kasser & A.D. Kanner (Eds.), *Psychology and consumer culture: The struggle for a good life in a materialistic world.* Washington, DC: American Psychological Association.

Kasser, T., & Ryan, R.M. (1993). A dark side of the American dream: Correlates of financial success as a central life aspiration. *Journal of Personality and Social Psychology, 65,* 410–422.

Katz, D. (1960). The functional approach to the study of attitudes. *Public Opinion Quarterly, 24,* 163–204.

Katz, D. (1967). The functional approach to the study of attitude. In M. Fishbein (Ed.), *Readings in attitude theory and measurement.* New York: Wiley.

Kausler, D.H. (1994). *Learning and memory in normal aging.* San Diego: Academic Press.

Kellaris, J.J., & Cox, A.D. (1989). The effects of background music in advertising: A reassessment. *Journal of Consumer Research, 16,* 113–118.

Keller, K.L. (1987). Memory factors in advertising: The effect of advertising retrieval cues on brand evaluations. *Journal of Consumer Research, 14,* 316–333.

Kent, R.J., & Allen, C.T. (1993). Does competitive clutter in television advertising 'interfere' with recall and recognition of brand names and ad claims? *Marketing Letters, 4,* 175–184.

Kent, R.J., & Allen, C.T. (1994). Competitive interference effects in consumer memory for advertising: The role of brand familiarity. *Journal of Marketing, 58,* 97–105.

Kestenbaum, G.I., & Weinstein, L. (1985). Personality, psychopathology and developmental issues in male adolescent video game use. *Journal of the American Academy of Child Psychiatry, 24,* 208–212.

Kids Health (2005). Overweight and obesity. Retrieved 10 October 2007 from http://www.kidshealth.org/parent/general/body/overweight_obesity.html

Kim, S., Goldstein, D., Hasher, L., & Zacks, R.T. (2005). Framing effects in younger and older adults. *Journal of Gerontology: Psychological Sciences, 60B,* 215–218.

Kimes, S.E., & Wirtz, J. (2003). Perceived fairness of revenue management in the US golf industry. *Journal of Revenue and Pricing Management, 1(4),* 332–344.

King, K.W., & Reid, L.N. (1990). Fear arousing anti-drinking and driving PSAs: do physical injury threats influence young adults? *Current Issues and Research in Advertising, 12,* 155–175.

King, T.R. (1989). Credibility gap: More consumers find celebrity ads unpersuasive. *Wall Street Journal,* July 5, p. B5.

Kirkeby, C. (2004). First commercial television broadcast July 1, 1941. Retreived June 14, 2008 from http://www.classbrain.com/artholiday/publish/article_349.shtml

Kisielius, J., & Sternthal, B. (1986). Examining the vividness controversy: An availability-valence interpretation. *Journal of Consumer Research, 12,* 418–431.

Klebber, J.M. (1985). Physiological measures of research: A review of brain activity, electro dermal response, pupil dilation, and voice analysis methods and studies. In J. Bryant & D. Zillmann, *Media effects: Advances in theory and research.* Hillsdale, NJ: Lawrence Erlbaum Associates.

Klees, D.M., Olson, J., & Wilson, R.D. (1988). An analysis of the content and organization of children's knowledge structures. In M.J. Houston (Ed.), *Advances in consumer research* (vol. 15, pp. 153–157). Provo, UT: Association of Consumer Research.

Kleine III, R.E., Kleine, S.S., & Kernan, J.B. (1993). Mundane consumption and the self: A social-identity perspective. *Journal of Consumer Psychology, 2,* 209–235.

Kleine, S.S., Kleine III, R.E., & Allen, C.T. (1995). How is a possession 'me' or 'not me'? Characterizing types and an antecedent of material possession attachment. *Journal of Consumer Research, 22,* 327–343.

Klimmt, C. (2003). Dimensions and determinants of the enjoyment of playing digital games: A three-level model. In M. Copier & J. Raessens (Eds.), *Level up: Digital games research conference* (pp. 246–257). Utrecht: Utrecht University Press.

Klinger, E. (1975). Consequences of commitment to and disengagement from incentives, *Psychological Review, 82,* 1–25.

Knez, I., & Niedenthal, S. (2007). Lighting in digital game worlds: Effects on affect and play performance. *CyberPsychology & Behavior, 11,* 129–137.

Ko, C.H., Yen, J.Y., Yen, C.F., Lin, H.C., & Yang, M.J. (2007). Factors predictive for incidence and remission of internet addiction in young adolescents: A prospective study. *Cyberpsychology and Behavior, 10,* 545–551.

Kohlberg, L. (1969). Stages and sequence: The cognitive-developmental approach to socialization. In D.A. Goslin (Ed.), *Handbook of socialization theory and research.* Chicago: Rand McNally.

Kohlberg, L. (1976). Moral stages and moralization: The cognitive-developmental approach. In T. Lickona (Ed.), *Moral development and behaviour.* New York: Holt, Rinehart and Winston.

Koolstra, C.M., van der Voort, T.H.A., & van der Kamp, L.J. (1997). Television's impact on children's reading comprehension and decoding skills: A 3-year panel study. *Reading Research Quarterly, 32,* 128–152.

Kortenhaus, C.M., & Demarest, J. (1993). Gender role stereotyping in children's literature: An update. *Sex Roles, 28,* 219–232.

Kotler, P. (1973). Atmospherics as a marketing tool. *Journal of Retailing, 49,* 48–64.

Kreshel, P.J. (1990). John B. Watson at J. Walter Thompson: The legitimation of 'science' advertising. *Journal of Advertising, 19,* 49–59.

Krishnan, H.S., & Chakravarti, D. (2003). A process analysis of the effects of humorous advertising executions on brand claims memory. *Journal of Consumer Psychology, 13,* 230–245.

Kroeber-Riel, W. (1986). Die inneren Bilder der Konsumenten: Messung, Verhaltenswirkung, Konsequenzen für das Marketing. *Marketing.ZFP, 8,* 81–96.

Krosnick, J.A., & Abelson, R.P. (1992). The case for measuring attitude strength in surveys. In J. Tanur (Ed.), *Questions about questions* (pp. 177–203). New York: Russell Sage Foundation.

Kruglanski, A.W. (1989). *Lay epistemics and human knowledge.* New York: Penguin.

Kruglanski, A.W., & Freund, T. (1983). The freezing and unfreezing of lay inferences: Effects on impressional primacy, ethnic stereotyping, and numerical anchoring. *Journal of Experimental Social Psychology, 19,* 448–468.

Krugman, H.E. (1965). The impact of television advertising: Learning without involvement. *Public Opinion Quarterly, 29,* 349–356.

Kubey, R. (1986). Television use in everyday life: Coping with unstructured time. *Journal of Communication, 36,* 108–123.

Kubey, R., & Csikszentmihalyi, M. (2002). Television addiction is no mere metaphor. *Scientific American, 286,* 74–80.

Kumkale, G.T., & Albarracín, D. (2004). The sleeper effect in persuasion: A meta-analytic review. *Psychological Bulletin, 130,* 143–172.

Kuna, D.P. (1976). The concept of suggestion in the early history of advertising psychology. *Journal of the History of the Behavioral Sciences, 12,* 347–353.

Kunkel, D., & Gantz, W. (1992). Children's television advertising in the multi-channel environment. *Journal of Communication, 42,* 134–152.

Kunkel, D. & Roberts, D. (1991). Young minds and marketplace values: Research and policy issues in children's television advertising. *Journal of Social Issues, 47,* 57–72.

Kwak, H. (2001). Web-based chatting: consumer communications and commercial communications. Unpublished doctoral dissertation, University of Georgia, Athens.

Lambert-Pandraud, R., Laurent, G., & Lapersonne, E. (2005). Repeat purchasing of new automobiles by older consumers: Empirical evidence and interpretations. *Journal of Marketing, 69,* 97–113.

Lang, A., Newhagen, J., & Reeves, B. (1996). Negative video as structure: Emotion, attention, capacity, and memory. *Journal of Broadcasting and Electronic Media, 40,* 460–477.

Lang, T., & Heasman, M. (2004). *Food wars: The global battle for mouths, minds and markets.* London: Earthscan.

Langer, E.J. (1989). *Mindfulness.* Reading, MA: Addison-Wesley.

Langlois, J.H. (1986). From the eye of the beholder to behavioural reality: Development of social behaviours and social relations as a function of physical attractiveness. In C.P. Herman, M.P. Zanna & E.T. Higgins (Eds.), *Appearance, stigma, and social behaviour: The Ontario symposium on personality and social psychology* (vol. 3 pp. 23–51). Hillsdale, NJ: Lawrence Erlbaum Associates.

LaPiere, R. (1934). Attitudes and actions. *Social Forces, 13,* 230–237.

Laroche, M., Toffoli, R., Zhang, Q., & Pons, F. (2001). A cross-cultural study of the persuasive effect of fear appeal messages in cigarette advertising: China and Canada. *International Journal of Advertising, 20,* 297–317.

Larson, R. (2001). Commentary. In D.R. Anderson, A.C. Huston, K.L. Schmitt, D.L. Linebarger & J.C. Wright, *Early childhood television viewing and adolescent behaviour.* Monographs of the Society for Research in Child Development, 66 (1, 264).

Larson, R.W., & Verma, S. (1999). How children and adolescents spend time across the world: Work, play, and developmental opportunities. *Psychological Bulletin, 125,* 701–736.

Lasn, K. (1999). *Culture jam: The uncoiling of America.* New York: Eagle Brook.

LaTour, M.S., & Zahra, S.A. (1989). Fear appeals as advertising strategy: Should they be used? *Journal of Consumer Marketing, 6,* 61–70.

Laurenceau, J.P., Barrett, L.F., & Pietromonaco, P.R. (1998). Intimacy as an interpersonal process: The importance of self-disclosure, partner disclosure, and perceived partner responsiveness in interpersonal exchanges. *Journal of Personality and Social Psychology, 74,* 1238–1251.

Lavinsky, D. (1993). When novelty wears off soft drinks clearly will fail. *Marketing News,* March 15, *27,* No. 6, 4.

Lawlor M.A., & Prothero A. (2003). Children's understanding of television advertising intent. *Journal of Marketing Management, 17,* 411–432.

Lea, S.E.G. (1999). Credit, debt and problem debt. In P.E. Earl & S. Kemp (Eds.), *The Elgar companion to consumer research and economic psychology.* Cheltenham: Edward Elgar Publishing Limited.

Lebergott, S. (1993). *Pursuing happiness: American consumers in the twentieth century.* Princeton, NJ: Princeton University Press.

Ledoux, J. (1998). *The emotional brain.* London: Weidenfeld & Nicolson.

Lee, A.Y. (2002). Effects of implicit memory on memory-based versus stimulus-based brand choice. *Journal of Marketing Research, 39,* 440–454.

Lee, J. (2005). That figures: women buy when ads get real. Retrieved February 15, 2005 from http://

www.smh.com.au/news/business/that-figures-women-buy-when-ads-get-real/2005/10/02/1128191605206.html

Lee, J.A. (2000). Adapting Triandis' model of subjective culture and social behavior relations to consumer behavior. *Journal of Consumer Psychology, 2,* 117–126.

Lehmann, D.R. (1998). Customer reactions to variety: too much of a good thing? *Journal of the Academy of Marketing Science, 26,* 62–65.

Leith, K.P., & Baumeister, R.F. (1996). Why do bad moods increase self-defeating behaviour? Emotion, risk taking, and self-regulation. *Journal of Personality and Social Psychology, 71,* 1250–1267.

Lenhart, A., Madden, M., & Hitlin, P. (2005). *Teens and Technology: Youth are leading the transition to a fully wired and mobile nation.* Washington, DC: Pew Internet & American Life Project.

Leonard-Barton, D. (1981). The diffusion of active-residential solar energy equipment in California. In A. Shama (Ed.), *Marketing solar energy innovations* (pp. 243–257). New York: Praeger.

Lepper, M.R. (1985). Microcomputers in education. *American Psychologist, 40,* 1–18.

Lepper, M.R., Greene, D., & Nisbett, R.E. (1973). Undermining children's intrinsic interest with extrinsic reward: A test of the over-justification hypothesis. *Journal of Personality and Social Psychology, 28,* 129–137.

Lerman, D. (2003). The effect of morphemic familiarity and exposure mode on recall and recognition of brand names. *Advances in Consumer Research, 30,* 80–81.

Lerner, J.S., & Keltner, D. (2000). Beyond valence: Toward a model of emotion-specific influences on judgement and choice. *Cognition and Emotion, 14,* 473–493.

Lerner, J.S., & Keltner, D. (2001). Fear, anger, and risk. *Journal of Personality & Social Psychology, 81,* 146–159.

Lerner, J.S., & Tiedens, L.Z. (2006). Portrait of the angry decision maker: How appraisal tendencies shape anger's influence on cognition. *Journal of Behavioral Decision Making, 19,* 115–137.

Leu, D.J., Coiro, J., Castek, J., Hartman, D., Henry, L.A., & Reinking, D. (2008). Research on instruction and assessment in the new literacies of online reading comprehension. In C. Collins Block, S. Parris & P. Afflerbach (Eds.). *Comprehension instruction: Research-based best practices.* New York: Guilford Press.

Leventhal, H., Watts, J.C., & Pagano, F. (1967). Effects of fear and instructions on how to cope with danger. *Journal of Personality and Social Psychology, 6,* 313–321.

Lever, J., Frederick, D.A., & Peplau, L.A. (2006). Does size matter? Men's and women's views on penis size across the lifespan. *Psychology of Men & Masculinity, 7,* 129–143.

Levin, I.P., & Gaeth, G.J. (1988). How consumers are affected by the framing of attribute information before and after consuming the product. *Journal of Consumer Research, 15,* 374–378.

Levine, M.W. (2000). *Levine and Shefner's fundamentals of sensation and perception* (3rd ed). Oxford: Oxford University Press.

Levinson, R. M. (1975). From Olive Oil to Sweet Polly Purebred: Sex role stereotypes and televised cartoons. *Journal of Popular Culture, 9,* 561–572.

Lewin, K. (1944). *Field theory in social science.* New York: Harper.

Lewin, K. (1947). Group decision and social change. In T.M. Newcomb & E.L. Hartley (Eds.), *Reading in social psychology* (pp. 330–344). New York: Holt.

Lewin, K., Dembo, T., Festinger, L., & Sears, P.S. (1944). Level of aspiration. In M.J. Hunt (Ed.), *Personality and the behavior disorders* (pp. 333–378). New York: Ronald Press.

Lewis, M. (1990). Self-knowledge and social development in early life. In L. Pervin (Ed.), *Handbook of personality: Theory and research* (pp. 277–300). New York: Guilford Press.

Lichtenstein, M., & Srull, T.K. (1985). Conceptual and methodological issues in examining the relationship between consumer memory and judgment. In L.F. Alwitt and A.A. Mitchell (Eds.), *Psychological processes and advertising effects: Theory, research, application* (pp. 113–128). Hillsdale, NJ: Lawrence Erlbaum Associates.

Light, L.L., LaVoie, D.J., Valencia-Laver, D., Albertson Owens, S.A., & Mead, G. (1992). Direct and indirect measures for memory for modality in young and older adults. *Journal of Experimental Psychology: Learning, Memory, and Cognition, 18,* 1284–1297.

Lin, Q., & Lee, J. (2004). Consumer information search when making investment decisions. *Financial Services Review, 13,* 319–332.

Lindridge, A.M., Hogg, M.K., & Shah, M. (2004). Imagined multiple worlds: How South Asian women in Britain use family and friends to navigate the 'border crossings' between household and social contexts. *Consumption, Markets and Culture, 7,* 211–238.

Lindstrom, M (2005). Sensing opportunity: Sensory appeal. *The Marketer, 10,* 6–11.

Linz, D.G., Donnerstein, E., & Penrod, S. (1988). Effects of long-term exposure to violent and sexually degrading depictions of women. *Journal of Personality and Social Psychology, 55,* 758–768.

Locke, E.A., Shaw, K.N., Saari, L.M., & Latham, G.P. (1981). Goal setting and task performance: 1969–1980. *Psychological Bulletin, 90,* 125–152.

Loken, B., Ross, I., & Hinkle, R.L. (1986). Consumer 'confusion' of origin and brand similarity perceptions. *Journal of Public Policy and Marketing, 5,* 195–211.

Lord, C.G. (1980). Schemas and images as memory aids: Two modes of processing social information. *Journal of Personality and Social Psychology, 38,* 257–269.

Lowe, M.R., & Butryn, M.L. (2007). Hedonic hunger: A new dimension of appetite? *Physiology & Behavior, 91,* 432–439.

Luchs, M., Walker Naylor, R., Irwin, J.R., & Raghunathan, R. (2008). Do consumers expect less from ethically superior products? Presentation made at the Society for Consumer Psychology conference, New Orleans, February.

Lumsdaine, A.A., & Janis, I.L. (1953). Resistance to 'counterpropaganda' produced by one-sided and two-sided 'propaganda' presentations. *Public Opinion Quarterly, 17,* 311–318.

Luna, D., Peracchio, L.A., & de Juan, M.D. (2003). The impact of language and congruity on persuasion in multicultural e-marketing. *Journal of Consumer Psychology, 13,* 41–45.

Lundy, R.F. Jr. (2008). Gustatory hedonic value: Potential function for forebrain control of brainstem taste processing. *Neuroscience & Biobehavioral Reviews, 32,* 1601–1606.

Luomala, H.T., & Laaksonen, M. (1997). Mood-regulatory self-gifts: Development of a conceptual framework. *Journal of Economic Psychology, 18,* 407–434.

Lupton, E. (1993). *Mechanical brides: Women and machines from home to office.* New York: Cooper-Hewitt Musem.

Luthar, S.S. (2003). The culture of affluence: Psychological costs of material wealth. *Child Development, 74,* 1581–1593.

Lyle, J., & Hoffman, H.R. (1972). Explorations in patterns of television viewing by preschool-age children. In E.A. Rubinstein, G.A. Comstock & J.P. Murray (Eds.), *Television and social behavior: Vol. 4. Television in day-to-day life: Patterns of use* (pp. 257–273). Washington, DC: U.S. Government Printing Office.

Lynch, J.G., & Srull, T.K. (1982). Memory and attentional factors in consumer choice: Concepts and research methods. *Journal of Consumer Research, 9,* 18–37.

MacGowan, K. (1928). Profiles: The adventures of the behaviorist. *The New Yorker, 4* (6 October), 30–32.

Machleit, K.A., & Powell Mantel, S. (2001). Emotional response and shopping satisfaction: Moderating effects of shopper attributions. *Journal of Business Research, 54,* 97–106.

MacInnis, D.J., Moorman, C., & Jaworski, B.J. (1991). Enhancing and measuring consumers' motivation, opportunity and ability to process brand information from ads. *Journal of Marketing, 55,* 32–53.

Macklin, M.C. (1996). Preschoolers' learning of brand names from visual cues. *Journal of Consumer Research, 23,* 251–261.

Magnusson, M.K., Arvola, A., Koivisto Hursti, U-K., Åberg, L., & Sjödén, P.O. (2001). Attitudes towards organic foods among Swedish consumers. *British Food Journal, 103,* 209–227.

Maheswaran, D., Mackie, D.M., & Chaiken, S. (1992). Brand name as a heuristic cue: The effects of task importance and expectancy confirmation on consumer judgments. *Journal of Consumer Psychology, 1,* 317–336.

Maio, G.R., & Olson, J.M. (1995). Relations between values, attitudes, and behavioural intentions: The moderating role of attitude function. *Journal of Experimental Social Psychology, 31,* 266–285.

Maison, D., Greenwald, A.G., & Bruin, R.H. (2004). Predictive validity of the implicit association test in studies of brands, consumer attitudes, and behaviour. *Journal of Consumer Psychology, 14*, 405–415.

Malamuth, N.M., & Donnerstein, E. (1982). The effects of aggressive-pornographic mass media stimuli. In L. Berkowitz (Ed.), *Advances in experimental social psychology* (vol. 15, pp. 104–136). New York: Academic Press.

Mandel, N., & Johnson, E.J. (2002). When web pages influence choice: Effects of visual primes on experts and novices. *Journal of Consumer Research, 29*, 235–245.

Mandel, N., Petrova, P.K., & Cialdini, R.B. (2006). Images of success and the preference for luxury brands. *Journal of Consumer Psychology, 16*, 57–69.

Mandler, G. (1975). *Mind and emotion.* New York: Wiley.

Mandler, G. (1982). The structure of value: Accounting for taste. In M.S. Clark & S.T. Fiske (Eds.), *Affect and cognition: The 17th Annual Carnegie Symposium on cognition* (pp. 3–36). Hillsdale, NJ: Lawrence Erlbaum Associates.

Mandler, G. (1984). *Mind and body: Psychology of emotion and stress.* New York: Norton.

Mano, H., & Oliver, R.L. (1993). Assessing the dimensionality and structure of the consumption experience: Evaluation, feeling and satisfaction. *Journal of Consumer Research, 13*, 418–430.

Mares, M., & Woodard, E.H. (2001). Prosocial effects on children's social interactions. In D.G. Singer & J.L. Singer (Eds.), *Handbook of children and the media* (pp. 183–205). Thousand Oaks, CA: Sage.

Marketing (2005). ITV and the consumer society. *Marketing*, 9/21/2005 Supplement, Special section, pp. 1–4.

Marsh, H.W., Kong, C.K. & Hau, K.T. (2000). Longitudinal multilevel models of the big-fish-little-pond effect on academic self concept: Counterbalancing contrast and reflected-glory effects in Hong Kong schools. *Journal of Personality and Social Psychology, 78*, 337–349.

Martin, M.C., & Gentry, N.J. (1997). Stuck in the model trap: The effects of beautiful models in ads on female pre-adolescents and adolescents. *Journal of Advertising, 26*, 19–33.

Martin, M.C., & Kennedy, P.F. (1993). Advertising and social comparison: Consequences for female preadolescents and adolescents. *Psychology & Marketing, 10*, 513–529.

Maslow, A. (1970). *Motivation and Personality* (2nd ed.). New York: Harper and Row.

Matlin, M.W. (1998). *Cognition.* Orlando, FL: Harcourt Brace.

Mattes, J., & Cantor, J. (1982). Enhancing responses to television advertisements via the transfer of residual arousal from prior programming. *Journal of Broadcasting, 26*, 553–566.

Mattoon, A.T. (2000). Paper piles up. In L.R. Brown, M. Renner & B. Halweil (Eds.), *Vital signs, 2000: The environmental trends that are shaping our future* (pp. 64–65). New York: Norton.

Mayer, J.D., Gaschke, Y.N., Braverman, D.L., & Evans, T.W. (1992). Mood-congruent judgement is a general effect. *Journal of Personality & Social Psychology, 63*, 119–132.

McAlister, A.T., & Cornwell, T.B. (2008). Preschool children's brand symbolism understanding: Links to social and cognitive development. Paper presented at the Society for Consumer Psychology Conference, New Orleans, February.

McClure, S.M., Li, J., Tomlin, D., Cypert, K.S., Montague, L.M., & Montague, P.R. (2004). Neural correlates of behavioural preference for culturally familiar drinks. *Neuron, 44*, 379–387.

McCracken, G. (1990). *Culture and consumption.* Indianapolis: Indiana University Press.

McCrary, J.W. Jr, & Hunter, W.S. (1953). Serial position curves in verbal learning. *Science, 117*, 131–134.

McGuire, W.J. (1968). Personality and susceptibility to social influence. In E.F. Borgatta & W.W. Lambert (Eds.), *Handbook of personality: Theory and research* (pp. 1130–1187). Chicago: Rand McNally.

McIlwraith, R.D. (1998). I am addicted to television: The personality, imagination, and TV watching patterns of self-identified TV addicts. *Journal of Broadcasting & Electronic Media, 42*, 371–386.

McIntyre, J.S., & Craik, F.I.M. (1987). Age differences in memory for item and source information. *Canadian Journal of Psychology, 41*, 175–192.

McKenzie-Mohr, D. (2000). Fostering sustainable behaviour through community-based social marketing. *American Psychologist, 55*, 531–537.

McNeal, J.U. (1964). *Children as consumers.* Austin, TX: Bureau of Business Research.

McNeal, J.V. (1998). Tapping the three kids' markets. *American Demographics, 20,* 36.

McSweeney, F.K., & Bierley, C. (1984). Recent developments in classical conditioning. *Journal of Consumer Research, 11,* 619–631.

Mead, G.H. (1934). *Mind, self and society.* Chicago: University of Chicago Press.

Megaw, E.D., & Richardson, J. (1979). Target uncertainty and visual scanning strategies. *Human factors, 21,* 303–316.

Mehrabian, A., & Russell, J.A. (1974). *An approach to environmental psychology.* Cambridge, MA: MIT Press.

Menon, G., & Raghubir, P. (2003). Ease of retrieval as an automatic input in judgments: A mere-accessibility framework? *Journal of Consumer Research, 30,* 230–243.

Merikle, P.M. (1988). Subliminal auditory messages: An evaluation. *Psychology & Marketing, 5,* 355–372.

Meyers-Levy, J. (1989). The influence of a brand name's association set size and word frequency on brand memory. *Journal of Consumer Research, 16,* 197–207.

Meyers-Levy, J., & Tybout, A.M. (1989). Schema congruity as a basis for product evaluation. *Journal of Consumer Research, 16,* 39–54.

Michaelidou, N., Dibb, S., & Ali, H. (2008). The effect of health, cosmetic and social antismoking information themes on adolescents' beliefs about smoking. *International Journal of Advertising, 27,* 235–250.

Michaelis, L. (2003). Sustainable consumption and greenhouse gas mitigation. *Climate Policy, 3,* 135–146.

Michon, R., Chebat, J., & Turley, L.W. (2005). Mall atmospherics: The interaction effects of the mall environment on shopping behaviour. *Journal of Business Research, 58,* 576–583.

Mikellides, B. (1990). Color and physiological arousal, *Journal of Architectural and Planning Research, 1,* 13–19.

Milgram, S. (1965). Some conditions of obedience and disobedience to authority. *Human Relations, 18,* 57–76.

Miller, G. (1956). The magical number seven, plus or minus two: Some limits on our capacity for processing information. *Psychological Review, 63,* 81–87.

Milliman, R.E. (1982). Using background music to affect the behaviour of supermarket shoppers. *Journal of Marketing, 46,* 86–91.

Milliman, R.E. (1986). The influence of background music on the behaviour of restaurant patrons. *Journal of Consumer Research, 13,* 286–289.

Mills, J., & Aronson, E. (1965). Opinion change as a function of the communicator's attractiveness and desire to influence. *Journal of Personality and Social Psychology, 1,* 173–177.

Milotic, D. (2003). The impact of fragrance on consumer choice. *Journal of Consumer Behaviour, 5,* 222–234.

Mitchell, K.J., Becker-Blease, K. & Finkelhor, D. (2005). Inventory of problematic Internet experiences encountered in clinical practice. *Professional Psychology: Research & Practice, 36*(5), 498–509.

Mitchell, T.R., Thompson, L., Peterson, E., & Cronk, R. (1997). Temporal adjustment in the evaluation of events: The 'rosy view'. *Journal of Experimental Social Psychology, 33,* 421–448.

Molnar, V., & Lamont, M. (2002). Social categorization and group identification: How African Americans shape their collective identity through consumption. In K. Green, A. McMeekin, M. Tomlinson & V. Walsh (Eds.), *An interdisciplinary approach to the study of demand and its role in innovation* (pp. 88–111). Manchester: Manchester University Press.

Montagu, A. (1986). *Touching: The human significance of the skin* (3rd ed.). New York: Harper & Row Publishers.

Montemayor, R., & Eisen, M. (1977). The development of self-conceptions from childhood to adolescence. *Developmental Psychology, 13,* 314–319.

Moon, Y. (2000). Intimate exchanges: Using computers to elicit self-disclosure from consumers. *Journal of Consumer Research, 26,* 324–340.

Moon, Y. (2003). Don't blame the computer: When self-disclosure moderates the self-serving bias. *Journal of Consumer Psychology, 13,* 125–137.

Moore, D.J., Mowen, J.C., & Reardon, R. (1994). Multiple sources in advertising appeals: When product endorsers are paid by the advertising sponsor. *Journal of the Academy of Marketing Science, 22,* 234–243.

Moore, T.E. (1992). Subliminal perception: Facts and fallacies. *Skeptical Inquirer, 16,* 273–281.

Morlock, H., Yando, T., & Nigolean, K., (1985). Motivation of video game players. *Psychological Reports, 57,* 247–250.

Morrin, M., & Ratneshwar, S. (2000). The impact of ambient scent on evaluation, attention, memory for familiar and unfamiliar brands. *Journal of Business Research, 49,* 157–165.

Morton, F.S., Zettelmeyer, F., & Silva Russo, J. (2001). Internet car retailing. *The Journal of Industrial Economics, 4,* 501–519.

Morwitz, V.G., Greenleaf, E.A., & Johnson, E.J. (1998). Divide and prosper: Consumers' reactions to partitioned prices. *Journal of Marketing Research, 35,* 453–463.

Moscovitch, M., & Wincour, G. (1992). The neuropsychology of memory and aging. In F.I.M. Craik & T.A. Salthouse (Eds.), *The handbook of aging and cognition* (pp. 315–372). Hillsdale, NJ: Lawrence Erlbaum Associates.

Moser, P.W. (1989). Double vision: Why do we never match up to our mind's ideal? *Self Magazine,* January, pp. 51–52.

Muehling, D.D. & Bozman, C.S. (1990). An examination of factors influencing effectiveness of 15-second advertisements. *International Journal of Advertising, 9,* 331–344.

Muehling, D.D., & Laczniak, R.N. (1988). Advertising's immediate and delayed influence on brand attitudes: Considerations across message-involvement levels. *Journal of Advertising, 17,* 23–43.

Muñiz, A.M., Jr., & O'Guinn, T.C. (2001). Brand community. *Journal of Consumer Research, 27,* 412–432.

Murphy, S.T., & Zajonc, R.B. (1993). Affect, cognition, and awareness: Affective priming with optimal and suboptimal stimulus exposures. *Journal of Personality and Social Psychology, 64,* 723–739.

Murray, H.A. (1951). Some basic psychological assumptions and conceptions. *Dialectica, 5,* 266–292.

Murray, K.B., & Häubl, G. (2002). The fiction of no friction: A user skills approach to cognitive lock-in. *Advances in Consumer Research, 29,* 8–9.

Murray, K.B., & Häubl, G. (2003). A human capital perspective of skill acquisition and interface loyalty. *Communications of the ACM, 46,* 272–278.

Mussweiler, T., & Förster, J. (2000). The sex-aggression link: A perception-behavior dissociation. *Journal of Personality and Social Psychology, 79,* 507–520.

Myers, D.G. (2004). *Psychology* (7th ed.). New York: Worth Publishers.

Myers, D.G., & Diener, E. (1996). The pursuit of happiness. *Scientific American,* 54–56.

Myers, E. (1985). Phenomenological analysis of the importance of special possessions: An exploratory study. In A.C. Hirschman & M.B. Holbrook (Eds.), *Advances in consumer research* (vol. 12). Provo, UT: Association for Consumer Research.

Myers-Levy, J. & Peracchio, L.A. (1995). Understanding the effects of color: How the correspondence between available and required resources affects attitudes. *Journal of Consumer Research, 22,* 121–138.

Nass, C.I., & Moon, Y. (2000). Machines and mindlessness: Social responses to computers. *Journal of Social Issues, 56,* 81–103.

Nastasi, B.K., & Clements, D.H. (1993). Motivational and social outcomes of cooperative computer education environments. *Journal of Educational Computing Research, 4,* 15–43.

National Statistics (2007). Retail sales: Slowdown in volume of sales. Retrieved 14 June 2008 from http://www.statistics.gov.uk/cci/nugget.asp?id=256

National Statistics (2008a). Consumer durables: Consumer durables ownership increases. Retrieved 5 March 2008 from http://www. statistics.gov.uk

National Statistics (2008b). Car access: 3 in 4 households have access to a car. Retrieved 5 March, 2008 from http://www. statistics.gov.uk

Nelson, J.E. (1987). Comment on humor and advertising effectiveness after repeated exposures to a radio commercial. *Journal of Advertising, 16*, 63–65.

Nelson, M.R., Brunel, F.F., Supphellen, M., & Manchanda, R.V. (2006). Effects of culture, gender, and moral obligations on responses to charity advertising across masculine and feminine cultures. *Journal of Consumer Psychology, 16*, 45–56.

Neuner, M., Raab, G., & Reisch, L.A. (2005). Compulsive buying in maturing consumer societies: An empirical re-inquiry. *Journal of Economic Psychology*, 509–522.

Nevid, J.S. (1981). Effects of brand labelling on ratings of product quality. *Perceptual and Motor Skills, 53*, 407–410.

Newell, A., & Simon, H.A. (1972). *Human problem solving.* Englewood Cliffs, NJ: Prentice Hall.

Newhouse, N. (1990). Implications of attitude and behaviour research for environmental conservation. *The Journal of Environmental Education, 22*, 26–32.

Nisbett, R.E., & Ross, L. (1980). *Human inference: Strategies and shortcomings of social judgment.* Englewood Cliffs, NJ: Prentice Hall.

Nixon, H.K. (1924). Attention and interest in advertising. *Archives of Psychology, 72*, 5–67.

Nixon, H.K. (1926). *An investigation of attention to advertisements.* New York: Columbia University Press.

Norman, K.A., & Schachter, D.L. (1997). False recognition in younger and older adults: Exploring the characteristics of illusory memories. *Memory & Cognition, 25*, 838–848.

North, A.C., & Hargreaves, D.J. (1998). The effect of music on atmosphere and purchase intentions in a cafeteria. *Journal of Applied Social Psychology, 28*, 2254–2273.

North, A.C., Hargreaves, D.J., & McKendrick, J. (1999). The influence of in-store music on wine selections. *Journal of Applied Psychology, 84*, 271–276.

Northcraft, G.B., & Neale, M.A. (1987). Experts, amateurs, and real estate: An anchoring and adjustment perspective on property pricing decisions. *Organizational Behavior and Human Decision Processes, 39*, 84–97.

Nunes, J.C., & Dreze, X. (2006). The endowed progress effect: How artificial advancement increases effort. *Journal of Consumer Research, 32*, 504–512.

Nunes, P.F., & Cespedes, F.V. (2003). The customer has escaped. *Harvard Business Review, 81*, 96–105.

Odin, Y., Odin, N., & Valette-Florence, P. (2001). Conceptual and operational aspects of brand loyalty: An empirical investigation. *Journal of Business Research, 53*, 75–84.

Ofcom (2007). Ofcom research identifies changing nature of children's programming. Retrieved 3 November 2007 from http://www.ofcom.org.uk/media/news/2007/10/nr_20071003

Ogilvie, D. (1987). The undesired self: A neglected variable in personality research. *Journal of Personality and Social Psychology, 52*, 379–385.

Okada, E.M. (2005). Justification effects on consumer choice of hedonic and utilitarian goods. *Journal of Marketing Research, 42*, 43–53.

Okagaki, L., & Frensch, P.A. (1994). Effects of video game playing on measures of spatial performance: Gender effects in late adolescence. *Journal of Applied Developmental Psychology, 15*, 33–58.

Oliver, R.L. (1994). Conceptual issues in the structural analysis of consumption emotion, satisfaction, and quality. In C.T. Allen & D.R. John (Eds.), *Advances in consumer research* (vol. 21). Provo, UT: Association for Consumer Research.

Oliver, R.L. (1996). *Satisfaction: A behavioral perspective on the consumer.* New York: McGraw-Hill.

Olsen, G.D. (2002). Salient stimuli in advertising: The effect of contrast interval length and type on recall. *Journal of Experimental Psychology: Applied, 8*, 168–179.

Ortega, B. (1993). Jewelers bet honest image, price cut and gimmicks will make sales glitter. *Wall Street Journal*, December 6, B1, B10.

Oskamp, S. (1977). *Attitudes and opinions.* Englewood Cliffs, NJ: Prentice Hall.

Oskamp, S. (2000). A sustainable future for humanity? How can psychology help? *American Psychologist, 55*, 496–508.

Packard, V. (1957). *Hidden persuaders.* New York: Penguin Books.

Padgham, C.A., & Saunders, J.E. (1975). *The perception of light and colour.* London: G. Bell & Sons Ltd.

Palmeri, T.J. & Gauthier, I. (2004). Visual object understanding. *Nature Reviews Neuroscience, 5,* 291–303.

Parasuraman, R. (1986). Vigilance, monitoring and search. In K.R. Boff, L. Kaufman & J.P. Thomas (Eds.), *Handbook of perception and human performance.* New York: Wiley.

Park, D.C., Royal, D., Dudley, W., & Morrell, R. (1988). Forgetting of pictures over a long retention interval in old and young adults. *Psychology and Aging, 3,* 94–95.

Park, D.C., Smith, A.D., Morrell, R.W., Puglisi, J.T., & Dudley, W.N. (1990). Effects of contextual integration on recall of pictures in older adults. *Journal of Gerontology: Psychological Sciences, 45,* 52–58.

Pavelchak, M.A., Antil, J.H., & Munch, J.M. (1988). The Super Bowl: An investigation into the relationship among program context, emotional experience, and ad recall. *Journal of Consumer Research, 15,* 360–367.

Pavlov, I.P. (1927). *Conditioned reflexes.* London: Clarendon Press.

Payne, J.W., Bettman, J.R. & Johnson, E.J. (1992). Behavioral decision research: A constructive processing perspective. *Annual Review of Psychology, 43,* 87–131.

Payne, J.W., Bettman, J.R., & Johnson, E.J. (1993). *The adaptive decision maker.* Sydney: Cambridge University Press.

Peck, J. (1999). Extraction of haptic properties: Individual characteristics and stimulus characteristics. Unpublished doctoral dissertation, University of Minnesota.

Peck, J., & Childers, T. (2003a). To have and to hold: The influence of haptic information on product judgements. *Journal of Marketing, 67,* 35–48.

Peck, J., & Childers, T. (2003b). Individual differences in haptic information processing: The 'need for touch scale'. *Journal of Consumer Research, 30,* 430–442.

Peracchio, L.A., & Tybout, A.M. (1996). The moderating role of prior knowledge in schema-based product evaluation. *Journal of Consumer Research, 23,* 177–193.

Peters, E., & Slovic, P. (2000). The springs of action: Affective and analytical information processing in choice. *Personality and Social Psychology Bulletin, 26,* 1465–1475.

Peterson, H.C. (1939). *Propaganda for war: The campaign against American neutrality, 1914–1917.* Norman: University of Oklahoma Press.

Petty, R.E. (1995). Attitude change. In A. Tesser (Ed.), *Advanced social psychology* (pp. 195–255). New York: McGraw-Hill.

Petty, R.E., & Cacioppo, J.T. (1981). *Attitudes and persuasion: Classic and contemporary approaches.* Dubuque: Wm. C. Brown.

Petty, R.E., & Cacioppo, J.T. (1986a). The elaboration likelihood model of persuasion. *Advances in Experimental Social Psychology, 19,* 123–205.

Petty, R.E., & Cacioppo, J.T. (1986b). *Communication and persuasion: Central and peripheral routes to attitude change.* New York: Springer Verlag.

Petty, R.E., & Krosnick, J.A. (1995). *Attitude strength: Antecedents and consequences.* Mahwah, NJ: Lawrence Erlbaum Associates.

Petty, R.E., & Wegener, D. (1998). Attitude change: Multiple roles for persuasion variables. In D.T. Gilbert, S.T. Fiske & G. Lindzey (Eds.), *The handbook of social psychology* (4th ed., vol. 2, pp. 323–390). New York: McGraw-Hill.

Pham, M.T. (1998). Representativeness, relevance, and the use of feelings in decision-making. *Journal of Consumer Research, 25,* 144–159.

Pham, M.T., & Avnet, T. (2004). Ideals and oughts and the weighting of affect versus substance in persuasion. *Journal of Consumer Research, 30,* 503–518.

Phillips, H., & Bradshaw, R. (1993). How customers actually shop: Customer interaction at the point of sale. *Journal of Market Research, 35,* 51–62.

Piaget, J. (1932). *The moral judgement of the child.* Harmondsworth: Penguin.

Piaget, J. (1936). *The origin of intelligence in the child.* London: Routledge & Kegan Paul.

Piaget, J. (1951). *Play, dreams, and imitation in childhood.* London: Routledge & Kegan Paul.

Pieters, R.G.M. (1991). Changing garbage disposal patterns of consumers: Motivation, ability, and performance. *Journal of Public Policy and Marketing, 10,* 59–76.

Pinto, M.B., & Leonidas, L. (1994). The impact of office characteristics on satisfaction with medical care: A 'before and after' study. *Health Marketing Quarterly, 12,* 43–54.

Platt, J. (1973). Social traps. *American Psychologist, 28,* 641–651.

Plummer, J.T. (1985). How personality makes a difference. *Journal of Advertising Research, 24,* 27–31.

Poffenberger, A.T. (1925). *Psychology in advertising.* New York: A.W. Shaw.

Poffenberger, A.T. (1927). *Applied psychology: Its principles and methods.* New York: D. Appleton.

Pollay, R.W. (1983). Measuring the cultural values manifest in advertising. In J.H. Leigh, & C.R. Martin (Eds.), *Current issues and research in advertising* (pp.71–92). Ann Arbor: University of Michigan Press.

Potter, W.J. (1991). The linearity assumption in cultivation research. *Human Communication Research, 17,* 562–583.

Povinelli, D.J. (1994). A theory of mind is in the head, not the heart. *Behavioral and Brain Sciences, 17,* 573–574.

Pratkanis, A.R. (1992). The cargi-cult science of subliminal persuasion. *Skeptical Inquirer, 16,* 260–272.

Pratkanis, A.R., Greenwald, A.G., Leippe, M.R. & Baumgardner, M.H. (1988). In search of reliable persuasion effects: III. The sleeper effect is dead. Long live the sleeper effect. *Journal of Personality and Social Psychology, 54,* 203–218.

Premack, D. (1959). Toward empirical behaviour laws: I. Positive reinforcement. *Psychological Review, 66,* 219–233.

Priester, J., Nayakankuppam, D., Fleming, M.A., & Godek, J. (2004). The A2SC2 model: The influence of attitudes and attitude strength on consideration and choice. *Journal of Consumer Research, 30,* 574–587.

Priester, J.R., & Petty, R.E. (1995). Source attributions and persuasion: Perceived honesty as a determinant of message scrutiny. *Personality and Social Psychology Bulletin, 21,* 637–654.

Priester, J.R., & Petty, R. (2003). The influence of spokesperson trustworthiness on message elaboration, attitude strength, and advertising effectiveness. *Journal of Consumer Psychology, 13,* 408–421.

Provenzo, E.F. (1991). *Video kids: Making sense of Nintendo.* Cambridge, MA: Harvard University Press.

Qrius (2005). *Jongeren 2005.* Amsterdam: Qrius.

Raacke, J.R., & Bonds-Raacke, J. (2008). MySpace and Facebook: Applying the uses and gratifications theory to exploring friend-networking sites. *CyberPsychology & Behavior, 11,* 169–174.

Raghunathan, R., & Pham, M.T. (1999). All negative moods are not equal: Motivational influences of anxiety and sadness on decision making. *Organizational Behavior and Human Decision Processes, 79,* 56–77.

Raghunathan, R., & Trope, Y. (2002). Walking the tightrope between feeling good and being accurate: Mood as a resource in processing persuasive messages. *Journal of Personality and Social Psychology, 83,* 521–525.

Ratchford, B.T. (2001). The economics of consumer knowledge. *Journal of Consumer Research, 27.*

Ray, M.L., & Wilkie, W.L. (1970). Fear: The potential of an appeal neglected by marketing. *Journal of Marketing, 34,* 54–62.

Reeves, B., & Nass, C.I. (1996). *The media equation.* Cambridge: Cambridge University Press.

Regan, D.T., & Fazio, R.H. (1977). On the consistency of attitudes and behaviour: Look to the method of attitude formation. *Journal of Experimental Social Psychology, 13,* 38–45.

Reichel, D.A., & Geller, E.S. (1980). Group vs. individual contingencies to conserve transportation energy. Paper presented at the Southeastern Psychological Association meeting, Washington, DC.

Reichert, T., & Alvaro, E. (2001). The effects of sexual information on ad and brand processing and recall. *Southwestern Mass Communication Journal, 17,* 9–17.

Reichert, T., Heckler, S.E., & Jackson, S. (2001). The effects of sexual social marketing appeals on cognitive processing and persuasion. *Journal of Advertising, 30,* 13–27.

Reingen, P.H. (1982). Test of a list procedure for inducing compliance with a request to donate money. *Journal of Applied Psychology, 67,* 110–118.

Rhodes, N., & Wood, W. (1992). Self-esteem and intelligence affect influenceability: The mediating role of message reception. *Psychological Bulletin, 111*, 156–171.

Rice, M.L., Huston, A.C., Truglio, R.T., & Wright, J.C. (1990). Words from Sesame Street: Learning vocabulary while viewing. *Developmental Psychology, 26*, 421–428.

Richins, M.L. (1991). Social comparison and the idealized images of advertising. *Journal of Consumer Research, 18*, 71–83.

Richins, M.L. (1994). Special possessions and the expression of material values. *Journal of Consumer Research, 21*, 522–533.

Richins, M.L. (1997). Measuring emotions in the consumption experience. *Journal of Consumer Research, 24*, 127–146.

Richins, M.L., & Dawson, S. (1992). A consumer values orientation for materialism and its measurement: Scale development and validation. *Journal of Consumer Research, 19*, 303–316.

Rindfleisch, A., Burroughs, J.E., & Denton, F. (1997). Family structure, materialism, and compulsive consumption. *Journal of Consumer Research, 23*, 312–325.

Roberts, D.F., Foehr, U.G., Rideout, U.T., & Brodie, M. (1999). *Kids and the media at the new millennium.* Menlo Park, CA: Kaiser Family Foundation.

Robertson, T.S., & Rossiter, J.R. (1974). Children and commercial persuasion: An attribution theory analysis. *Journal of Consumer Research, 1*, 13–20.

Rochberg-Halton, E. (1984). Object relations, role models and cultivation of the self. *Environment and Behavior, 16*, 335–368.

Roche, J. (1994). *The international cotton trade.* Cambridge: Woodhead Publishing Limited.

Rock, I. (1986). The description and analysis of object and event perception. In K.R. Boff, L. Kaufman & J.P. Thomas (Eds.), *Handbook of perception and human performance* (vol. 2, pp. 33–1 to 33–71). New York: Wiley.

Roehm, M.L. (2001). Instrumental vs. vocal versions of popular music in advertising. *Journal of Advertising Research, 41*, 49–58.

Rogers, R. (1983). Cognitive and physiological processes in fear appeals and attitude change: A revised theory of protection motivation. In J.T. Cacioppo & R.E. Petty (Eds.), *Social psychophysiology: A sourcebook* (pp. 153–176). New York: Guilford Press.

Rogers, W.A., & Fisk, A.D. (2000). Human factors. In F.I.M. Craik & T.A. Salthhouse (Eds.), *The handbook of aging and cognition* (2nd ed., pp. 559–591). Mahwah, NJ: Erlbaum.

Roggeveen, A.B., Kingstone, A., & Enns, J.T. (2003). Symmetry relations influence target-distractor comparison in visual search, *Journal of Vision, 3*, 229.

Rokeach, M. (1973). *The nature of human values.* New York: Free Press.

Roodman, D.M. (1999). Building a sustainable society. In L.R. Brown & C. Flavin (Eds.), *State of the world, 1999* (pp. 169–188). New York: Norton.

Rook, K.S. (1986). Encouraging preventive behaviour for distant and proximal health threats: Effects of vivid versus abstract information. *Journal of Gerontology, 41*, 526–534.

Rose, P. (2007). Mediators of the association between narcissism and compulsive buying: The roles of materialism and compulsive control. *Psychology of Addictive Behaviors, 21*, 576–581.

Rosenkoetter, L.J., Rosenkoetter, S.E., Ozretich, R.A., & Acock, A.C. (2004). Mitigating the harmful effects of violent television. *Journal of Applied Developmental Psychology, 25*, 25–47.

Rosenthal, R., & Jacobson, L.F. (1968). *Pygmalion in the classroom.* New York: Holt, Rinehart & Winston.

Roskos-Ewoldsen, D.R., & Fazio, R.H. (1992). On the orienting value of attitudes: Attitude accessibility as a determinant of an object's attraction of visual attention. *Journal of Personality and Social Psychology, 63*, 198–211.

Ross, R.P., Campbell, T., Wright, J.C., Huston, A.C., Rice, M.L., & Turk, P. (1984). When celebrities talk, children listen: An experimental analysis of children's responses to TV ads with celebrity endorsement. *Journal of Applied Developmental Psychology, 5*, 185–202.

Ross, W.T., & Creyer, E.H. (1992). Making inferences about missing information: The effects of existing information. *Journal of Consumer Research, 19*, 14–25.

Rossiter, J., & Percy, L. (1997). *Advertising, communications and promotion management.* New York: McGraw-Hill.

Rossiter, J.R. (1976). Visual and verbal memory in children's product information utilization. In B.B. Anderson (Ed.), *Advances in consumer research* (vol. 3, pp. 572–576). Ann Arbor, MI: Association for Consumer Research.

Roth, I. (1986). An introduction to object perception. In I. Roth & J.P. Frisby (Eds.), *Perception and representation: A cognitive approach.* Milton Keynes: Open University Press.

Rothschild, M.L., & Gaidis, W.C. (2002). Behavioral learning theory: Its relevance to marketing and promotions. In G.R. Foxall (Ed.), *Consumer behaviour analysis: Critical perspectives on business and management* (pp. 82–91). London: Routledge.

Rubin, A.M. (1978). Child and adolescent television use and political socialization. *Journalism Quarterly, 55,* 125–129.

Ruiter, R.A.C., Abraham, C., & Kok, G. (2001). Scary warnings and rational precautions: A review of the psychology of fear appeals. *Psychology and Health, 16,* 613–630.

Ruskin, G. (1999). Why they whine: How corporations pry on our children. *Mothering, 97,* 41–50.

Ryan, B., Jr. (1991). *It works! How investment spending in advertising pays off.* New York: American Association of Advertising Agencies.

Salovey, P., & Birnbaum, D. (1989). Influence of mood on health-related cognitions. *Journal of Personality and Social Psychology, 57,* 539–551.

Salthouse, T.A. (1996). The processing-speed theory of adult age differences in cognition. *Psychological Review, 103,* 403–428.

Schachtel, E.G. (1959). *Metamorphosis,* New York: Basic Books.

Schachter, S. (1951). Deviation, rejection and communication. *Journal of Abnormal and Social Psychology, 46,* 190–207.

Schaie, K.W. (2005). *Developmental influences on adult intelligence: The Seattle longitudinal study.* New York: Oxford University Press.

Schau, H., & Gilly, M. (2003). We are what we post: Self-presentation in personal Web space. *Journal of Consumer Research, 30,* 385–404.

Schechter, D. (2000). Eye on the media: Television finds new ways to beam violence at us. *Newsday,* May 10, p. A46.

Scherhorn, G., Reisch, L.A., & Raab, G. (1990). Addictive buying in West Germany: An empirical study. *Journal of Consumer Policy, 13,* 355–387.

Schlosser, A.E. (2003). Computers as situational cues: Implications for consumers' product cognitions and attitudes. *Journal of Consumer Psychology, 13,* 103–112.

Schlosser, A.E., Barnett-White, T., & Lloyd, S.M. (2006). Converting web site visitors into buyers: how web site investments increase consumer trusting beliefs and online purchase intentions. *Journal of Marketing, 70,* 2.

Schmitt, K.L., Anderson, D.R., & Collins, P.A. (1999). Form and content: Looking at visual features of television. *Developmental Psychology, 35,* 1156–1167.

Schneider, D. (1997). The rising seas. *Scientific American, 276,* 112–117.

Schoenbachler, D.D., & Whittler, T.E. (1996). Adolescent processing of social and physical threat communications. *Journal of Advertising, 25,* 37–54.

Schuller, R.A., Smith, V.L., & Olson, J.M. (1994). Jurors' decisions in trials of battered women who kill: The role of prior beliefs and expert testimony. *Journal of Applied Social Psychology, 24,* 316–337.

Schultz, D.P., & Schultz, S.E. (2004). *A history of modern psychology.* Belmont, CA: Wadsworth.

Schutte, N.S., Malouff, J.M., Post-Gorden, J.C. & Rodasta, A.L. (1988). Effects of playing video games on children's aggressive and other behaviours. *Journal of Applied Social Psychology, 18,* 454–460.

Schwartz, B. (2004). *The paradox of choice: Why more is less.* New York: HarperCollins.

Schwartz, B., Ward, A., Monterosso, J., Lyubomirsky, S., White, K., & Lehman, D.R. (2002). Maximizing versus satisficing: Happiness is a matter of choice. *Journal of Personality and Social Psychology, 83,* 1178–1197.

Schwartz, N., & Kurz, E. (1989). What's in a picture? The impact of face-ism on trait attribution. *European Journal of Social Psychology, 19*, 311–316.

Schwartz, S.H. (1992). Universals in the content and structure of values: Theoretical advances and empirical tests in 20 countries. In M.P. Zanna (Ed.), *Advances in experimental social psychology* (vol. 25, pp. 1–65). San Diego: Academic Press.

Schwartz, S.H., & Bilsky, W. (1987). Toward a universal psychological structure of human values. *Journal of Personality and Social Psychology, 53*, 550–562.

Schwarz, N. (1990). Feelings as information: Informational and motivational functions of affective states. In E.T. Higgins & R. Sorrentino (Eds.), *Handbook of motivation and cognition: Foundations of social behaviour* (vol. 2, pp. 527–561). New York: Guilford Press.

Schwarz, N. (2001). Feelings as information: Implications for affective influences on information processing. In L.L. Martin & G.L. Clore (Eds.), *Theories of mood and cognition: A user's guidebook* (pp. 159–179). Mahwah, NJ: Erlbaum.

Schwarz, N. (2004). Metacognitive experiences in consumer judgment and decision making. *Journal of Consumer Psychology, 14*, 332–348.

Schwarz, N., Bless, H., Strack, F., Klumpp, G., Rittenauerschatka, H., & Simons, A. (1991). Ease of retrieval as information: Another look at the availability heuristic. *Journal of Personality and Social Psychology, 61*, 195–202.

Schwarz, N., & Clore, G.L. (1983). Mood, misattribution and judgments of well-being: Informative and directive functions of affective states. *Journal of Personality and Social Psychology, 45*, 513–523.

Schwarz, N., & Clore, G.L. (1996). Feelings and phenomenal experiences. In E.T. Higgins & A.W. Kruglanski (Eds.), *Social psychology: Handbook of basic principles* (pp. 433–465). New York: Guilford Press.

Schwarz, N., & Vaughn, L.A. (2002). The availability heuristic revisited: Ease of recall and content of recall as distinct sources of information. In T. Gilovich, D.W. Griffin & D. Kahneman (Eds.), *Heuristics and biases: The psychology of intuitive judgment* (pp. 103–119). Cambridge: Cambridge University Press.

Scott, C., Klein, D.M., & Bryant, J. (1990). Consumer response to humor in advertising: A series of field studies using behavioural observation. *Journal of Consumer Research, 16*, 498–501.

Scott, W.D. (1903). *Theory of advertising.* Boston: Small, Maynard, & Co.

Sedikides C., & Brewer, M. (Eds.), (2001). *Individual self, relational self, collective self.* New York: Psychology Press.

Sedikides, C., Gregg, A.P., Cisek, S., & Hart, C.M. (2007). The I that buys: Narcissists as consumers. *Journal of Consumer Psychology, 17*, 254–257.

Shah, A.K., & Oppenheimer, D.M. (2008). Heuristics made easy: An effort-reduction framework. *Psychological Bulletin, 134*, 207–222.

Shammas, C. (1990). *The preindustrial consumer in England and America.* Oxford: Basil Blackwell.

Shapiro, S., Lindsey, C., & Krishnan, H.S., (2006). Intentional forgetting as a facilitator for recalling new product attributes. *Journal of Experimental Psychology: Applied, 12*, 251–263.

Shavitt, S. (1990). The role of attitude objects in attitude functions. *Journal of Experimental Social Psychology, 26*, 124–148.

Shavitt, S., Lee, A.Y., & Johnson, T.P. (2008). Cross-cultural consumer psychology. In C.P. Haugtvedt, P.M. Herr & F.R. Kardes (Eds.), *Handbook of consumer psychology* (pp. 1103–1132). New York: Lawrence Erlbaum Associates.

Shavitt, S., Swan, S., Lowrey, T.M., & Wänke, M. (1994). The interaction of endorser attractiveness and involvement in persuasion depends on the goal that guides message processing. *Journal of Consumer Psychology, 3*, 137–162.

Sheehan, M.O. (2001). Making better transportation choices. In L.R. Brown, C. Flavin & H. French (Eds.), *State of the world, 2001: A Worldwatch Institute report on progress toward a sustainable society* (pp. 103–122). New York: Norton.

Sherman, S.J., Zehner, K.S., Johnson, J., & Hirt, E.R. (1983). Social explanation: The role of timing, set and recall on subjective likelihood estimates. *Journal of Personality and Social Psychology, 44*, 1127–1143.

Sheth, J.N., & Sisodia, R.S. (1999). Revisiting marketing's lawlike generalizations. *Journal of Academy of Marketing Science, 27*, 71–87.

Shiv, B., Carmon, Z., & Ariely, D. (2005). Placebo effects of marketing actions: Consumers may get what they pay for. *Journal of Marketing Research, 42*, 383–393.

Signorielli, N. (1984). The measurement of violence in television programming: Violence indices. In J.R. Dominic & J.E. Fletcher (Eds.), *Broadcasting research methods*. Boston: Allyn and Bacon.

Signorielli, N. (1991). *A sourcebook on children and television*. New York: Greenwood.

Signorielli, N., & Lears, M. (1992). Children, television, and conceptions about chores: Attitudes and behaviours. *Sex Roles, 27*, 157–170.

Singer, D.G., Singer, J.L., & Zuckerman, D.M. (1990). *The parents' guide: Use TV to your child's advantage*. Reston: Acropolis.

Siomos, K.E., Dafouli, E.D., Braimiotis, D.A., Mouzas, O.D., & Angelopoulos, N.V. (2008). Internet addiction among Greek adolescent students. *Cyberpsychology & Behavior, 11*, 653–657.

Skinner, B.F. (1953). *Science and human behavior*. New York: Free Press.

Skowronski, J.J., & Carlston, D.E. (1987). Social judgement and social memory: The role of cue diagnosticity in negativity, positivity, and extremity biases. *Journal of Personality and Social Psychology, 52*, 689–699.

Skurnik, I., Yoon, C., Park, D.C., & Schwarz, N. (2005). How warnings about false claims become recommendations. *Journal of Consumer Research, 31*, 713–724.

Smith, A.D., Park, D.C., Cherry, K., & Berkovsky, K. (1990). Age differences in memory for concrete and abstract pictures. *Journal of Gerontology: Psychological Sciences, 45*, P205–P209.

Smith, E.R., Fazio, R.H., & Cejka, M.A. (1996). Accessible attitudes influence categorization of multiply categorizable objects. *Journal of Personality and Social Psychology, 71*, 888–898.

Smith, G.H., & Engle, R. (1968). Influence of a female model on perceived characteristics of an automobile. *Proceedings of the 76th Annual Convention of the American Psychological Association, 3*, 681–682.

Smith, K.H., & Stutts, M.A. (2003). Effects of short-term cosmetic versus long-term health fear appeals in anti-smoking advertisements on the smoking behaviour of adolescents. *Journal of Consumer Behaviour, 3*, 157–177.

Smith, M.B., Bruner, J.S., & White, R.W. (1956). *Opinions and personality*. New York: Wiley.

Smith, R.E., & Swinyard, W.R. (1983). Attitude-behavior consistency: The impact of product trial versus advertising. *Journal of Marketing Research, 20*, 257–267.

Smith, S.M., & Shaffer, D.R. (1991). Celerity and cajolery: Rapid speech may promote or inhibit persuasion through its impact on message elaboration, *Personality and Social Psychology Bulletin, 17*, 663–669.

Smith, S.M., & Shaffer, D.R. (1995). Speed of speech and persuasion: Evidence for multiple effects. *Personality and Social Psychology Bulletin, 21*, 1051–1060.

Smith, S.M., & Shaffer, D.R. (2000). Vividness can undermine or enhance message: The moderating role of vividness congruency. *Personality and Social Psychology Bulletin, 26*, 769–779.

Snyder, M. (1974). Self-monitoring of expressive behaviour. *Journal of Personality and Social Psychology, 30*, 526–537.

Snyder, M. (1979). Self-monitoring processes. In L. Berkowitz (Ed.), *Advances in experimental social psychology* (vol. 12, pp. 86–131). New York: Academic Press.

Snyder, M., & DeBono, K.G. (1985). Appeals to images and claims about quality: Understanding the psychology of advertising. *Journal of Personality and Social Psychology, 49*, 586–597.

Snyder, M., & DeBono, K.G. (1989). Understanding the functions of attitudes: Lessons for personality and social behaviour. In A.R. Pratkanis, S.J. Breckler & A.G. Greenwald (Eds.), *Attitude structure and function* (pp. 339–359). Hillsdale, NJ: Lawrence Erlbaum Associates.

Snyder, M.L., Stephan, W.G., & Rosenfield, D. (1978). Attributional egotism. In J.H. Harvey, W. Ickes & R.F. Kidd (Eds.), *New directions in attribution research* (vol. 2, pp. 91–120). Hillsdale, NJ: Lawrence Erlbaum Associates.

Solomon, M.R. (1983). The role of products as social stimuli: A symbolic interactionism perspective. *Journal of Consumer Research, 10*, 319–329.

Solomon, M.R., Drenan, S., & Insko, C.A. (1981). Popular induction: When is consensus information informative? *Journal of Personality, 49*, 212–224.

Soper, W.B., & Miller, M.J. (1983). Junk time junkies: An emerging addiction among students. *School Counsellor, 31*, 40–43.

Spangenberg, E.R., Crowley, A.E., & Henderson, P.W. (1996). Improving the store environment: Do olfactory cues affect evaluations and behaviours? *Journal of Marketing, 60*, 67–80.

Speck, P.S. (1991). The humorous ads. In. J.H. Leigh & C.R. Martin, Jr. (Eds.), *Current issues and research in advertising.* (pp. 1–44). Ann Arbor, MI: University of Michigan Press.

Sperling, G. (1960). The information available in brief visual presentations. *Psychological Monographs, 74*, 1–29.

Spotts, H.E., Weinberger, M.G., & Parsons, A.L. (1997). Assessing the use and impact of humor on advertising effectiveness: A contingency approach. *Journal of Advertising, 26*, 17–32.

Sprott, D.E., & Shimp, T.A. (2004). Using product sampling to augment the perceived quality of store brands. *Journal of Retailing, 80*, 305–315.

Srull, T.K. (1983). Affect and memory: The impact of affective reactions in advertising on the representation of product information in memory. In R.P. Bagozzi & A. Tybout (Eds.), *Advances in consumer research* (vol. 10). Ann Arbor, MI: Association for Consumer Research.

Srull, T.K. (1984). The effects of subjective affective states on memory and judgment. In T.C. Kinnear (Ed.), *Advances in consumer research* (Vol. 11). Provo, UT: Association for Consumer Research.

Starch, D. (1914). *Advertising: Its principles, practice and technique.* New York: Scott, Foresman.

Starch, D. (1923). *Principles of advertising,* New York: McGraw-Hill.

Statistics Norway (2007). Survey of consumer expenditure 2004–2006. Retrieved 10 June 2008 from http://www.ssb.no/fbu_en

Stern, B., & Resnik, A. (1978). Children's understanding of a televised commercial disclaimer. In S. Jain (Ed.), *Research frontiers in marketing: Dialogues and directions* (pp. 332–336). Chicago: American Marketing Association.

Stern, P.C. (2000). Psychology, sustainability, and the science of human–environment interactions. *American Psychologist, 55*, 523–530.

Stern, P.C., Dietz, T., Ruttan, V.W., Socolow, R.H., & Sweeney, J.L. (1997). *Environmentally significant consumption.* Washington, DC: National Academy Press.

Sternthal, B., & Craig, C.S. (1982). *Consumer behaviour: An information processing perspective.* Englewood Cliffs, NJ: Prentice-Hall.

Stone, M., Hobbs, M., & Khaleeli, M. (2002). Multichannel customer management: The benefits and challenges. *Journal of Database Marketing, 10*, 39–52.

Strahan, E.J., Spencer, S.J., & Zanna, M.P. (2002). Subliminal priming and persuasion: Striking while the iron is hot. *Journal of Experimental Social Psychology, 38*, 556–568.

Stunkard, A., Sorensen, T., & Schulsinger, F. (1980). Use of the Danish Adoption Register for the study of obesity and thinness. In S. Kety (Ed.), *The genetics of neurological and psychiatric disorders* (pp. 115–120). New York: Raven Press.

Suls, J., & Wheeler, L. (Eds.), (2000). *Handbook of social comparison: Theory and research.* New York: Kluwer/Plenum.

Sum, S., Mathews, R.M., Hughes, I., & Campbell, A. (2008). Internet use and loneliness in older adults. *CyberPsychology & Behavior, 11*, 208–211.

Supphellen, M., & Nelson, M.R. (2001). Developing, exploring, and validating a typology of private philanthropic decision making. *Journal of Economic Psychology, 22*, 573–603.

Swann, W.B., & Miller, L.C. (1982). Why never forgetting a face matters: Visual imagery and social memory. *Journal of Personality and Social Psychology, 43*, 457–480.

Sweeney, J.C., & Wyber, F. (2002). The role of cognitions and emotions in the music-approach-avoidance behaviour relationship. *The Journal of Services Marketing, 16*, 51–69.

Syme, G.J., Seligman, C., Kantola, S.J., & Macpherson, D.K. (1987). Evaluating a television campaign to promote petrol conservation. *Environment and Behavior, 19*, 444–461.

Tajfel, H. (1981). *Human groups and social categories: Studies in social psychology.* Cambridge: Cambridge University Press.

Tajfel, H., & Wilkes, A.L. (1963). Classification and quantitative judgement. *British Journal of Psychology, 54*, 101–114.

Tanner, C., & Jungbluth, N. (2003). Evidence for the coincidence effect in environmental judgments: Why isn't it easy to correctly identify environmentally friendly food products? *Journal of Experimental Psychology: Applied, 9*, 3–11.

Tatzel, M. (2003). The art of buying: Coming to terms with money and materialism. *Journal of Happiness Studies, 4*, 405–435.

Taylor, S.E., & Thompson, S.C. (1982). Stalking the elusive 'vividness' effect. *Psychological Review, 89*, 155–181.

Thayer, S.E., & Ray, S. (2006). Online communication preferences across age, gender, and duration of Internet use. *CyberPsychology & Behavior, 9*, 432–40.

The Information Centre (2006). Statistics on obesity, physical activity and diet: England, 2006. Retrieved 12 January 2008 from http://www.ic.nhs.uk/webfiles/publications/opan06/OPAN%20bulletin%20finalv2.pdf

Theus, K.T. (1994). Subliminal advertising and the psychology of processing unconscious stimuli: A review. *Psychology & Marketing, 11*, 271–290.

Thøgersen, J. (1993). Wasteful food consumption: Trends in food and packaging waste. In W.F. van Raaij & G. Bamossy (Eds.), *European Advances in Consumer Research 1* (pp. 434–439). Provo, UT: Association for Consumer Research.

Thompson, J.K., Heinberg, L.J., Altabe, M., & Tantleff-Dunn, S. (1999). *Exacting beauty: Theory, assessment and treatment of body image disturbance*. Washington, DC: American Psychological Association.

Tietje, B., & Brunel, F. (2005). Towards a unified theory of implicit consumer brand cognitions. In F.R. Kardes, P.M. Herr & J. Natel (Eds.), *Applying social cognition consumer-focused strategy*. Mahwah, NJ: Erlbaum.

Tinsley, B.R. (2002). *How children learn to be healthy*. New York: Cambridge University Press.

Tipper, S.P. & Driver, J. (2000). Negative priming between pictures and words in a selective attention task: Evidence for semantic processing of ignored stimuli. In M.S. Gazzaniga (Ed.), *Cognitive neuroscience: A reader* (pp 176–187). Maiden, MA: Blackwell Publishers Inc.

Tolman, E.C. (1932). *Purposive behaviour in animals and men*. New York: Century Books.

Tom, G. (1990). Marketing with music. *Journal of Consumer Marketing, 7*, 49–53.

Trappey, C. (1996). A meta-analysis of consumer choice and subliminal advertising. *Psychology & Marketing, 13*, 517–530.

Trope, Y., & Pomerantz, E.M. (1998). Resolving conflicts among self-evaluative motives: Positive experiences as a resource for overcoming defensiveness. *Motivation and Emotion, 22*, 53–72.

Tulving, E. (1972). Episodic and semantic memory. In E. Tulving & W. Donaldson (Eds.), *Organisation of memory*. London: Academic Press.

Tulving, E. (1983). Synergistic ecphory in recall and recognition. *Canadian Journal of Psychology, 36*, 130–147.

Tulving, E., & Psotka, J. (1971). Retroactive inhibition in free recall: Inaccessibility of information available in the memory store. *Journal of Experimental Psychology, 87*, 1–8.

Tulving, E., & Thomson, D.M. (1973). Encoding specificity and retrieval processes in episodic memory. *Psychological Review, 80*, 352–373.

Tun, P.A., Wingfield, A., Rosen, M.J., & Blanchard, L.S. (1998). Response latencies for false memories: Association, discrimination, and normal aging. *Psychology and Aging, 14*, 230–241.

Turley, L.W., & Milliman, R.E. (2000). Atmospheric effects on shopping behaviour: A review of the experimental evidence. *Journal of Business Research, 49*, 193–211.

Tversky, A. (1972). Elimination by aspects: A theory of choice. *Psychological Review, 79*, 281–299.

Tversky, A., & Kahneman, D. (1973). Availability: A heuristic for judging frequency and probability. *Cognitive Psychology, 5*, 207–232.

Tversky, A., & Kahneman, D. (1974). Judgement under uncertainty: Heuristics and biases. *Science, 185*, 1124–1131.

Tversky, A., & Kahneman, D. (1982). Causal schemas in judgments under uncertainty. In D. Kahneman, P. Slovic & A. Tversky (Eds.), *Judgment under uncertainty: Heuristics and biases* (pp. 117–128). New York: Cambridge University Press.

Tversky, A., & Kahneman, D. (1983). Extensional versus intuitive reasoning: the conjunction fallacy in probability judgement. *Psychological Review, 90*, 293–315.

Twedt, D.W. (1965). Consumer psychology. *Annual Review of Psychology, 16*, 265–294.

United Nations (1998). *Human Development Report.* New York: Oxford University Press.

Unnava, H.R., & Burnkrant, R.E. (1991). Effects of repeating varied ad executions on brand name memory. *Journal of Marketing Research, 28*, 406–416.

Valkenburg P.M., & Peter, J. (2007). Preadolescents' and adolescents' online communication and their closeness to friends. *Developmental Psychology, 43*, 267–277.

Valkenburg, P.M., Peter, J., & Schouten A.P. (2006). Friend networking sites and their relationship to adolescents' well-being and social self-esteem. *CyberPsychology & Behavior, 9*, 584–590.

Van Boven, L. (2005). Experientialism, materialism, and the pursuit of happiness. *Review of General Psychology, 9*, 132–142.

Van Boven, L., Campbell, M.C., & Gilovich, T. (2008). Social costs of materialism: On stereotypes and impressions of materialistic versus experiential pursuits. Paper presented at the Conference for Society for Consumer Psychology, New Orleans, February.

Van Boven, L., & Gilovich, T. (2003). To do or to have? That is the question. *Journal of Personality and Social Psychology, 85*, 1193–1202.

Van den Broek, P. (1997). Discovering the element of the universe: The development of event comprehension from childhood to adulthood. In P. Van den Broek, P. Bauer & T. Bourg (Eds.), *Developmental spans in event comprehension: Bridging fictional and actual events* (pp. 321–342). Mahwah, NJ: Erlbaum.

Van den Broek, P., Lorch, E.P., & Thurlow, R. (1996). Children's and adults' memory for television stories: The role of causal factors, story-grammar categories, and hierarchical level. *Child Development, 67*, 3010–3028.

VanRullen, R., & Thorpe, S.J. (2001). Is it a bird? Is it a plane? Ultra-rapid visual categorisation of natural and artifactual objects. *Perception, 30*, 655–668.

Verhoef, P.C., Neslin, S.A., & Vroomen, B. (2007). Multichannel customer managements: Understanding the research-shopper phenomenon. *International Journal of Research in Marketing, 24*, 129–148.

Verplanken, B., & Aarts, H. (1999). Habit, attitude, and planned behaviour: Is habit an empty construct or an interesting case of automaticity? *European Review of Social Psychology, 10*, 101–134.

Verplanken, B., Hofstee, G., & Janssen, H.J.W. (1998). Accessibility of affective versus cognitive components of attitudes. *European Journal of Social Psychology, 28*, 23–35.

Victor, C., Scambler, S., Bond, J., & Bowling, A. (2000). Being alone in later life: Loneliness, social isolation and living alone. *Review of Clinical Gerontology, 10*, 407–417.

Vignoles, V.L., Regalia, C., Manzi, C., Golledge, J., & Scabini, E. (2006). Beyond self-esteem: The influence of multiple motives on identity construction. *Journal of Personality and Social Psychology, 90*, 308–333.

Vorkinn, M., & Riese, H. (2001). Environmental concern in a local context: The significance of place attachment. *Environment & Behavior, 33*, 249–263.

Wachtel, P. (1967). Conceptions of broad and narrow ability. *Psychological Bulletin, 68*, 417–429.

Wachtel, P.L (1983). *The poverty of affluence: A psychological portrait of the American way of life.* New York: Free Press.

Wackernagel, M., & Rees, W. (1996). *Our ecological footprint: Reducing human impact on the earth.* Philadelphia, PA: New Society.

Walker, J.M. (1979). Energy demand behavior in a master-meter apartment complex: An experimental analysis. *Journal of Applied Psychology, 64*, 190–196.

Wall, G. (1995). General versus specific environmental concern: A Western Canadian case. *Environment and Behavior, 27*, 294–316.

Wänke, M., Bohner, G., & Jurkowitsch, A. (1997). There are many reasons to drive a BMW – surely you know one: Ease of argument generation influences brand attitudes. *Journal of Consumer Research, 24*, 70–77.

Ward, S. (1972). Children's reactions to commercials. *Journal of Advertising Research, 12*, 37–45.

Ward, S., Wackman, D.B., & Wartella, E. (1977). *How children learn to buy.* Beverly Hills, CA: Sage Publications.

Wärneryd, K-E. (1999). Katona, George. In P.E. Earl & S. Kemp (Eds.), *The Elgar companion to consumer research and economic psychology.* Cheltenham: Edward Elgar Publishing Limited.

Warrington, E.K., & Shallice, T. (1972). Neuropsychological evidence of visual storage in short-term memory tasks. *Quarterly Journal of Experimental Psychology, 24*, 30–40.

Watson, J.B. (1913). Psychology as the behaviorist views it. *Psychological Review, 20*, 158–177.

Watson, J.B. (1919). *Psychology from the standpoint of a behaviorist.* Philadelphia, PA: Lippincott.

Watson, J.B. & Rayner, R. (1920). Conditioned emotional reactions. *Journal of Experimental Psychology, 3*, 1–14.

Watson, J.J. (2003). The relationship of materialism to spending tendencies, savings, and debt. *Journal of Economic Psychology, 24*, 723–739.

Weaver, J.B. & Laird, E.A. (1995). Mood management during the menstrual-cycle through selective exposure to television. *Journalism & Mass Communication Quarterly, 72*, 139–146.

Wegener, D.M., Petty, R.E., & Smith, S.M. (1995). Positive mood can increase or decrease message scrutiny: The hedonic contingency view of mood and message processing. *Journal of Personality and Social Psychology, 69*, 5–15.

Weinberger, M.G., & Campbell, L. (1991). The use and impact of humor in radio advertising. *Journal of Advertising Research, 31*, 44–52.

Weinberger, M.G., & Gulas, C.S. (1992). The impact of humor in advertising: A review. *Journal of Advertising, 21*, 35–59.

Weinberger, M.G., Spotts, H.E., Campbell, L., & Parsons, A.L. (1995). The use of humor in different advertising media. *Journal of Advertising Research, 35*, 44–56.

Weinstein, C.S. (1991). The classroom as a social context for learning. *Annual Review of Psychology, 42*, 493–525.

Weir, W. (1984). Another look at subliminal 'facts'. *Advertising Age*, 15 October, p. 46.

Weiss, J., & Brown, P. (1977). Self-insight error in the explanation of mood. Unpublished manuscript, Harvard University.

Wells, W.D. (Ed.), (1997). *Measuring advertising effectiveness.* Mahwah, NJ: Erlbaum.

Wenzel, B.M. (1979). Obituary: Albert Theodore Poffenberger (1885–1977). *American Psychologist, 34*, 88–90.

Wertheimer, M. (1923). Principles of perceptual organisation. In D.C. Beardslee & M. Wertheimer (Eds.), *Readings in Perception.* Princeton, NJ: Van Nostrand.

Westbrook, R.A., & Oliver, R.L. (1991). The dimensionality of consumption emotion patterns and consumer satisfaction. *Journal of Consumer Research, 18*, 84–91.

Wheeler, L. (1991). A brief history of social comparison theory. In J. Suls & T.A. Wills (Eds.), *Social comparison: Contemporary theory and research* (pp. 3–21). Hillsdale, NJ: Lawrence Erlbaum Associates.

Wickens, C.D. (1992). *Engineering psychology and human performance* (2nd ed.). New York: HarperCollins.

Wickens, C.D., & Hollands, J.G. (2000). *Engineering psychology and human performance* (3rd ed.). Upper Saddle River, NJ: Prentice Hall Inc.

Wickens, D.D. (1972). Characteristics of word encoding. In A.W. Melton & E. Martin (eds.), *Coding processes in human memory* (pp. 191–215). Washington, DC: Winston/Wiley.

Wicklund, R.A., & Gollwitzer, P.M. (1982). *Symbolic self-completion.* Hillsdale, NJ: Lawrence Erlbaum Associates.

Wigfield, A., & Eccles, J. S. (2000). Expectancy – value theory of motivation. *Contemporary Educational Psychology, 25*, 68–81.

Wilk, R. (1997). A critique of desire: Distaste and dislike in consumer behaviour. *Consumption, Markets & Culture, 1*, 175–196.

Wilkinson, J.B., Mason, J., & Paksoy, C.H. (1982). Assessing the impact of short-term supermarket strategy variables. *Journal of Marketing Research, 14*, 72–86.

Wills, T.A. (1981). Downward comparison principles in social psychology. *Psychological Bulletin, 90*, 245–271.

Wilson, J.R., & Wilson, S.L.R. (1998). *Mass media/mass culture* (4th ed.). New York: McGraw-Hill.

Wilson, T.D., & Brekke, N.C. (1994). Mental contamination and mental correction: Unwanted influences on judgements and evaluations. *Psychological Bulletin, 116*, 117–142.

Wilson, T.D., Houston, C.E., & Meyers, J.M. (1998). Choose your poison: Effects of lay beliefs about mental processes on attitude change. *Social Cognition, 16*, 1124–1132.

Wilson, T.D., Lindsey, S., & Schooler, T.Y. (2000). A model of dual attitudes. *Psychological Review, 107*, 101–126.

Wimmer, H., & Perner, J. (1983). Beliefs about beliefs: representations and constraining fuction of wrong beliefs in young children's understanding of deception. *Cognition, 13*, 103–128.

Winell, M. (1987). Personal goals: The key to self-direction in adulthood. In M.E. Ford & D.H. Ford (Eds.), *Humans as self-constructing living systems: Putting the framework to work* (pp. 261–287). Hillsdale, NJ: Lawrence Erlbaum Associates.

Winkel, M., Novak, D.M., & Hopson, H. (1987). Personality factors, subject gender and the effects of aggressive video games on aggression in adolescents. *Journal of Research in Personality, 21*, 211–223.

Winkler, J.R., & Bromberg, W. (1939). *The mind explorers.* New York: Reynald and Hitchcock, Advertising Publications, Inc.

Wolak, J., Mitchell, K.J., & Finkelhor, D. (2003). Escaping or connecting? Characteristics of youth who form close online relationships. *Journal of Adolescence, 26*, 105–119.

Wolf, N., & Feldman, E., (1991). *Plastics: America's packaging dilemma.* Environmental Action Coalition. Washington, DC: Island Press.

Wood, J.V. (1989). Theory and research concerning social comparisons of personal attributes. *Psychological Bulletin, 106*, 231–248.

Wood, S.L., & Bettman, J.R. (2007). Predicting happiness: How normative feeling rules influence (and even reverses) durability bias. *Journal of Consumer Psychology, 17*, 188–201.

Worldwatch Institute (2004). *State of the world 2004: Consumption by the numbers.* Retrieved 16 June 2008 from http://www.worldwatch.org/node/1783

Wright, J.C., Huston, A.C., Alvarez, M., Truglio, R., Fitch, M., & Piemyat, S. (1995). Perceived television reality and children's emotional and cognitive responses to its social content. *Journal of Applied Developmental Psychology, 16*, 231–251.

Wright, J.C., Huston, A.C., Murphy, K.C., St. Peters, M., Pinon, M., Scantlin, R., et al. (2001). The relations of early television viewing to school readiness and vocabulary of children from low-income families: The early window project. *Child Development, 72*, 1347–1366.

Wyer, R.S. (2004). *Social comprehension and judgment: The role of situation models, narratives, and implicit theories.* Mahwah, NJ: Erlbaum.

Yalch, R.F. (1991). Memory in a jingle jungle: Music as a mnemonic device in communicating advertising slogans. *Journal of Applied Psychology, 76*, 268–275.

Yalch, R.F., & Spangenberg, E.R. (2000). The effects of music in a retail setting on real and perceived shopping times. *Journal of Business Research, 49*, 139–147.

Yang, B., & Lester, D. (2004). Attitudes toward buying online. *CyberPsychology & Behavior, 7*, 85–91.

Yankelovich Partners & Harris Interactive (2001). Business-to-Business media study: Final report. Retrieved 22 September 2002 from http://www.americanbusinessmedia.com/images/abm/pdfs/resources/yankelovich_fullreport.pdf

Yeung, C.W.M., & Wyer, R.S. (2004). Affect, appraisal and consumer judgements. *Journal of Consumer Research, 31*, 412–424.

Yoon, C., Lee, M.P., & Danziger, S. (2007). The effects of optimal time of day on persuasion processes in older adults. *Psychology & Marketing, 5*, 475–495.

Young, K.S. (1996). Internet addiction: The emergence of a new clinical disorder. Paper presented at the 104th annual convention of the American Psychological Association, Toronto.

Yurchisin, J., & Johnson, K.P.P. (2004). Compulsive buying behaviour and its relationship to perceived social status associated with buying, materialism, self-esteem, and apparel-product involvement. *Family and Consumer Sciences Research Journal, 32*, 291–314.

Zahavi, A. (1975). Mate selection – A selection for a handicap. *Journal of Theoretical Biology, 53*, 205–214.

Zaichkowsky, J.L. (1985). Measuring the involvement construct in marketing. *Journal of Consumer Research, 12*, 341–352.

Zajonc, R.B. (2000). Feeling and thinking: Closing the debate of the independence of affect. In J.P. Forgas (Ed.), *Feeling and thinking: The role of affect in social cognition.* New York: Cambridge University Press.

Zajonc, R.B., & Markus, H. (1982). Affective and cognitive factors in preferences. *Journal of Consumer Research, 9*, 123–131.

Zanna, M.P., & Rempel, J.K. (1988). Attitudes: A new look at an old concept. In D. Bar-Tal & A.W. Kruglanski (Eds.), *The social psychology of attitudes* (pp. 315–334). New York: Cambridge University Press.

Zauberman, G. (2002). Lock-in over time: Time preferences, prediction accuracy and the information cost structure. *Advances in Consumer Research, 29*, 9–10.

Zhang, Y., & Gelb, B. (1996). Matching advertising appeals to culture: The influence of products' use conditions. *Journal of Advertising, 25*, 29–46.

Zhang, Y., & Zinkhan, G.M. (2006). Responses to humorous ads. *Journal of Advertising, 35*, 113–127.

Zhu, R., & Meyers-Levy, J. (2005). Distinguishing between the meanings of music: When background music affects product perceptions. *Journal of Marketing Research, 42*, 333–345.

Zill, N., Davies, E., & Daly, M. (1994). *Viewing of Sesame Street by preschool children in the United States and its relationship to school readiness.* Rockville: Westat.

Zillmann, D. (1971). Excitation transfer in communication-mediated aggressive behaviour. *Journal of Experimental Social Psychology, 7*, 419–434.

Zillmann, D. (1978). Attribution and misattribution of excitatory reactions. In J.H. Harvey, W. Ickes & R.F. Kidd (Eds.), *New directions in attribution research* (vol. 2, pp. 335–368). Hillsdale, NJ: Lawrence Erlbaum Associates.

Zillmann, D., & Bryant, J. (1984). Effects of massive exposure to pornography. In N.M. Malamuth & E. Donnerstein (Eds.), *Pornography and sexual aggression* (pp. 115–138). New York: Academic Press.

Zinkhan, G.M., Kwak, H., Morrison, M., & Peters, C.O. (2003). Web-based chatting: Consumer communication in cyberspace. *Journal of Consumer Psychology, 13*, 17–27.

Zinkhan, G., Kwak, H., & Pitt, L. (2001). Global and cultural perspectives on web-based chatting: An exploratory study. In P. Tidwell & T. Muller (Eds.), *Asia Pacific advances in consumer research* (vol. 4, pp. 243–250). Valdosta: Association for Consumer Research.

Zuckerman, M. (1994). *Behavioral expression and biosocial bases of sensation seeking.* New York: Cambridge University Press.

Zuckerman, M. (2000). Are you a risk-taker? *Psychology Today* (Nov/Dec), 54–87.

Author index

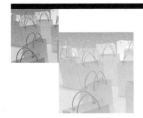

Subject index

Related books from Open University Press
Purchase from www.openup.co.uk or order through your local bookseller

SOCIAL PSYCHOLOGY
Wendy Stainton-Rogers

This introductory social psychology textbook is unique. It acknowledges the two very different approaches being taken to social psychology – experimental and critical – and presents them together in a single, coherent text. No attempt is made to find a cosy 'integration' between them; rather, students explore the benefits and drawbacks of each.

The book encourages students to develop their skills of critical analysis by addressing such questions as:

- What is social psychology: a natural science, a social science, a human science or something else?
- How should social psychology be studied: by doing experiments or by analysing discourse?

The book has a number of features that provide a broad context for addressing these questions:

- An introduction to the experimental approach, including the study of social influence, attitudes, attribution, groups, language and communication
- An introduction to the critical approach, including semiotics, social constructionist and grounded theories, and discourse and narrative analyses
- An exploration of the historical origins and development of the two approaches, their philosophical bases and the contrasting 'logics of enquiry' they use to pursue empirical research

By studying experimental and critical approaches presented together rather than separately, students gain a richer and deeper understanding of what social psychology in the 21st century is about, where it is going and the issues it must address.

Contents
Part one: Starting points – *What is social psychology?* – *Social psychology's two paradigms* – *Methods and analytics* – ***Part two: Topics in social psychology*** – *Communication and language* – *Understanding the social world* – *Values and attitudes* – *Constructing the social world* – *Selves and identities* – *Groups* – *Where next for social psychology?* – *Glossary* – *References* – *Index*

2003   384pp
978–0–335–21126–5 (Paperback)

ATTITUDES, PERSONALITY AND BEHAVIOUR
SECOND EDITION

Icek Ajzen

A very strong text on a key area of social psychology.

Dr. Jim Golby, University of Teesside

- Why do people say one thing and do another?
- Why do people behave inconsistently from one situation to another?
- How do people translate their beliefs and feelings into actions?

This thoroughly revised and updated edition describes why and how beliefs, attitudes and personality traits influence human behaviour. Building on the strengths of the previous edition, it covers recent developments in existing theories and details new theoretical approaches to the attitude-behaviour relationships. These novel developments provide insight into the predictability – and unpredictability – of human behaviour.

The book examines:

- Recent innovations in the assessment of attitudes and personality
- The implications for prediction of behaviour of these innovations
- Differences between spontaneous and reasoned processes
- The most recent research on the relations between intentions and behaviour

While the book is written primarily for students and researchers in social, personality, and organizational psychology, it also has wide-reaching appeal to students, researchers and professionals in the fields of health and social welfare, marketing and consumer behaviour.

Contents
Preface – Attitudes and personality traits – Consistency in human affairs – From dispositions to actions – The principle of compatibility – From intentions to actions – Explaining intentions and behaviour– Conclusion – References – Author index – Subject index

2005   192pp
978–0–335–21703–8 (Paperback)